MENTOR'S GUIDE **Capstone** Curriculum

Urban Mission

Focus *on* Reproduction

Church Growth:

REPRODUCING IN NUMBER *and* QUALITY

Planting Urban Churches:

SOWING

Planting Urban Churches:

TENDING

Planting Urban Churches:

REAPING

This curriculum is the result of thousands of hours of work by The Urban Ministry Institute (TUMI) and should not be reproduced without their express permission. TUMI supports all who wish to use these materials for the advance of God's Kingdom, and affordable licensing to reproduce them is available. Please confirm with your instructor that this book is properly licensed. For more information on TUMI and our licensing program, visit *www.tumi.org* and *www.tumi.org/license*.

Capstone Module 12: Focus on Reproduction Mentor's Guide

ISBN: 978-1-62932-032-8

© 2005, 2011, 2013, 2015. The Urban Ministry Institute. All Rights Reserved.
First edition 2005, Second edition 2011, Third edition 2013, Fourth edition 2015.

Copying, redistribution and/or sale of these materials, or any unauthorized transmission, except as may be expressly permitted by the 1976 Copyright Act or in writing from the publisher is prohibited. Requests for permission should be addressed in writing to: The Urban Ministry Institute, 3701 E. 13th Street, Wichita, KS 67208.

The Urban Ministry Institute is a ministry of World Impact, Inc.

All Scripture quotations, unless otherwise noted, are from The Holy Bible, English Standard Version, copyright © 2001 by Crossway Bible, a division of Good News Publishers. Used by permission. All Rights Reserved.

Contents

Course Overview
- 3   About the Instructor
- 5   Introduction to the Module
- 7   Course Requirements

13   Lesson 1
Church Growth: Reproducing in Number and Quality

57   Lesson 2
Planting Urban Churches: Sowing

99   Lesson 3
Planting Urban Churches: Tending

143   Lesson 4
Planting Urban Churches: Reaping

185   Appendices

295   Mentoring the Capstone Curriculum

- 303   Lesson 1 Mentor's Notes
- 311   Lesson 2 Mentor's Notes
- 315   Lesson 3 Mentor's Notes
- 321   Lesson 4 Mentor's Notes

About the Instructor

Rev. Dr. Don L. Davis is the Executive Director of The Urban Ministry Institute and a Senior Vice President of World Impact. He attended Wheaton College and Wheaton Graduate School, and graduated summa cum laude in both his B.A. (1988) and M.A. (1989) degrees, in Biblical Studies and Systematic Theology, respectively. He earned his Ph.D. in Religion (Theology and Ethics) from the University of Iowa School of Religion.

As the Institute's Executive Director and World Impact's Senior Vice President, he oversees the training of urban missionaries, church planters, and city pastors, and facilitates training opportunities for urban Christian workers in evangelism, church growth, and pioneer missions. He also leads the Institute's extensive distance learning programs and facilitates leadership development efforts for organizations and denominations like Prison Fellowship, the Evangelical Free Church of America, and the Church of God in Christ.

A recipient of numerous teaching and academic awards, Dr. Davis has served as professor and faculty at a number of fine academic institutions, having lectured and taught courses in religion, theology, philosophy, and biblical studies at schools such as Wheaton College, St. Ambrose University, the Houston Graduate School of Theology, the University of Iowa School of Religion, the Robert E. Webber Institute of Worship Studies. He has authored a number of books, curricula, and study materials to equip urban leaders, including *The Capstone Curriculum*, TUMI's premiere sixteen-module distance education seminary instruction, *Sacred Roots: A Primer on Retrieving the Great Tradition*, which focuses on how urban churches can be renewed through a rediscovery of the historic orthodox faith, and *Black and Human: Rediscovering King as a Resource for Black Theology and Ethics*. Dr. Davis has participated in academic lectureships such as the Staley Lecture series, renewal conferences like the Promise Keepers rallies, and theological consortiums like the University of Virginia Lived Theology Project Series. He received the Distinguished Alumni Fellow Award from the University of Iowa College of Liberal Arts and Sciences in 2009. Dr. Davis is also a member of the Society of Biblical Literature, and the American Academy of Religion.

Introduction to the Module

Greetings, dearest friends, in the strong name of Jesus Christ!

As 21st century disciples of Jesus in the cities of America, we desire to be fruitful in the work of God–ministering to the lost, and advancing the Kingdom of Christ (John 15.8,16). In module 12, *Focus on Reproduction*, we concentrate our attention on the need to evangelize, equip, and empower the lost in order that they might become salt and light in the communities where they live and work.

In our first lesson, ***Church Growth: Reproducing in Number and Quality***, we affirm the single most critical concept in understanding mission in the city: the lordship of Jesus Christ. As risen Lord and God's Anointed Messiah, Jesus has been exalted to the position of head over all things to the Church and Lord of the harvest. In this lesson we survey his call to make disciples of all nations, to *Evangelize*, as well as to affirm that radical discipleship is proven in Christian community. Jesus has called us to evangelize the lost, equip new disciples to live the Christian life, and to empower his Church to reproduce itself, all for the glory of God.

Next, in our second lesson, ***Planting Urban Churches: Sowing*** we introduce the important concept of *oikos* in urban evangelism. Here we show how an *oikos* is that web of common kinship relationships, friendships, and associations that make up a person's larger social circle. Beginning with an outline of *oikos* in the NT, we then explore the meaning of this critical idea for urban cross-cultural evangelism.

In lesson three we further outline the second main phase of church planting, *Equipping*, through the idea of *follow-up*, or incorporating new disciples into the Church. Arguing that the Church is God's means of bringing new Christians to maturity, we provide key elements and tips in the practice of following up new believers in Christ. In this lesson we will also look closely at the practice of discipling growing believers. Examining the role of the discipler as model, mentor, and friend, we will offer practical advice in how to help new Christians grow to maturity.

Finally, in lesson four, we will consider our role in helping new churches progress toward independence through *Empowerment* and the final phase of urban church planting: transition. We will define the purpose, plan, and perspectives related to empowering through four biblical aspects of godly urban church leadership. Without a doubt, godly, servant leadership is critical to ensure a dynamic growing church in the city. We conclude our module study with a blueprint of a godly urban church, those characteristics that represent a healthy, reproducing church in the city that is an agent of change and freedom in its community, in Jesus' name.

My sincere prayer is that God will grant you grace to understand his will for reproducing fruit and making disciples of the Kingdom in the city. May his Spirit grant you the power and desire to make disciples where you live, and so multiply his Church, to the glory of his great name!

In his Grasp,

- Rev. Dr. Don L. Davis

Course Requirements

Required Books and Materials

- Bible (for the purposes of this course, your Bible should be a translation [ex. NIV, NASB, RSV, KJV, NKJV, etc.], and not a paraphrase [ex. The Living Bible, The Message]).

- Each Capstone module has assigned textbooks which are read and discussed throughout the course. We encourage you to read, reflect upon, and respond to these with your professors, mentors, and fellow learners. Because of the fluid availability of the texts (e.g., books going out of print), we maintain our *official* Capstone Required Textbook list on our website. Please visit *www.tumi.org/books* to obtain the current listing of this module's texts.

- Paper and pen for taking notes and completing in-class assignments.

Suggested Readings

- Bakke, Ray. *A Theology as Big as the City.* Downers Grove, IL: InterVarsity, 1997.

- ------. *Urban Christian.* Downer Grove, IL: InterVarsity, 1987.

- Conn, Harvie, ed. *Planting and Growing Urban Churches: From Dream to Reality.* Grand Rapids: Baker, 1997.

- Greenway, Roger S. and Timothy M. Monsma. *Cities: Missions' New Frontier.* 2nd ed. Grand Rapids: Baker Book House, 2000.

- Hesselgrave, David J. *Planting Churches Cross-Culturally*, 2nd. ed. Grand Rapids: Baker Books, 2001.

- Perkins, John M. *Beyond Charity: The Call to Christian Community Development.* Grand Rapids: Zondervan, 1993.

- Silvoso, Ed. *That None Should Perish: How to Reach Entire Cities for Christ through Prayer Evangelism.* Ventura, CA: Regal Books, 1994.

Summary of Grade Categories and Weights

Attendance & Class Participation	30%	90 pts
Quizzes	10%	30 pts
Memory Verses	15%	45 pts
Exegetical Project	15%	45 pts
Ministry Project	10%	30 pts
Readings and Homework Assignments.	10%	30 pts
Final Exam	10%	30 pts
Total:	100%	300 pts

Course Requirements

Grade Requirements

Attendance at each class session is a course requirement. Absences will affect your grade. If an absence cannot be avoided, please let the Mentor know in advance. If you miss a class it is your responsibility to find out the assignments you missed, and to talk with the Mentor about turning in late work. Much of the learning associated with this course takes place through discussion. Therefore, your active involvement will be sought and expected in every class session.

Attendance and Class Participation

Every class will begin with a short quiz over the basic ideas from the last lesson. The best way to prepare for the quiz is to review the Student Workbook material and class notes taken during the last lesson.

Quizzes

The memorized Word is a central priority for your life and ministry as a believer and leader in the Church of Jesus Christ. There are relatively few verses, but they are significant in their content. Each class session you will be expected to recite (orally or in writing) the assigned verses to your Mentor.

Memory Verses

The Scriptures are God's potent instrument to equip the man or woman of God for every work of ministry he calls them to (2 Tim. 3.16-17). In order to complete the requirements for this course you must select a passage and do an inductive Bible study (i.e., an exegetical study) upon it. The study will have to be five pages in length (double-spaced, typed or neatly hand written) and deal with one of the aspects of Christian mission and reproduction in urban evangelism and church planting which are highlighted in this course. Our desire and hope is that you will be deeply convinced of Scripture's ability to change and practically affect your life, and the

Exegetical Project

Ministry Project

lives of those to whom you minister. As you go through the course, be open to finding an extended passage (roughly 4-9 verses) on a subject you would like to study more intensely. The details of the project are covered on pages 10-11, and will be discussed in the introductory session of this course.

Our expectation is that all students will apply their learning practically in their lives and in their ministry responsibilities. The student will be responsible for developing a ministry project that combines principles learned with practical ministry. The details of this project are covered on page 12, and will be discussed in the introductory session of the course.

Class and Homework Assignments

Classwork and homework of various types may be given during class by your Mentor or be written in your Student Workbook. If you have any question about what is required by these or when they are due, please ask your Mentor.

Readings

It is important that the student read the assigned readings from the text and from the Scriptures in order to be prepared for class discussion. Please turn in the "Reading Completion Sheet" from your Student Workbook on a weekly basis. There will be an option to receive extra credit for extended readings.

Take-Home Final Exam

At the end of the course, your Mentor will give you a final exam (closed book) to be completed at home. You will be asked a question that helps you reflect on what you have learned in the course and how it affects the way you think about or practice ministry. Your Mentor will give you due dates and other information when the Final Exam is handed out.

Grading

The following grades will be given in this class at the end of the session, and placed on each student's record:

A - Superior work   D - Passing work

B - Excellent work   F - Unsatisfactory work

C - Satisfactory work   I - Incomplete

Letter grades with appropriate pluses and minuses will be given for each final grade, and grade points for your grade will be factored into your overall grade point average. Unexcused late work or failure to turn in assignments will affect your grade, so please plan ahead, and communicate conflicts with your instructor.

Exegetical Project

Purpose

As a part of your participation in the Capstone *Focus on Reproduction* module of study, you will be required to do an exegesis (inductive study) on one of the following passages:

- ❏ Matthew 28.18-20
- ❏ Acts 1.1-8
- ❏ Luke 24.44-48
- ❏ 2 Timothy 2.1-2
- ❏ Romans 10.12-18
- ❏ Matthew 5.13-16
- ❏ Titus 2.11-15
- ❏ Luke 4.16-21

The purpose of this exegetical project is to give you an opportunity to do a detailed study of a major passage on the issue of Christian evangelism and reproduction. Our hope is that in thinking through step by step the insights presented in one of the texts above you will be able to explain critically how God wants us to conceive and conduct ministry that advances his Kingdom in the city. As God-called and enabled men and women, God's desire is that we go forward through the power of the Spirit to bear witness to Christ and his Kingdom where he has placed us. Understanding the nature of this call is fundamental to fulfilling it in the urban community, or wherever God has currently positioned you. As you study one of the above texts (or a text which you and your Mentor agree upon which may not be on the list), our hope is that your analysis of your selected text will make more clear to you how God intends you to bear fruit in ministry, and fruit that remains. We also desire that the Spirit will give you insight as to how you can relate its meaning directly to your own personal walk of discipleship, as well as to the leadership role God has given to you currently in your church and ministry.

Outline and Composition

This is a Bible study project, and, in order to do *exegesis*, you must be committed to understand the meaning of the passage in its own setting. Once you know what it meant, you can then draw out principles that apply to all of us, and then relate those principles to life. A simple three step process can guide you in your personal study of the Bible passage:

1. What was *God saying to the people in the text's original situation*?

2. What principle(s) does *the text teach that is true for all people everywhere*, including today?

3. What is *the Holy Spirit asking me to do with this principle here, today*, in my life and ministry?

Once you have answered these questions in your personal study, you are then ready to write out your insights for your *paper assignment*.

Here is a *sample outline* for your paper:

1. List out what you believe is *the main theme or idea* of the text you selected.

2. *Summarize the meaning* of the passage (you may do this in two or three paragraphs, or, if you prefer, by writing a short verse-by-verse commentary on the passage).

3. *Outline one to three key principles or insights* this text provides on Christian evangelism and church reproduction.

4. Tell how one, some, or all of the principles may relate to *one or more* of the following:

    a. Your personal spirituality and walk with Christ

    b. Your life and ministry in your local church

    c. Situations or challenges in your community and general society

As an aid or guide, please feel free to read the course texts and/or commentaries, and integrate insights from them into your work. Make sure that you give credit to whom credit is due if you borrow or build upon someone else's insights. Use in-the-text references, footnotes, or endnotes. Any way you choose to cite your references will be acceptable, as long as you 1) use only one way consistently throughout your paper, and 2) indicate where you are using someone else's ideas, and are giving them credit for it. (For more information, see *Documenting Your Work: A Guide to Help You Give Credit Where Credit Is Due* in the Appendix.)

Make certain that your exegetical project, when turned in meets the following standards:

- It is legibly written or typed.
- It is a study of one of the passages above.
- It is turned in on time (not late).
- It is 5 pages in length.
- It follows the outline given above, clearly laid out for the reader to follow.
- It shows how the passage relates to life and ministry today.

Do not let these instructions intimidate you; this is a Bible study project! All you need to show in this paper is that you *studied* the passage, *summarized* its meaning, *drew out* a few key principles from it, and *related* them to your own life and ministry.

Grading

The exegetical project is worth 45 points, and represents 15% of your overall grade, so make certain that you make your project an excellent and informative study of the Word.

Ministry Project

Purpose

The Word of God is living and active, and penetrates to the very heart of our lives and innermost thoughts (Heb. 4.12). James the Apostle emphasizes the need to be doers of the Word of God, not hearers only, deceiving ourselves. We are exhorted to apply the Word, to obey it. Neglecting this discipline, he suggests, is analogous to a person viewing our natural face in a mirror and then forgetting who we are, and are meant to be. In every case, the doer of the Word of God will be blessed in what he or she does (James 1.22-25).

Our sincere desire is that you will apply your learning practically, correlating your learning with real experiences and needs in your personal life, and in your ministry in and through your church. Therefore, a key part of completing this module will be for you to design a ministry project to help you share some of the insights you have learned from this course with others.

Planning and Summary

There are many ways that you can fulfill this requirement of your study. You may choose to conduct a brief study of your insights with an individual, or a Sunday School class, youth or adult group or Bible study, or even at some ministry opportunity. What you must do is discuss some of the insights you have learned from class with your audience. (Of course, you may choose to share insights from your Exegetical Project in this module with them.)

Feel free to be flexible in your project. Make it creative and open-ended. At the beginning of the course, you should decide on a context in which you will share your insights, and share that with your instructor. Plan ahead and avoid the last minute rush in selecting and carrying out your project.

After you have carried out your plan, write and turn in to your Mentor a one-page summary or evaluation of your time of sharing. A sample outline of your Ministry Project summary is as follows:

1. Your name
2. The place where you shared, and the audience with whom you shared
3. A brief summary of how your time went, how you felt, and how they responded
4. What you learned from the time

Grading

The Ministry Project is worth 30 points and represents 10% of your overall grade, so make certain to share your insights with confidence and make your summary clear.

Lesson 1

Church Growth
Reproducing in Number and Quality

page 303

Lesson Objectives

page 304

Welcome in the strong name of Jesus Christ! After your reading, study, discussion, and application of the materials in this lesson, you will be able to:

- Defend the idea that the single most critical concept in understanding evangelism, discipleship, and church planting is the lordship of Jesus Christ.

- Show biblically how Jesus as the risen Lord and God's Anointed Messiah has been exalted to the position of head over all things to the Church and Lord of the harvest.

- Recite Scripture that supports that Jesus himself serves as the ground of all missionizing activity, who alone is the Lord who calls his servants to the field and empowers them with his Spirit, determining where he will send them.

- Explain how Jesus as Lord determines what his servants must endure for his name's sake, and how Jesus promises to stand with them to the end of their task.

- Affirm how in all mission, teaching, preaching, and outreach, we must appeal to our Lord Jesus, for he alone enables us to win souls and plant churches in the city.

- Demonstrate from the Bible the way in which radical discipleship is produced and authenticated in Christian community.

- Articulate the three integrated steps of urban church planting: evangelizing the lost, equipping the new disciples to live the Christian life in the context of Christian community – the Church, and empowering the leaders and the community to reproduce itself and associate with other like-minded churches.

- Highlight the ten critical principles drawn from a church planting model from Acts, and apply them to your own church planting efforts in the city.

We Must Obey God Rather Than Men

Acts 5.27-32 - And when they had brought them, they set them before the council. And the high priest questioned them, [28] saying, "We strictly charged you not to teach in this name, yet here you have filled Jerusalem with your teaching, and you intend to bring this man's blood upon us." [29] But Peter and the apostles answered, "We must obey God rather than men. [30] The God of our fathers raised Jesus, whom you killed by hanging him on a tree. [31] God exalted him at his right hand as Leader and Savior, to give repentance to Israel and forgiveness of sins. [32] And we are witnesses to these things, and so is the Holy Spirit, whom God has given to those who obey him."

By whose authority do we have any right to talk to those who do not believe in the "outlandish" claims of Jesus of Nazareth? In a day of political correctness and at a time when religious intolerance is producing horrific acts of violence and terrorism, shouldn't all decent people sort of "simmer down," so to speak, and let everyone merely believe what they believe, without our interference or judgment? Is the time of sharing your faith for the purpose of persuading others to follow your view outmoded, outdated, and simply wrong?

The example of the Apostles is instructive for all men and women called to represent the interests and reputation of our risen Lord before others. In the face of horrible opposition and the threat of severe bodily harm if they continued to share the good news of Christ and his Kingdom, the Apostles remained unmoved. Peter and the Apostles are clear in the face of intimidation and threat: "We must obey God rather than men. The God of our fathers raised Jesus, whom you killed by hanging him on a tree. God exalted him at his right hand as Leader and Savior, to give repentance to Israel and forgiveness of sins. And we are witnesses to these things, and so is the Holy Spirit, whom God has given to those who obey him."

"We must obey God, rather than men." The Great Commission of our Lord, while given to the excited company of witnesses who heard the risen Lord's command to go into all the world and preach the Good News, is a generational command. Until the appearing of our Lord, every Christian generation goes forth into its own Jerusalems, Judeas, and Samarias with the Gospel of the Kingdom. All of us are responsible to share the Gospel to the ends of the earth. Nothing can detract us or intimidate us, for the very same Jesus of Nazareth crucified in Jerusalem so many centuries ago has been exalted. "The God of our fathers raised Jesus, whom you killed by hanging him on a tree. God exalted him at his right hand as Leader and Savior, to give repentance to Israel and forgiveness of sins." Exalted at the right hand of God as Leader and Savior, now repentance and forgiveness is preached to the entire world. To this, both the Apostles and the Holy Spirit testify.

What is the ground of our ministry? Why can we remain unmoved in the face of severe persecution and rejection? Why must we go, even if no one responds? Our God has exalted the Messiah to be Lord and Savior, and in obedience to his command, members of the Church have been going for centuries. Many have died, many have suffered, and many have been persecuted. But not one has been defeated. "God exalted him at his right hand as Leader and Savior . . ."(.) This great Commander will guide us until we die. Until then, we must obey God, rather than men.

Nicene Creed and Prayer

After reciting and/or singing the Nicene Creed (located in the Appendix), pray the following prayer:

God, our heavenly Father, who revealed your love by sending your only Son into the world that all might live through him: grant that by the power of the Spirit your Church may fulfil the command to proclaim to all men the good news of Jesus Christ, and strengthen us in our resolution to work and witness for his kingdom, through Jesus Christ our Lord.

~ The Church of the Province of South Africa. **Minister's Book for Use With the Holy Eucharist and Morning and Evening Prayer**. Braamfontein: Publishing Department of the Church of the Province of South Africa. p. 114.

Quiz

No quiz this lesson

Scripture Memorization Review

No Scripture memorization this lesson

Assignments Due

No assignments due this lesson

Marketing and Godliness Do Mix

In a leader's meeting at a local urban church which was determined to grow, one of the head deacons commented that although their church is a godly church, it simply doesn't know how to market itself to those in the neighborhood. "Let's face it," he says, "the reason that many of the churches in the suburbs are growing is that they are constantly sharing their message and programs with others–they get the word out. And, what's good for the goose is good for the gander. If we want to grow as a church, we are going to have to get better marketing strategies. We can start small, but that's where we have to start. I believe, and you should too, that marketing and godliness do mix." Is this brother correct? What role does marketing play in growing the Church of Jesus Christ?

page 305 4

Not Ready Yet

Hosea is a bright and wonderful new Christian in your church of twenty two years who expresses a deep passion to share the Good News with others. After service one morning you find him looking discouraged. When you ask what is going on, he says in a dejected way, "Oh, its about my feelings lately. Ever since I gave my heart to the Lord about two years ago, I have had this deep burden to be in the Lord's ministry. Not a day goes by without my heart being stirred about the lost. I can't sleep, I cry all the time; early in the morning I am up, pacing, asking the Lord to tell me what he wants me to do. I believe he has called me to the ministry. I shared my burden with Deacon Wilson, and he told me that I was not old enough in the Lord to be put in a position to share the Gospel with others. Not yet, at least. I needed more time in the Word and in the church to prepare myself. I know he is right, but this burden nearly consumes me. What should I do?" How would you answer Hosea?

The Church Turns People Off

You hear of a new Bible study group formed by members of the church who are disgruntled with the way things are going in the church. While they don't intend to leave the church, nor lead a campaign to replace the pastor, they simply don't believe that the church is adequate to bring new converts in. The music is old-fashioned, the services are dry, and the people seem unfriendly. This group formed itself with the intent on being more inviting and appealing to new members. As one of its members recently said, "Our church loves the Lord and the Word, but its got some problems. I fear that new people are going to find us too stiff and unattractive. We formed this church to bring in some excitement. The church turns people off, and we are going to help it out." What do you think about this member's opinion and the formation of the new group?

CONTENT

Church Growth: Reproducing in Number and Quality

Segment 1: The Lordship of Christ Jesus

Rev. Dr. Don L. Davis

Summary of Segment 1

Of all the concepts involved in kingdom work, the single most critical concept in understanding evangelism, discipleship, and church planting is the lordship of Jesus Christ. As Lord of the harvest, our exalted Lord Jesus Christ calls, empowers, and deploys his servants throughout the earth to bear witness to his kingdom reign.

Our objective for this segment, *The Lordship of Christ Jesus*, is to enable you to see that:

- The single most critical concept in understanding evangelism, discipleship, and church planting is the lordship of Jesus Christ.

- Jesus as the risen Lord and God's Anointed Messiah has been exalted to the position of head over all things to the Church and Lord of the harvest.

- Our Lord Jesus himself serves as the ground of all missionizing activity, and he alone is the Lord who calls his servants to the field and empowers them with his Spirit, determining where he will send them.

- The servants of Jesus are called to endure suffering for his name's sake, and Jesus promises to stand with them to the end of their task.

- In all mission, teaching, preaching, and outreach, we appeal to our Lord Jesus, for he alone enables us to win souls and plant churches in the city.

I. **The Ground of Evangelism and Church Growth Is the Risen and Living Lord Jesus Christ (Authority).**

Video Segment 1 Outline

   A. All authority in heaven and earth has been bestowed upon the risen Christ.

      1. Jesus has been *endowed with all authority on high*, Matt. 28.18-20.

      2. The authority of Christ is *total and exhaustive*, Phil. 3.20-21.

      3. He now has assumed *a position of power and prominence* at the Father's right hand, Heb. 1.1-4.

      4. Implications for evangelism and church planting: Messiah Jesus is the *uncontested Lord of the entire universe*, possessing all authority over heaven and earth.

   B. The Father's pleasure is to exalt Jesus to supreme rank and authority.

      1. Jesus has ascended to a position of exaltation because of his voluntary humiliation, Phil. 2.5-11; cf. Phil. 2.9-11.

      2. The Father's good pleasure is that all the fullness of God dwell in the person of Messiah Jesus, Col. 1.15-19.

      3. Jesus' name and glory will be unequaled in this age, as well as the Age to come, Eph. 1.20-23.

4. Implications for evangelism and church planting: Messiah Jesus' high place grows out of *God's intent to exalt him above all others*, save himself.

C. Messiah Jesus has been given absolute authority over the harvest field and the work: he is Lord of the harvest.

1. He alone sends out laborers into the harvest field of God.

    a. Matt. 9.35-38

    b. Matt. 10.1

2. Jesus sends out his workers and laborers with the same kind of mandate, calling, and burden that he had when the Father called him, John 20.20-21.

    a. They are sent with the same *agency and representative authority*.

    b. They are sent with the same *stigma and scandal*.

    c. They are sent with the same *Spirit of power*.

3. Christ's calling is closely associated with his intercession and consultation with the Father, Luke 6.12-13.

4. Implications for evangelism and church planting: church planting and ministry is not a *science of well-schooled techniques*; rather, evangelism and church planting is *a divine calling and burden*.

II. Exalted Now as Lord of the Harvest, Messiah Jesus Determines Who Will Represent Him (Calling).

A. He calls whomsoever he wills.

1. No one can go unless he sends them into his field, Rom. 10.14-15.

2. Apostleship (the gift of evangelism and church planting) is a gift of grace, not an act of effort and scientific mimicry.

    a. Luke 24.46-47

    b. Acts 26.17-18

    c. Rom. 1.5

    d. Titus 1.3

3. Jesus underwrites, sustains, and stands by every person whom he has called to the gospel ministry; *the call guarantees the provision*, 2 Tim. 4.17.

4. Implication for evangelism and church planting: *receiving the call from Jesus Christ is the only assurance the church planter needs of his resources and leading*.

B. The calling and gifts of Messiah Jesus are irrevocable.

1. He never rescinds or takes back his call, Rom. 11.29.

2. He will be faithful to his called ones because of his perfect and impeccable character: *he never turns his back on his promise*, 2 Tim. 2.11-13.

3. Not in a million years will the Lord Jesus fail to empower us with his own presence until the job of church planting is done, Matt. 28.19-20.

4. Implication for evangelism and church planting: Messiah Jesus is both loyal and sovereign; *he never reneges on a promise or turns his back on his servants*.

C. Messiah Jesus ensures that his servants possess all the necessary gifts, opportunities, and grace to accomplish their apostolic and prophetic task.

1. The servant of Christ learns by experience that whatever they need, Messiah Jesus will provide, Phil. 4.11-13.

2. The evangelist and church planter receive the necessary power to accomplish their task only as they stay connected to the Lord Jesus in obedience and communion.

   a. John 15.4-5

   b. John 5.19

3. Through faith in Jesus Christ, God ensures that his servants have all they need to fulfill his will in mission and ministry.

a. Acts 1.8

b. Mic. 3.8

c. Zech. 4.6

d. Luke 10.19

4. Implication for evangelism and church planting: *God calls a woman or man to no task without granting them the power, authority, and ability to accomplish it.*

The Holy Spirit Guides the Apostles' Witness

The same commission introduces a factor of profound importance for the **apostolate**: *the coming of the Spirit. Curiously enough, this is most fully treated in John 14–17, which does not use the word 'apostle' at all. This is the great commissioning discourse of the Twelve (***apostello** *and* **pempo** *are used without discrimination): their commission from Jesus is as real as his from God (cf. John 20.21); they are to bear witness from their long acquaintance with Jesus, yet the Spirit bears witness of him (John 15.26–27). He will remind them of the words of Jesus (John 14.26), and guide them into all the truth (a promise often perverted by extending its primary reference beyond the apostles) and show them the age to come (of the church) and Christ's glory (John 16.13–15). Instances are given in the Fourth Gospel of this process, where the significance of words or actions was recalled only after Christ's 'glorification' (John 2.22; 12.16; cf. 7.39).* **That is, the witness of the apostles to Christ is not left to their impressions and recollections, but to the guidance of the Holy Spirit, whose witness it is also—a fact of consequence in assessing the recorded apostolic witness in the Gospels** *[emphasis mine].*

~ D. R. W. Wood. **New Bible Dictionary**. 3rd ed. Downers Grove, IL: InterVarsity Press, 1996. p. 58.

III. As Lord of the Harvest, Jesus Precisely Determines Where His Messengers Must Go (Location).

A. As Commander-in-chief of the host of God's armies, Messiah Jesus sets apart his own for the work he has called them to do.

1. He selects specific servants among all his servants to do a particular mission, task, or service in his name, Acts 13.1-3.

2. The call of the Lord simultaneously includes a *call to suffering for his name's sake*, Acts 9.13-16.

3. Godly workers are set apart by the Lord for the work of the ministry; evangelism and church planting begin with the Lord's intent.

    a. Acts 22.21

    b. Rom. 1.1

    c. Rom. 10.15

    d. Gal. 1.15

    e. Gal. 2.8-9

4. Jesus supervises the campaign of his submitted servants step by step, Phillip and the Ethiopian eunuch, Acts 8.26-40; cf. Acts 8.26-29.

5. Implication: *our willingness to go* means nothing at all in the spiritual realm *if God does not intend for us to go.*

B. Messiah Jesus exercises authority over places, people, and dominions which have in the past been ravaged by the enemy.

1. The Lord Jesus came to destroy the works of the devil.

    a. 1 John 3.8

    b. Gen. 3.15

    c. Mark 1.24

    d. Rom. 16.20

    e. Heb. 2.14

2. Messiah Jesus can direct his workers wherever he will because he has disarmed and shamed all demonic opposition.

    a. Col. 2.15

    b. Ps. 68.18

    c. Matt. 12.29

d. Luke 10.18

e. John 12.31

3. Jesus is directing his men and women into specific cities, towns, territories, and places to testify of his kingdom reign and proclaim deliverance to the captives.

   a. Acts 1.8

   b. Luke 24.46-49

4. Implication: *as Lord of the harvest, Jesus paves the way by undermining the demonic forces seeking to inhibit his kingdom proclamation to a particular neighborhood, community, town, or city.*

C. Jesus delegates workers to particular people and places at different times at his own bidding and purpose.

1. Jesus' intelligence on the status of his workers is "live:" up-to-the-minute and second, (even nano-second!), Acts 18.5-11.

2. Jesus' leadership of his servants is never based on memory; he is with them, right at the crucial moment of opposition or movement.

   a. 2 Cor. 12.9

   b. 2 Tim. 4.17

c. Acts 23.11

d. Acts 27.23-24

3. Jesus is Lord: his oversight cannot be preempted or questioned, John 21.18-21; cf. v. 21-22.

4. Implication: *Jesus' leadership of the workers of the harvest is personal, absolute, and sufficient.*

IV. As Lord of the Harvest, Jesus Determines What His Messengers Must Endure (Suffering).

A. The servant of Jesus is not greater than Jesus himself (i.e., *the servant can expect hardship because Jesus endured hardship*).

1. The servant is not greater than the one who sent him.

   a. Matt. 10.24-25

   b. Luke 6.40

   c. John 13.16

2. As representatives of Messiah Jesus, we will receive the same response and treatment he would have received if he were there, John 15.20.

3. If the ones to whom we go hate Messiah Jesus, they will hate us as well, John 15.18-25.

4. The ministry of church planting is about being conformed to the image of Jesus, Heb. 12.2-4.

5. Implication: *Jesus alone has called us to endure such suffering, and will enable us to bear much fruit in his name*, John 15.16; 1 Cor. 4.1-5.

B. Those who are chosen to represent Messiah Jesus are appointed to endure suffering for his sake.

1. We are appointed to testify (*maturia*) to the name of Jesus and his Kingdom, *and* to suffer for his name's sake, Acts 9.15.

2. It is given to us who believe not only to believe in Messiah Jesus, but also to suffer for his name's sake.

   a. Phil. 1.29-30

   b. Acts 5.41

   c. Rom. 5.3

   d. 1 Pet. 4.13

3. Everyone living godly in Messiah Jesus will endure suffering.

a. 2 Tim. 3.12

b. Matt. 5.10-12

c. John 17.14

d. Acts 14.22

C. As representatives of Christ and his Kingdom, we must arm ourselves with a mind to suffer on behalf of Messiah Jesus and the Good News.

1. We are to suffer hardship as good soldiers of Jesus Christ, 2 Tim. 2.3.

2. Our sense of sacrifice is informed by our Lord's own willingness to become nothing, to become poor on our behalf.

   a. 2 Cor. 8.9

   b. Phil. 2.5-8

3. In the same way our Lord suffered in his ministry, we are called to arm ourselves with the same attitude and disposition, 1 Pet. 4.1-2.

4. Implication: *we possess the high honor of enduring suffering for the sake of Messiah Jesus and the Good News.*

Conclusion

» God has exalted Jesus as Lord, and as Lord, he alone provides meaning to every phase of our work in evangelism, discipleship, and church planting.

» As the risen Lord and God's Anointed Messiah, Jesus has been exalted to the position of head over all things to the Church and Lord of the harvest.

Segue 1

Student Questions and Response

page 305 5

Please take as much time as you have available to answer these and other questions that the video brought out. The lordship of Jesus Christ is the foundation for all ministry in the city; no other power, idea, concept, or truth can serve as the appropriate ground that authorizes us to share the Good News with our neighbors. A clear understanding of this principle is essential for any biblically-based urban ministry. Be clear and concise in your answers, and where possible, support with Scripture!

1. Why is it so significant for us to affirm that our Lord Jesus Christ is risen and exalted? In what ways does the authority of Jesus make it possible for us to continue the work of witness that started with the Apostles?

2. What does it mean to say that "Messiah Jesus is the uncontested Lord of the entire universe, possessing all authority over heaven and earth"?

3. How would you define the relationship of the Father to Jesus' current rank and authority in heaven? Why is it so critical for us to know and affirm this as we enter into urban ministry?

4. How does Jesus' position as "Lord of the harvest" shape and condition what we are to do in urban ministry today?

5. In what way does Jesus determine who will represent him in kingdom ministry? What is the relationship between being called by Christ to ministry and the assurance that you will have what you need to minister? Explain your answer.

6. What assurances can we have in ministry knowing that Jesus is Lord of the harvest? In other words, what promises about the ministry can we claim as we go forward in obedience to Christ's call to go into all the world and preach the Gospel?

7. What is the relationship of the call of Jesus to minister and the certainty of suffering and persecution with that call? Is it possible to be called to ministry by Christ and not have to endure persecution and suffering of some kind? Explain.

8. In light of the lordship of Jesus Christ over all things today, what kind of implications exist for the man or woman of God as they go forward in their work to evangelize, disciple, and plant churches in the city? What is your level of confidence regarding your own life, your calling, and the lordship of Jesus where you are?

From his study of church planters from several Protestant denominations, Charles Ridley developed a helpful process for determining the probability that a person will succeed in church planting. Denominations across North America use his work to assess their planter candidates. Ridley determined that most successful church planters share thirteen behavioral characteristics. It is the Ridley assessment to which most people refer when they speak of a church-planter assessment.

The Ridley Categories

1. *Visionizing Capacity* is the ability to imagine the future, to persuade other persons to become involved in that dream, and to bring the vision into reality.

2. *Intrinsically Motivated* means that one approaches ministry as a self-starter, and commits to excellence through hard work and determination.

3. *Creates Ownership of Ministry* suggests that one instills in others a sense of personal responsibility for the growth and success of the ministry and trains leaders to reproduce other leaders.

4. *One Who Relates to the Unchurched* develops rapport and breaks through barriers with unchurched people, encouraging them to examine and to commit themselves to a personal walk with God. As an additional outcome, new believers become able to lead others to salvation in Jesus Christ.

5. *Spousal Cooperation* describes a marital partnership by which church planting couples agree on ministry priorities, each partner's role and involvement, and the integration and balance of ministry with family life.

6. *Effectively Builds Relationships* is the skill to take initiative in meeting people and deepen relationships as a basis for more effective ministry.

7. *Starters Committed to Church Growth* value congregational development as a means for increasing the number and quality of disciples. Through this commitment they increase numerical growth in the context of spiritual and relational growth.

8. *Responsiveness to the Community* describes abilities to adapt one's ministry to the culture and needs of the target area residents.

9. *One who Utilizes Giftedness of Others* equips and releases other people to minister on the basis of their spiritual giftedness.

10. *A starter who is Flexible and Adaptable* can adjust to change and ambiguity, shift priorities when necessary, and handle multiple tasks at the same time. This leader can adapt to surprises and emergencies.

11. *Builds Group Cohesiveness* describes one who enables the group to work collaboratively toward common goals, and who skillfully manages divisiveness and disunifying elements.

12. *A Starter who Demonstrates Resilience* shows the ability to sustain himself or herself emotionally, spiritually, and physically through setbacks, losses, disappointments, and failures.

13. *One who Exercises Faith* translates personal convictions into personal and ministry decisions and resulting actions.

Church Growth: Reproducing in Number and Quality

Segment 2: How to Plant an Urban Church that Reproduces: An Overview

Rev. Dr. Don L. Davis

Summary of Segment 2

As disciples called to obey Christ's commission to go and make disciples of all nations, we know that radical discipleship is produced and authenticated only in Christian community. To plant churches is to fulfill the Great Commission, which involves three integrated steps: *Evangelizing* (winning the lost), *Equipping* (establishing new disciples in the Church), and *Empowering* (outfitting leaders and the church to reproduce itself in fellowship with other like-minded churches).

Our objective for this segment, *How to Plant an Urban Church that Reproduces: an Overview*, is to enable you to see that:

- The Word of God teaches that radical discipleship is produced and authenticated only in the context of Christian community.

- To fulfill the Great Commission of the risen Lord Jesus we must plant healthy, Christ-honoring churches among all the peoples of the earth.

- Church planting is made up of three integrated steps of kingdom ministry. The first step is *Evangelize*, where we evangelize the lost by sharing in word and deed the good news of the Kingdom in Jesus Christ.

- The second step is *Equip*, which is establishing new disciples to live the Christian life in the context of Christian community – the Church.

- The third step is *Empower*, which involves resourcing and outfitting the leaders and the congregation of the newly formed church to reproduce itself and associate with other like-minded churches.

- Ten critical principles exist to guide us in our church planting efforts, which are drawn from the apostolic ministry in Acts, and can be readily applied to our own church planting efforts in the city.

- By *evangelizing* the lost, *equipping* new Christians to grow as disciples of Jesus, and *empowering* leaders and churches to reproduce, we can see dozens of solid, healthy churches planted throughout the cities of our nation and world.

I. Evangelize: Share the Good News of Christ and His Kingdom in the Community.

Video Segment 2 Outline

Mark 16.15-18 - And he said to them, "Go into all the world and proclaim the gospel to the whole creation. [16] Whoever believes and is baptized will be saved, but whoever does not believe will be condemned. [17] And these signs will accompany those who believe: in my name they will cast out demons; they will speak in new tongues; [18] they will pick up serpents with their hands; and if they drink any deadly poison, it will not hurt them; they will lay their hands on the sick, and they will recover."

Our work of ministry builds upon the Apostles' work. "The Twelve were chosen that they might be with Christ (Mark 3.14), and this personal association qualified them to act as his witnesses (Acts 1.8); they were from the first endowed with power over unclean spirits and diseases (Matt. 10.1), and this power was renewed and increased, in a more general form, when the promise of the Father (Luke 24.49) came upon them in the gift of the Holy Spirit (Acts 1.8); on their first mission they were sent forth to preach (Mark 3.14), and in the great commission they were instructed to teach all nations (Matt. 28.19). They thus received Christ's authority to evangelize at large. But they were also promised a more specific function as judges and rulers of God's people (Matt. 19.28; Luke 22.29–30), with power to bind and to loose (Matt. 18.18), to remit and to retain sins (John 20.23)."
~D. R. W. Wood. New Bible Dictionary. 3rd ed. Downers Grove, IL: InterVarsity Press, 1996. p. 202.

A. Importance of Evangelism in reproducing urban churches

1. Evangelism is the *centerpiece* of all Christian mission and outreach; the Good News is the power of God to salvation to all who believe, Rom. 1.6-17.

2. No church or church plant that refuses to work tirelessly in sharing the Gospel will be dynamic or healthy.

3. Demonstrating both the power of the Spirit as well as proclaiming the Word of God is essential for effective disciple-making in urban communities.

   a. Signs and wonders of the Holy Spirit, Rom. 15.18-20 "For I will not venture to speak of anything except what Christ has accomplished through me to bring the Gentiles to obedience—by word and deed, [19] by the power of signs and wonders, by the power of the Spirit of God—so that from Jerusalem and all the way around to Illyricum I have fulfilled the ministry of the Gospel of Christ; [20] and thus I make it my ambition to preach the Gospel, not where Christ has already been named, lest I build on someone else's foundation"

   b. Good works which reveal the power of the Kingdom, Matt. 5.13-16

   c. Clear, bold presentations of the good news of the grace of God, Gal. 3.1ff.; 1 Thess. 1.5ff.

B. Keys to *Evangelizing the Lost*

1. Evangelism is *being a herald: it is boldly declaring through word and deed that Jesus is the Messiah, the risen Lord of the Kingdom!*

2. A boldness to engage neighbors with the lifestyle and witness of the Gospel

3. A willingness to befriend and serve the community where God has placed you

4. A focused, unbroken intercessory team that undergirds all the efforts with fervent, faith-filled prayer

C. Stage One: Prepare - *lay the initial foundation for responsible mission and outreach through your prayer, your team, your selection of your target area, and your understanding of the context.*

1. Key texts

    a. Luke 24.46-49

    b. Matt. 28.19-20

2. Basic principle: spend the appropriate time seeking the mind of the Lord and preparing yourselves before you enter into the community to begin your work.

3. Form a church-plant team.

4. Pray.

5. Select a target area and population.

6. Do demographic and ethnographic studies.

D. Stage Two: Launch - *in the name of Jesus, enter into the community to learn, to serve, and to witness of the good news of Christ and his Kingdom in your target area.*

1. Key texts

   a. Acts 1.8

   b. Gal. 2.7-10

2. Basic principles: filled with the Holy Spirit, with knowledge of one another and the people and place to whom God has called them, the team goes forth into the community serving and witnessing in the name of Jesus.

3. Recruit and train volunteers.

4. Conduct evangelistic events and door-to-door evangelism.

II. Equip: Gather the New Disciples into an Assembly and Grow Them to Maturity.

Eph. 4.11-16 - And he gave the apostles, the prophets, the evangelists, the pastors and teachers, [12] to equip the saints for the work of ministry, for building up the body of Christ, [13] until we all attain to the unity of the faith and of the knowledge of the Son of God, to mature manhood, to the measure of the stature of the fullness of Christ, [14] so that we may no longer be children, tossed to and fro by the waves and carried about by every wind of doctrine, by human cunning, by craftiness in deceitful schemes. [15] Rather, speaking the truth in love, we are to grow up in every way into him who is the head, into Christ, [16] from whom the whole body, joined and held together by every joint with which it is equipped, when each part is working properly, makes the body grow so that it builds itself up in love.

A. Importance of *Equipping* in reproducing urban churches

1. The goal is *discipleship*, not conversion, Matt. 28.18-20.

2. Believers grow only as their gifts function together under the direction of the Holy Spirit.

    a. 1 Cor. 12.3-11

    b. 1 Pet. 4.10-11

    c. Rom. 12.3-8

    d. Eph. 4.9-16

3. The Jesus movement is a *communal commitment and journey*, not an individual religion.

4. No relationship to God is sustainable without the body of Christ.

B. Keys to *Equipping believers*

1. Equipping is *parenthood: raising spiritual children to maturity*.

2. Form deep convictions of its importance and place in reproduction.

3. Develop a clear plan on how to proceed.

4. Cultivate a flexible approach that allows the members to meet their own needs through solid leadership and the functioning of the gifts of the Spirit.

C. Stage Three: Assemble - *gather the new converts and small groups together to form a local assembly, announcing to the community the presence of a new Christ-centered fellowship in the neighborhood.*

1. Key texts

    a. Acts 2.41-47

    b. Heb. 10.24-25

2. Basic principle: new and immature believers must gather together as a local assembly to ensure their protection, feeding, fellowship, and care.

3. Form cell groups, Bible studies, etc. to follow up new believers, to continue evangelism, and to identify and train emerging leaders.

4. Announce the birth of a new church to the neighborhood and meet regularly for public worship, instruction and fellowship.

D. Stage Four: Nurture - *through small groups and individual discipleship, strengthen the disciples of Jesus in the basics of the Christian life, Christian community, and church growth.*

1. Key texts

    a. 1 Thess. 2.5-9

    b. 1 Cor. 4.14-15

2. Basic principle: through small groups and individual friendships, corporate worship, and solid teaching and fellowship, new believers are nurtured and equipped to live as disciples of Jesus in the body of Christ.

3. Develop individual and group discipleship.

4. Fill key roles in the church: identify and use spiritual gifts.

III. Empower: Commission Leaders for the Church and Train Them to Reproduce.

Acts 20.28 - Pay careful attention to yourselves and to all the flock, in which the Holy Spirit has made you overseers, to care for the church of God, which he obtained with his own blood.

Acts 20.32 - And now I commend you to God and to the word of his grace, which is able to build you up and to give you the inheritance among all those who are sanctified.

A. Importance of *Empowerment* in reproducing urban churches

1. Reproduction is largely a matter of *laying the right foundation* for the church's ongoing growth and development.

2. Empowerment is *investment*; it involves providing the growing church with all the tools that it needs in order to "take the baton" and continue on the journey.

3. To define empowerment in terms of abandonment is to ensure that it will never go further than its bitterness against those who started the effort.

4. The Holy Spirit must show you who plant the church the difference between *avoiding harmful dependence* and *being stingy and patronizing*.

B. Keys to *Empowering churches to reproduce*

1. Empowerment is investment: identifying, investing in, and releasing leaders to accomplish their own God-given dreams and tasks in the Lord.

a. Investing in *people*

b. Investing in *structures*

c. Investing in *facilities*

d. Investing in *relationships*

2. Seek the mind of the Spirit as to what the best *times* and *means* are to turn the church's affairs over to its leaders.

3. Challenge the assembly from the very beginning that *reproduction*, not *survival* is the goal of the kingdom activity there.

4. Celebrate the church's growth and its right to *fall on its own face for God!*

C. Transition

1. Key texts

a. Titus 1.4-5

b. Acts 14.21-23

2. Basic principle: transferring authority, leadership, and direction over to the leaders and congregation of the church in order that they may continue to reproduce, and associate with other like-minded assemblies for fellowship and challenge

3. Transfer leadership to indigenous leaders so they become self-governing, self-supporting and self-reproducing (appoint elders and pastors).

4. Finalize decisions about denominational or other affiliations.

5. Commission the church.

6. Foster association with World Impact and other urban churches for fellowship, support and mission ministry.

IV. The Pauline Cycle: Hesselgrave's Model of Planting Churches Cross-Culturally

Pauline Precedents from Acts: The Pauline Cycle (The "Pauline Cycle" terminology and stages are taken from David J. Hesselgrave, *Planting Churches Cross-Culturally*. 2nd ed. [Grand Rapids: Baker Book House, 2000]).

A. The importance of Acts in cross-cultural missions

1. The Apostles were the *first cross-cultural urban missionaries.*

2. The churches of the cities of Asia minor were *urban cross-cultural church plants.*

3. The epistles from the Apostles were the *first urban follow-up materials.*

B. The steps to cross-cultural church planting *(note: see how our three principles of "Evangelize, Equip, and Empower" correspond to Hesselgrave's steps)*

1. Missionaries Commissioned: Acts 13.1-4; 15.39-40; Gal. 1.15-16

2. Audience Contacted: Acts 13.14-16; 14.1; 16.13-15; 17.16-19

3. Gospel Communicated: Acts 13.17-41; 16.31; Rom. 10.9-14; 2 Tim. 2.8

4. Hearers Converted: Acts 13.48; 16.14-15; 20.21; 26.20; 1 Thess. 1.9-10

5. Believers Congregated: Acts 13.43; 19.9; Rom. 16.4-5; 1 Cor. 14.26

6. Faith Confirmed: Acts 14.21-22; 15.41; Rom 16.17; Col. 1.28; 2 Thess. 2.15; 1 Tim. 1.3

7. Leadership Consecrated: Acts 14.23; 2 Tim. 2.2; Titus 1.5

8. Believers Commended: Acts 14.23; 16.40; 21.32 (2 Tim. 4.9 & Titus 3.12 by implication)

9. Relationships Continued: Acts 15.36; 18.23; 1 Cor. 16.5; Eph. 6.21-22; Col. 4.7-8

10. Sending Churches Convened: Acts 14.26-27; 15.1-4

C. Ten Principles of cross-cultural urban church planting

1. *Jesus is Lord*. (Matt. 9.37-38) All church plant activity is made effective and fruitful under the watch care and power of the Lord Jesus, who himself is the Lord of the harvest.

2. *Evangelize, Equip, and Empower unreached people to reach people.* (1 Thess. 1.6-8) Our goal in reaching others for Christ is not only for solid conversion but also for dynamic multiplication; those who are reached must be trained to reach others as well.

3. *Be inclusive: whosoever will may come.* (Rom. 10.12) No strategy should forbid any person or group from entering into the Kingdom through Jesus Christ by faith.

4. *Be culturally neutral: come just as you are.* (Col. 3.11) The Gospel places no demands on any seeker to change their culture as a prerequisite for coming to Jesus; they may come just as they are.

5. *Avoid a fortress mentality.* (Acts 1.8) The goal of missions is not to create an impregnable castle in the midst of an unsaved community, but a dynamic outpost of the Kingdom which launches a witness for Jesus within and unto the very borders of their world.

6. *Continue to evangelize to avoid stagnation.* (Rom. 1.16-17) Keep looking to new horizons with the vision of the Great Commission in mind; foster an environment of aggressive witness for Christ.

7. *Cross racial, class, gender, and language barriers.* (1 Cor. 9.19-22) Use your freedom in Christ to find new, credible ways to communicate the kingdom message to those farthest from the cultural spectrum of the traditional church.

8. *Respect the dominance of the receiving culture.* (Acts 15.23-29) Allow the Holy Spirit to incarnate the vision and the ethics of the Kingdom of God in the words, language, customs, styles, and experience of those who have embraced Jesus as their Lord.

9. *Avoid dependence.* (Eph. 4.11-16) Neither patronize nor be overly stingy towards the growing congregation; do not underestimate the power of the Spirit in the midst of even the smallest Christian community to accomplish God's work in their community.

10. *Think reproducibility.* (2 Tim. 2.2; Phil. 1.18) In every activity and project you initiate, think in terms of equipping others to do the same by maintaining an open mind regarding the means and ends of your missionary endeavors.

V. Last Word: the Fastest, Most Productive, and Most Biblical Method of World Evangelization and Discipleship Is to Plant Churches Cross-Culturally!

Conclusion

» Planting churches in obedience to the Great Commission of Christ involves three basic stages: *Evangelize*, *Equip*, and *Empower*.

» As we *evangelize* the lost, we share the Good News with those who have not heard of God's saving work in Jesus.

» We *equip* new disciples to live the Christian life by laying a foundation for solid Christian community for years to come.

» We *empower* leaders and the church for independence, helping them to reproduce themselves while associating with other like-minded churches.

Segue 2

Student Questions and Response

The following questions were designed to help you review the material in the second video segment. The Great Commission of the Lord Jesus means that we are called to go to all nations making disciples in his name. We fulfill the Great Commission as we plant healthy, viable churches among the various people groups of the world. We accomplish this through *Evangelizing*, *Equipping*, and *Empowering*. Your ability to understand and apply these principles can be all the difference in ministering effectively in urban poor communities, so your ability to understand and articulate them is important. Answer the questions thoroughly, and always support your thinking with Scripture.

1. Why can it be said that "evangelism is the centerpiece of all Christian mission and outreach?" Why is merely demonstrating the Gospel in good deeds not entirely sufficient to kingdom ministry?

2. What role did signs and wonders of the Holy Spirit play in the ministry of the apostles in testifying to the grace of God? What role can or should they play in our work today in the city?

3. What precisely is the Gospel that we are called to bear witness to in our ministry? How did your lesson summarize the church planting process through the acrostic PLANT? What do the letters refer to?

4. What is the definition of the "Prepare" step of church planting in the *Evangelism* stage? Correspondingly, what is the meaning of the "Launch" phase of church planting in the *Evangelism* stage? What is included in each, and what are the kinds of activities associated with each of these stages?

5. Why is equipping new Christians in the faith such a critical step in all true disciple making? What role does the local church play in the discipling of the new convert to Christ? What are the keys to equipping believers to live the Christian life?

6. Explain the "Assemble" and "Nurture" phases of church planting in urban ministry, and correlate how these phases enables us to *Equip* new believers to grow in Christ. How are they the same, how do they differ, and what is involved in each?

7. Why is it important for churches to constantly seek to reproduce themselves through continued evangelism and equipping of others? What is the relationship between spiritual health and spiritual fruit?

8. Explain the "Transition" phase of *Empowerment*. How is empowerment essentially an "investment" in the leadership and membership of the new church?

9. What are the three "selfs" of the "Transition" phase of urban church planting? Outline briefly Hesselgrave's model of planting churches cross-culturally. How do the three-self understanding, in the Hesselgrave model, and the three E's of church planting connect to one another?

10. Summarize briefly the ten principles of cross-cultural church planting. Do you agree with the statement that "the fastest, most productive, and most biblical method of world evangelization and discipleship is to plant churches cross-culturally?" Explain your answer.

CONNECTION

Summary of Key Concepts

page 306 6

This lesson focuses upon providing you with a general overview of the critical theology, methodology, and perspective in doing effective urban ministry. In order to be most effective in advancing the Kingdom of God in the city, we as his called servants must understand carefully and precisely what God is doing in the world through the proclamation of the Gospel. The Father has exalted Jesus to his right hand as Lord and Savior, and now, through the Spirit, the Gospel is bring proclaimed throughout the earth. As we plant healthy, viable churches of Jesus Christ in the city through *evangelism*, *equipping*, and *empowerment* we can see men and women, boys and girls be converted, grow, and become fruitful witnesses of the Kingdom of Christ where they live, play, and work.

- The most foundational theological concept that grounds all of our understanding of evangelism, discipleship, and church planting in the city is the lordship of Jesus Christ.

- Because Jesus has been exalted to the Father's right hand as risen Lord and anointed Messiah, he now holds the position of head over all things, not only to the Church but also to the advance of the Kingdom in the world, as Lord of the harvest.

- The primacy of Jesus' position ensures that Jesus alone serves as the final ground of all missionizing activity. As the Lord of heaven, the exalted Jesus is he who calls men and women to represent his Kingdom throughout the earth. He calls them to the particular fields of service where they live and work, and he alone empowers them with his Spirit.

- As Lord of all, Jesus is in charge of every dimension of his servant's ministry, determining where he will send them, as well as what his servants must endure for his name's sake. He has assured his servants that he will stand with and by them to the end of their task.

- In every phase and dimension of mission, teaching, preaching, and outreach, we must appeal to our Lord Jesus for aid and direction, for he alone can enable us to win souls and plant churches in the city.

- The Great Commission of Christ is a call to go and make disciples of the nations, and this radical discipleship cannot be produced and proven valid apart from the Christian community.

- An effective church planting strategy can be summarized in the PLANT acrostic: prepare, launch, assemble, nurture, and transition. These phases are included within three integrated stages: *evangelizing* the lost, *equipping* the new disciples to live the Christian life in the church, and *empowering* the leaders and the community to reproduce itself and associate with other like-minded churches.

- The principles of cross-cultural church planting underwrite our efforts to minister among the poor in the city. Drawn from the apostles' experience outlined in Acts, these principles make plain the critical insights of effective urban ministry. They include affirming that Jesus is Lord, the challenge to evangelize, equip, and empower unreached people to reach people, and the need to be inclusive, culturally neutral, and to cross racial, class, gender, and language barriers to make the Gospel of the Kingdom plain to those who we seek to reach.

Student Application and Implications

page 307 7

Now is the time for you to discuss with your fellow students your questions about church growth and reproduction. To grapple with these concepts, we must seek the integrated nature of effective urban ministry. We evangelize with a mind to equip the new believers in the faith, and equip with a commitment to empower these same growing Christians to share their faith with others. As you reflect on these stages and ideas, what particular questions have come to mind? Explore your own questions, as you reflect on those below.

* Why is the teaching regarding the lordship of Christ so extremely foundational for any valid perspective of ministry or outreach of the Gospel? What is your understanding and application of this important doctrine in your life today? Explain.

* Have you sensed from the Lord a call to minister the Gospel? How and in what way? If you have sensed such a call, when did you first realize that he had called you to such a ministry?

* How would you describe your ability to trust in the lordship of Christ during times of difficulty, persecution, and trouble? Are you a worrier, that is, do you fret over the various dimensions of your life and ministry? How might an application of the doctrine of Christ help you overcome your fears and anxieties in these areas?

* What about the PLANT process seems most clear to you? What in the acrostic seems least clear? Have you ever considered the possibility that God might want you to be involved in planting new churches for him? Why or why not?

* Discuss the truthfulness and biblical validity of the following statement: "The fastest, most productive, and most biblical method of world evangelization and discipleship is to plant churches cross-culturally." Do you agree with this statement? Why or why not?

* Of the three broad areas of urban ministry (*Evangelize, Equip*, and *Empower*), which do you feel most drawn to and gifted to do? Are you part of a fellowship that emphasizes these principles in a practical way in your worship, life, and fellowship together?

* Do you feel comfortable in crossing barriers (class, race, gender, language, etc.) in sharing the good news of Christ and his Kingdom with others?

* How burdened are you to share the Gospel with your family, friends, and coworkers? What is the greatest obstacle for you to overcome in being a better witness for Christ among those with whom you live and work?

* Which of the ten cross-cultural principles most directly affects and influences your life situation right now? How might you apply this principle more directly in your own life and ministry today?

Giving People a Little More Incentive

page 308 8

(Adapted from a true story) One church, in an effort to get more people interested and involved in their growing church, determined to give visitors a little more incentive to come to their Sunday services. The church began to advertise to the public that every Sunday after service they would be conducting a raffle where the lucky winner could win as much as $800! When asked about the advisability of such a tactic, those involved said, "Why shouldn't we use any means at our disposal to lure and woo people to a service that will not merely promise a handful of dollars but the eternal treasures of life in Jesus Christ?" Not only was the raffle successful, increasing the number of worshipers in the service, it has emboldened the church to think of even bigger and better "lures" to get the lost to come hear the Good News. What is right or wrong in such an approach to church growth?

God Is in This

Without the authorization of any parent church or ministry, a dear couple determined to follow through on a burden they had had for some time. In an act of courage and faith, they began a Bible study with an intent to plant a church that would be self-sufficient and godly. God has blessed their effort; in less than two years they have grown to a robust congregation of 300 active members, all who love the Lord and the "first family" of the pastor with their whole hearts. A gentle strife has been brewing lately, because a group feels more and more that the authority of the pastor and his wife seem almost absolute and dictatorial; nothing can be done or decided in the church without their involvement and endorsement. Some are suggesting that this goes against the teaching of the Bible on the lordship of Jesus, who is the Church's one true and only head. If the church asked you to give a teaching on this, how would you advise them to apply the lordship of Jesus to their situation?

Let's Start Our Own Service

In a growing but small urban church, the young people are completely frustrated with the traditional congregational services. Although the pastor's teaching is fresh and edifying, and the believers in the church are loving and caring, the styles embraced in the services are so traditional and old fashioned that many of the young people coming to the church feel left out and alienated. The pastor, affirming our freedom in Christ, wants the young people to start their own service. His argument is clear: "Since the Gospel can overcome any barrier of culture or class or race, there is no reason why we can't overcome barriers of custom, music, and tradition, too." Some think this kind of teaching will lead to a compromise of the Gospel, and soon the leadership team will begin to discuss this possibility. How would you advise the leadership team to approach this issue in the church?

Charity Begins at Home

The senior pastor has been in ongoing discussion with the leaders of the church about a new proposal that is causing much discussion throughout the church. Rather than moving to a larger building outside of the "needy neighborhood" where the church has been for the last ten years, the pastor wants to stay. His proposal is not to go to a bigger building, but rather equip members of the church to go and plant another church in the same neighborhood. The pastor, explaining the power of church planting to win new disciples to Christ, affirms his belief that no method is more biblical or faster. Those on the other side, while not rejecting church planting, want to have a strong, central church that can be better able to plant new churches if the "mother church" is strong. After all, they argue, charity should begin at home. If you were the associate pastor of the church, how would you seek to resolve the brewing conflict over methods?

The most foundational theological concept that grounds all of our understanding of evangelism, discipleship, and church planting in the city is the lordship of Jesus Christ. Because Jesus has been exalted to the Father's right hand as risen Lord and anointed Messiah, he now holds the position of head over all things, not only to the Church but also to the advance of the Kingdom in the world, as Lord of the harvest. Every dimension of ministry is subject to his direction and power.

The Great Commission of Christ is a call to go and make disciples of the nations, and this radical discipleship cannot be produced and proven valid apart from the Christian community. We can summarize that process for church planting in the PLANT acrostic: prepare, launch, assemble, nurture, and transition. Three stages connect these phases: evangelizing the lost, equipping new disciples to live the Christian life in the Church, and empowering leaders and the congregation to reproduce itself and associate with other like-minded churches.

Restatement of the Lesson's Thesis

page 308 9

The wisdom of the principles drawn from the apostles' experience outlined in Acts provide us with critical insights for effective urban ministry. They include affirming that Jesus is Lord, the challenge to evangelize, equip, and empower unreached people to reach people, and the need to be inclusive, culturally neutral, and to cross racial, class, gender, and language barriers to make the Gospel of the Kingdom plain to those whom we seek to reach.

Resources and Bibliographies

If you are interested in pursuing some of the ideas of *Church Growth: Reproducing in Number and Quality*, you might want to give these books a try:

Ellul, Jacques. *The Presence of the Kingdom*. New York: Seabury Press, 1967.

Garrison, David. *Church Planting Movements*. Bangalore, India: WIGTake Resources, 2004.

Hopler, Thom. *A World of Difference*. Downers Grove, IL: InterVarsity Press, 1981.

Pippert, Rebecca Manley. *Out of the Saltshaker and Into the World*. Downers Grove, IL: InterVarsity Press, 1979.

Ministry Connections

Now is your time to address the meaning of these doctrinal and theological insights to your own personal life situation as well as to your own very real practical ministry connection. Think in terms of what you want to meditate on, reconsider, and pray for throughout this upcoming week.

Specifically, what does it appear that the Holy Spirit is stirring within you as a result of your reflection, study, and discussion on the nature of the lordship of Christ, the Great Commission to go and make disciples of all the nations, and your own contribution to that? In what way do you feel called to contribute today to the call to make disciples of Jesus, in your family, in your church, in the neighborhood, or on the job? Do you sense a more formal calling to the Gospel ministry in your life, in other words, has or is God calling you to make the ministry your full time vocation? With whom might you share this desire and burden? What specifically have you done so far to articulate your burden to your pastor and spiritual leaders, to your husband or wife, to your friends and relatives? How might you personally give time, talent, or treasure to the mission of planting churches, both in your community, through your church, or even overseas? Is God calling you to consider a change in your employment, your schedule or life direction to pursue something more in sync and in line with presenting the Gospel to the lost?

If God is not suggesting these kinds of changes to you, how might you so apply these teachings to your life so you can become a more effective disciple maker for the Lord Jesus? Is the Holy Spirit placing a particular situation on your mind regarding how you might apply this teaching in your life today? Think prayerfully about these and related questions, and ask the Spirit to make plain to you his challenges for you to consider and respond to on this lesson topic.

As we seek our part in this great work of fulfilling the Great Commission, it will be necessary for us to be prayerful, even practicing the discipline of fasting and meditation in order to give God the opportunity to speak to our hearts more clearly. Make sure that you ask your mentor and colleagues to pray for specific leading and direction in your life as you pursue more and more practical ways in which you can join this grand effort to make Jesus known in all the places which have yet to hear of his loving grace and coming Kingdom. Set aside time to pray specifically to the Lord for guidance and wisdom as you pursue your calling under Christ to advance his Kingdom in the place and position where you are now. Be open to a new journey and a new future, even as you yield to the leading of the Spirit on these issues.

Counseling and Prayer

page 309 10

ASSIGNMENTS

Matthew 28.18-20 and Acts 1.8

Scripture Memory

To prepare for class, please visit *www.tumi.org/books* to find next week's reading assignment, or ask your mentor.

Reading Assignment

Your work begins in earnest for the next lesson, so do not procrastinate or seek to cram your work at the last minute. Give yourself enough time to concentrate on the reading so you can glean the concepts we will consider next week. Furthermore,

Other Assignments

page 309 11

stay up on your memorization work, and review carefully the materials from this week in preparation for your upcoming quiz. Again, your quiz next session will concentrate upon *the actual video content and outline covered in this lesson*. So, make certain that you spend time covering your notes, especially focusing on the main ideas of the lesson.

Please read the assigned reading, and summarize each reading with no more than a paragraph or two for each. Keep your summary concise and simple; please give your best understanding of what you think was the main point in each of the readings. Do not be overly concerned about giving detail, but rather write out what you consider to be the main point discussed in that section of the book. Please bring these summaries to class next week. (Please see the "Reading Completion Sheet" at the end of this lesson.)

Looking Forward to the Next Lesson

In this lesson we examined how the lordship of Jesus Christ conditions and provides meaning to every phase of our work in evangelism, discipleship, and church planting. We also looked at the PLANT process of urban church planting, summarized in the three stages of church planting: *Evangelizing*, *Equipping*, and *Empowering*. In our next lesson, we will turn again to evangelism, and speak about how to win urbanites in the context of their circle of influence and family, *the principle of oikos*, or household evangelism. An *oikos* is that web of common kinship relationships, friendships, and associations that make up a person's larger social circle. We will see how revolutionary this concept can be as we strive to make impacts on the lost in the city.

Capstone Curriculum

Module 12: Focus on Reproduction
Reading Completion Sheet

Name _____

Date _____

For each assigned reading, write a brief summary (one or two paragraphs) of the author's main point. (For additional readings, use the back of this sheet.)

Reading 1

Title and Author: _____ Pages _____

Reading 2

Title and Author: _____ Pages _____

LESSON 2

Planting Urban Churches
Sowing

page 311

Lesson Objectives

Welcome in the strong name of Jesus Christ! After your reading, study, discussion, and application of the materials in this lesson, you will be able to:

- Recite and defend with Scripture the most significant concept in urban evangelism today: *the principle of oikos*, or household evangelism, including the idea of an *oikos* as that web of common kinship relationships, friendships, and associations that make up a person's larger social circle.

- List out clearly the more difficult challenges involved in urban evangelism (including broken family units, economic underdevelopment, alienation and loneliness, drug abuse, violence, housing shortages, and general despair).

- Demonstrate the concept of *oikos* in the NT, and explain how this concept was critical in the early church's conception of penetrating larger social units with the Gospel.

- Explore the relationship of *oikos* to identity as members of the family of God, and examine the significance of the relationship of *oikos* to evangelism and church planting in the New Testament.

- Detail the kind of *oikos* relationships (i.e., that web of common kinship relationships, friendships, and associations that make up a person's larger social circle) that exist in our urban communities, and how critical this concept is for penetrating the circle of influence of city residents today.

- Articulate the central benefits for *oikos* evangelism in the city, and relate these strategies to our evangelistic methods as we launch incarnationally into the community with the Gospel.

Devotion

You and Your Household

page 312

Acts 16.19-34 - But when her owners saw that their hope of gain was gone, they seized Paul and Silas and dragged them into the marketplace before the rulers. [20] And when they had brought them to the magistrates, they said, "These men are Jews, and they are disturbing our city. [21] They advocate customs that are not lawful for us as Romans to accept or practice." [22] The crowd joined in attacking them, and the magistrates tore the garments off them and gave orders to beat them with rods. [23] And when they had inflicted many blows upon them, they threw them into prison, ordering the jailer to keep them safely. [24] Having received this order, he put them into the inner prison and fastened their feet in the stocks. [25] About midnight Paul and Silas were praying and singing hymns to God, and the prisoners were listening to them, [26] and suddenly there was a great earthquake, so that the foundations of the prison were shaken. And immediately all the doors were opened, and everyone's bonds were unfastened. [27] When the jailer woke and saw that the prison doors were open, he drew his sword and was about to kill himself, supposing that the prisoners had escaped. [28] But Paul cried with a loud voice, "Do not harm yourself, for we are all here." [29] And the jailer called for lights and rushed in, and trembling with fear he fell down before Paul and Silas. [30] Then he brought them out and said, "Sirs, what must I do to be saved?" [31] And they said, "Believe in the Lord Jesus, and you will be saved, you and your household." [32] And they spoke the word of the Lord to him and to all who were in his house. [33] And he took them the same hour of the night and washed their wounds; and he was baptized at once, he and all his family. [34] Then he brought them up into his house and set food before them. And he rejoiced along with his entire household that he had believed in God.

This story is the last episode of Paul and Silas' witness in the region of Macedonia, and in the leading city of that region, Philippi. As a result of their effective ministry there, with the first convert in Europe (Lydia and her "household," *oikos*, Acts 16.14ff.), they ran into trouble with false accusations of religious profiteers, and were thrown into prison. After being beaten by the jailer with "many blows," they were thrown into prison with feet bound in stocks. Around midnight they were praying and singing hymns of praise to God, with prisoners listening on, and suddenly a great earthquake shook the foundations of the prison house. All the doors opened and everyone's chains were unfastened – the power of prayer and praise of God's servants in trouble!

When the jailer awoke and saw all this and was about to draw his sword (he thought to kill himself thinking that the prisoners had escaped), Paul cried out with a loud voice for him not to harm himself for "we are all here!" The jailer called for lights, fell before Paul and Silas, and after bringing them out of the prison, asked them what he needed to do to be saved. Paul and Silas' answer is as potent today as those centuries ago: "Believe in the Lord Jesus, and you will be saved, you and your household."

Simple faith in the risen Lord Jesus is sufficient to deliver us from wrath, break the power of condemnation and guilt, justify us before God as righteous, and ensure us of eternal life, commencing from the moment we declare Jesus Lord of all, and Lord over our lives. Paul and Silas spoke the word of God to the jailer, and to all the members of his *oikos*, that network of family, friends, and associates connected to the jailer through trusting relationships and ongoing contact. Not only did the jailer repent and believe on the Lord Jesus, being baptized by Paul and Silas, but "all his household" as well. They ate together that night, rejoicing as an *oikos* that they had believed in God. In one meeting, the entire family, friendship, and associate network of the jailer entered the Kingdom through faith in Jesus Christ.

This incident is the safe, easiest, and most effective way for the Gospel to spread. Every human being is connected by birth, proximity, and relationship to a network of people who know them, are associated with them, and who recognize them. These networks represent the "fabric of our lives," the web of relationships that provide us with identity, friendship, and connection. This story illustrates the power of the Gospel to penetrate society, and reveals how the Good News spreads through the work of the apostles. Through their web of influence, their network of relationships, the Good News touched every strata of society, every corner of the Roman empire. We marvel at the work of God through the apostles, as we should. We also should look carefully at the natural, spontaneous, and very real way the Gospel spreads–along the lines of real family, friendships, and associates.

Who is in your *oikos* network today? Of what family are you a part? Who are those neighbors and friends you know who need the Savior? What coworkers and associates do you know need the love of God in their lives? As we walk with Christ, may he give us courage, grace, and opportunity to speak with those kinfolk, friends, neighbors, and coworkers who belong to our *oikos*, and may he grace us, that salvation will have not only come to us, but to us and our households, to the glory of God through Jesus Christ.

After reciting and/or singing the Nicene Creed (located in the Appendix), pray the following prayer:

> *Almighty God, your blessed Son before his passion prayed for his disciples that they might be one, as you and he are one. Grant that your church, being bound together in love and obedience to you, may be united in one body by the one Spirit, that the world may believe in him whom you have sent, your Son Jesus Christ our Lord; who lives and reigns with you in the unity of the Holy Spirit, one God, now and forever. Amen.*
>
> ~ Presbyterian Church (U.S.A.) and Cumberland Presbyterian Church. The Theology and Worship Ministry Unit. **Book of Common Worship**. Louisville: Westminister/John Knox Press, 1993. p. 337.

Nicene Creed and Prayer

Put away your notes, gather up your thoughts and reflections, and take the quiz for Lesson 1, *Church Growth: Reproducing in Number and Quality*.

Quiz

Review with a partner, write out and/or recite the text for last class session's assigned memory verses: Matthew 28.18-20 and Acts 1.8.

Scripture Memorization Review

Turn in your summary of the reading assignment for last week, that is, your brief response and explanation of the main points that the authors were seeking to make in the assigned reading (Reading Completion Sheet).

Assignments Due

CONTACT

A Prophet Is Honored, Except at Home

Some have believed and taught, based on the saying of our Lord's teaching in Matthew 13.57 - "And they took offense at him. But Jesus said to them, 'A prophet is not without honor except in his hometown and in his own household.'" Their application goes something like this: the hardest people to reach with the Gospel are those members of our own families and those in our own households. Because they have seen us as we are, they find it doubly difficult to listen to us share the transformation that our Lord has brought in our lives. Do you believe this particular argument? Would you say that this is a correct teaching of Scripture regarding the difficulty of reaching those in our own families with the Gospel of Christ?

Effective Evangelism: Which Method Works Best?

> While many churches spend many dollars and hours investing in methods that focus on contacting "strangers" with the Gospel through programs, visitation, and outreaches, the evidence shows more and more that the vast majority of people come to Christ through those who are nearby–friends, family, and associates. What is your opinion about using methods of evangelism that emphasize contact with people who are "total strangers," rather than seeking to help members share the Good News with people in their "webs of influence?"

I Don't Know Anybody around Here

> More and more urban communities are disconnected in terms of friendships and contacts. It is common to find people living in a neighborhood and not a single person in their *relational network* live in the physical community where they live. Most of their significant relationships, those who make up their web of kinship, friendship, and affiliation and association, do not actually live on their block or even in their community. What should these facts about the pattern of relationships that are becoming so common in urban communities suggest about what we think about when we want to plant a *neighborhood* church, or encourage members to ask their *family, friends, and neighbors* to come to their church? How might we need to change the way in which we think about "church" and "outreach" for our urban church members?

CONTENT ▶ Planting Urban Churches: Sowing

Segment 1: Introducing the Concept of *Oikos* in Urban Evangelism

Rev. Dr. Don L. Davis

Summary of Segment 1

God has granted us his wisdom in pursuing effective evangelistic strategies in the city. In connection to the various ways we can win others to Christ in the most natural and personal way, one of the key concepts deals with *the principle of oikos*, or household evangelism. An *oikos* is a web of common kinship relationships, friendships, and associations that make up a person's larger social circle. Winning others in the context of their *oikos* is an effective means to share the Good News with the lost in the city.

Our objective for this segment, *Introducing the Concept of **Oikos** in Urban Evangelism*, is to enable you to see that:

- In regard to outreach and methods of sharing the Good News in the city, one of the key concepts deals with *the principle of oikos*, or household evangelism. An *oikos* is a web of common kinship relationships, friendships, and associations that make up a person's larger social circle.

- Urban communities are faced with difficult challenges that must be taken into account as we strategize to engage in urban evangelism (including broken family units, economic underdevelopment, alienation and loneliness, drug abuse, violence, housing shortages, and general despair).

- The concept of *oikos* in the NT is significant, explaining not only the Church of God as the *family of God* but also as the most common term for *family unit*.

- The meaning of *oikos* is fuller than our modern day notion of family (i.e., father, mother, and children), but included blood relatives, other dependents (including slaves, employees, and "clients," among others), as well as those whom the head of the household patronized and protected.

- The outreach in the NT expanded along the lines of the *oikos*; evangelism was done in conjunction with this structure, and became the primary structure for worship, discipleship, and outreach. The *oikos* was actually considered a "church" if its members came to faith in the Lord Jesus.

- In the same way that the *oikos* laid the foundation for evangelism in the early church, it likewise can become a key to spreading the Gospel in the urban community.

I. Go and Make Disciples . . . in the 'Hood'

Matt. 28.18-20 - And Jesus came and said to them, "All authority in heaven and on earth has been given to me. [19] Go therefore and make disciples of all nations, baptizing them in the name of the Father and of the Son and of the Holy Spirit, [20] teaching them to observe all that I have commanded you. And behold, I am with you always, to the end of the age."

Video Segment 1 Outline

A. The traits of today's urban poor neighborhoods: *communities of distrust and suspicion*

"Everybody's got a game, and if you don't watch out, they'll play it on you!"

1. Broken, disconnected, and disjointed family units

2. Economic underdevelopment

3. Alienation and loneliness

4. Violence and crime

5. Over crowding and shortage of affordable housing

6. General sense of despair and distrust

B. The challenge of urban cross-cultural church planting

1. The question of the hour: *how do we contact people within their own setting with credibility and openness in an environment saturated with distrust, fear, and alienation?*

2. The answer: *the natural penetration of the Gospel through the **oikos** of our neighbors*

C. The concept of Evangelism and *oikos*

1. The PLANT acrostic corresponds to the five stages of urban cross-cultural church planting (i.e., prepare, launch, assemble, nurture, transition).

2. Evangelism deals with the *Prepare* and *Launch* stages of the effort.

3. Awareness of the PLANT model is beneficial.

    a. It is *biblically informed*.

    b. It is *easy to memorize*.

    c. It is *reproducible*.

4. *Oikos* relates to the most effective way we can engage urban neighborhoods in credible and effective outreaches of the Gospel.

II. What Is "Family" Called in the New Testament?

A. *Patria*: the family of our historical descent, our physical and parental lineage

1. Joseph is of the *patria* of David, Luke 2.4.

2. All the families (*patria*) of the earth will be blessed in Abraham, cf. Acts 3.25.

3. God as Father, from whom the entire (*patria*) in heaven and earth are named Eph. 3.14-15

4. God has placed all human beings in a *patria*, a network of relationships and kinship that is constituted by our *physical and parental lineage*.

B. The Church of God as the family of God

Gal. 3.25-29 - But now that faith has come, we are no longer under a guardian, [26] for in Christ Jesus you are all sons of God, through faith. [27] For as many of you as were baptized into Christ have put on Christ. [28] There is neither Jew nor Greek, there is neither slave nor free, there is neither male nor female, for you are all one in Christ Jesus. [29] And if you are Christ's, then you are Abraham's offspring, heirs according to promise.

1. Our "natural" state before our sonship and daughterhood in the Father through Christ

    a. Children of the devil

        (1) John 8.44

        (2) 1 John 3.10

    b. Children of wrath, Eph. 2.1-3

    c. Children of disobedience, Col. 3.6

    d. Children of Adam, Rom. 5.12-21

2. We share in God's DNA: entrance into the family of God, John 1.12-13.

3. The living instrumentality of the Word of God as that by which we are born from above, 1 Pet. 1.22-25

4. The repentance and faith of the Christian *as the means by which we were born*, Acts 2.38-39

5. The regeneration (rebirth) of the Holy Spirit, Titus 3.4-7

6. Implication: *the picture of the family is one of the central figures of the Spirit to describe the process of repentance, faith, and new birth in Christ.*

C. *Oikos*: the most common term for "family"

1. *Oikos* (Greek) = *bayit* (Hebrew) = *familia* (Latin)

2. Family as household, as social unit, including blood relatives of the head of the house, as well as other dependents (i.e., slaves, employees, and "clients" [freedmen, friends, and others who looked to the head of the household for patronage, benefaction, advancement, or protection])

3. *Oikia* (plural of *oikos*) is also used to signify the property or substance of a particular household.

    a. Mark 10.29

    b. Mark 12.40

4. *Oikos* corresponds today to the entire network of relationships that we have in our immediate and extended families, our friendships, those connected to our web of contacts and associations.

III. What Is the Relationship of the Household (*Oikos*) to Evangelism and Church Planting in the New Testament?

A. *Oikia* is the most significant structure in early church development.

1. The Jerusalem church worshiped, was organized, and discipled in the *oikia*.

    a. Acts 2.46

    b. Acts 5.42

    c. Acts 12.12

2. Evangelism was done in conjunction with the presentation of the Gospel to the entire household (*oikos*), e.g., Cornelius and his household, Acts 10-11; cf. Acts 10.24.

B. The nucleus of most of Paul's missionary planted churches were made up of one or more households (*oikia*).

1. The households of Lydia and the jailer at Philippi

    a. Acts 16.15

    b. Acts 16.31-34

2. The households of Stephanas, Crispus, and Gaius at Corinth

    a. Acts 18.8

    b. Rom. 16.23

    c. 1 Cor. 1.14-16

    d. 1 Cor. 16.15

3. The households of Priscilla and Aquila, as well as Onesiphorus at Ephesus

    a. 1 Cor. 16.19

    b. 2 Tim. 1.16

    c. 2 Tim. 4.19

4. The household of Philemon at Colossae, Philem. 1.1-2

5. The household of Nympha at Laodicea, Col. 4.15-16

6. The household and Aristobolus, Narcissus, and others at Rome, Rom. 16.10-11

C. Evidence exists that households, once converted to Jesus and his Kingdom, could themselves constitute a church.

1. Note the Pauline language "the church (*ekklesia*) which meets in their house (*oikos*)," Rom.16.3-5

2. The different classifications included in the "household codes" in Ephesians and Colossians—husband and wife, parents and children, master and slave—are those who would be a part of a single New Testament *household*.

3. *Oikia* were stable enough to provide a nucleus or base out of which a wide group of believers could meet and live under its hospitality.

D. The structure of the household churches

1. Universal inclusiveness: Gentile and Jew are connected (literally, become "blood kin") on the basis of faith in Jesus Christ.

    a. Gal. 3.28

    b. Eph. 2.19

2. Leadership and authority: oversight of the business of the church lay in the hands of elders, who were *to be good managers of their own oikia, since they were called to care for the household of God*.

a. 1 Tim. 3.2-7

   b. 1 Tim. 3.12

   c. Titus 1.6

      (1) Leaders were always mentioned in the plural.

      (2) Leaders were always associated with households.

   d. Women are mentioned as heads of households and often before their husbands (e.g., Lydia, Nympha, and Priscilla); (does this suggest that women were in charge of the *churches in their houses*?)

3. Evangelism, worship, fellowship and discipleship occurred in the *oikos*.

   a. The household was the place of the church's ongoing life together as a community of the Lord.

   b. Preaching of the Good News took place through the "households."

      (1) Acts 5.42

      (2) Acts 20.20

   c. Baptism of new believers occurred in the *oikos*.

      (1) Acts 16.15

      (2) 1 Cor. 1.16

   d. The Lord's table (breaking of bread), Acts 2.46

e. Discipling new believers and bringing them into the church family occurred "house to house," Acts 20.20.

f. Christian education for children, Eph. 6.4

g. Discipling of young wives, 1 Cor. 14.35

Conclusion

» The ministry of evangelizing the lost, discipling believers, and planting churches was done in conjunction with the households (i.e., *oikia*) of the NT families!

» The early Church expanded through the structure of the *oikos*, or household evangelism. An *oikos* is that web of common kinship relationships, friendships, and associations that make up a person's larger social circle.

» This social network played a crucial role in every dimension of the spread of the Gospel in both apostolic evangelism and church planting in the NT.

Segue 1

Student Questions and Response

page 312 📖 *3*

Please take as much time as you have available to answer these and other questions that the video brought out. As we consider the best ways to penetrate the complex urban neighborhoods with the good news of the Kingdom, we ought to study afresh the ways in which the apostles carried forth the Word through the cities of the Roman empire. From a study of the book of Acts, it is clear that the early Church was impacted by and expanded the Word through the natural social structures of the *oikos*, or household evangelism. An *oikos* is that web of common kinship relationships, friendships, and associations that make up a person's larger social circle. We must make certain that we understand its dimensions and nature if we are to apply its wisdom to our situation today. Think through the following questions carefully, making certain that they are consistent with the teaching of Scripture.

1. What are some of the pressing problems that confront today's urban poor neighborhoods? How specifically do these problems impact our ability to

share the Gospel across the barriers of culture, class, race, and language, and gender?

2. Review again together the PLANT model of church planting. Why does such a rendering of church planting help us as we begin to seriously prepare to evangelize in urban neighborhoods unreached with the Gospel.

3. Describe the biblical concept of *oikos*. What is the biblical distinction between the term *patria* as it relates to the biblical idea of *oikos*?

4. How does the association of *oikos* with the concept of the "family of God" help us better understand how important this concept is to Christian discipleship?

5. In looking throughout Acts and the NT, what insights do we glean about the nature of *oikos* and the spread and development of the Kingdom in the early church's experience? List out five key insights you get from observing the many times the term *oikos* is used in conjunction with evangelism and church planting in the NT.

6. How was Christian discipleship and body life lived out in the actual structure of many of the household churches spoken of in the NT? How does their experience give us insight into the kinds of relationships early Christians experienced in the context of their *oikos*?

7. What kind of conclusions can we draw about the nature of evangelism and church planting from looking at the biblical data about the *oikos* and its role in the early church? To what extent are these conclusions valid for us as we begin to think seriously about how we might begin to target and penetrate urban communities with the Gospel today?

The rationale for more churches is that every person in an area will have an opportunity to hear and know the Gospel, and receive or reject Jesus Christ as their personal Savior through the witness of a reproducing church. God's number one chosen instrument to proclaim the Good News continues to be the Church. God's plan to reach the world continues through his Church.

Note the spread of the Good News through new churches in the Book of Acts. How many places can we suggest new churches were started from the Jerusalem and Antioch churches and listed in the Book of Acts according to the context and later references?

The Apostle Paul, the leader of the early church planting movement, planted many churches as a direct result of Pentecost. Most of the churches he started had their roots in the Day of Pentecost when some of the people from the cities and areas were present. This reminds us, once again, that when the Holy Spirit inspires us to plant a church or churches in a city or an area, he prepares the spiritual soil ahead of time.
~Marlin Mull. *A Biblical Church Planting Manual.* Eugene, OR: Wipf and Stock Publishers, 2003. pp. 56-57.

Chapter 1. Jerusalem

Chapter 2. Parthians (Iran), Elamites (east of Tigris and Euphrates Rivers), Mesopotamia (Babylon), Judea, Cappadocia (area north of Tarsus), Pontus (Turkey today), Asia (cities of Ephesus, Smyrna and Pergamos), Phrygia (moue area of Turkey), Pamphyllia (south Turk Egypt, Libya near Cyrene (north cost of AI in modern Libya), Rome, Cretans (isle Crete), and Arabs (between the Red Sea the Persian Gulf)

Chapter 4. Cypress

Chapter 6. Greece, Antioch

Chapter 8. Judea, Samaria, Ethiopia, Samaritan towns

Chapter 9. Damascus, Tarsus, Lydda, Sharon

Chapter 10. Caesarea

Chapter 11. Phoenicia (near Tyre), Cyprus, Antioch, Tarsus, Cyrene

Chapter 13. Salamis (in Cypress), Paphos (in Cypress), Perga, Pisidian Antioch

Chapter 14. Iconium, Lystra, Derbe

Chapter 15. Cypress, Syria, Cilicia

Chapter 16. Derbe, Lystra, Iconium, Phrygia, Galatia (center of Asia Minor), Philippi, Thyatira

Chapter 17. Thessalonica, Berea, Athens

Chapter 18. Corinth, Pontus, Ephesus, Achaia (Greece), Galatia, Phygia, Ephesus

Chapter 19. Ephesus, Macedonia (Philippi)

Chapter 20. Macedonia, Greece, Berea, Thessalonica, Derbe, province of Asia, Troas, Miletus

Chapter 21. Tyre, Ptolemais, Caesarea, Cyprus

Chapter 27. Thessalonia, Sidon

Chapter 28. Puteoli (port in Italy), Bay of Naples, Rome

Planting Urban Churches: Sowing

Segment 2: The *Oikos* and Urban Evangelism

Rev. Dr. Don L. Davis

In understanding the biblical conception of a relationship network, we see that the Gospel was shared and spread along the lines of the natural web of relationships that individuals had in their kinships, friendships, and associations. Today in our urban neighborhoods, we ought to develop strategies for evangelism and outreach that take seriously the natural social units, i.e., the *oikos*, of each person who we seek to reach. We must seek to win the entire *household* in the biblical sense, the web of influence represented in the network of the people we befriend, serve, and witness to.

Our objective for this segment, *The Oikos and Urban Evangelism*, is to enable you to see that:

- The roots of a relational network are grounded both in the Old and New Testament views of the *household*. Such networks included generational unity, kinship relationships, friendships, and associates with whom the head of the household protected and patronized.

- Those who live in the city today also have a *web of connection and influence* which could be considered a kind of modern day *oikos*. This includes family members, friendships, and affiliations with others based on work, living, interests, and associations.

- *Oikos* evangelism is effective, for a number of reasons. It is biblical, effective in terms of those who respond favorably to the Good News, and is based on contacts who are receptive to those within the network. Furthermore, in using those who have come to the Lord already, it both multiplies the workers who are sharing the Gospel, and emphasizes natural sharing (no cold calling) in the network. It greatly increases the number of possible positive contacts, and makes follow-up more personal.

- Evangelizing in the *oikos* does have challenges, especially when one person speaks for the entire *oikos*, the possibility of sharing can be closed if that person rejects the Lord. Nevertheless, we ought to do all we can to plan strategies which acknowledge and build upon the natural relationships that flow out of a person's *oikos*.

Summary of Segment 2

Video Segment 2 Outline

I. **Defining the Modern Day Urban *Oikos***

    A. Roots: biblical conceptions of a family network (*oikos*)

        1. The Old Testament view: "A household usually contained four generations, including men, married women, unmarried daughters, slaves of both sexes, persons without citizenship, and 'sojourners,' or resident foreign workers," Hans Walter Wolff, *Anthology of the Old Testament*.

            a. The place of *generational unity*: four generations

            b. The place of *kinship*: immediate and extended family

            c. The place of *commerce and livelihood*: included servants, workers, and slaves

            d. The place of *association*: sojourners, associates

        2. The New Testament view: the OT view extended into the intertestamental period, and during the life of Jesus.

        3. The Gospel in our NT narratives is described as coming through and to the various people *in the household where they resided*.

            a. Mark 5.19

b. Luke 19.9

c. John 1.41-45

d. John 4.53

e. Cornelius is a prime example of the role of household in evangelism, Acts 10-11.

B. Modern definition of *oikos*

"That natural web of relationships where individuals are recognized and embraced as a part of a larger social unit, based upon common kinship relationships, common friendships, and associations"

1. *Natural web of relationships*: an *oikos* is the most basic and natural web of identity and connection for people.

2. *Where individuals are recognized and embraced as a part of a larger social unit*: an *oikos* is that social unit where individuals are recognized and embraced as a significant member of a larger network of relationships.

   a. The family or group to which the individual belongs

   b. Where their associations and connections are based

   c. Includes place of origin, family background, neighborhood, larger network of friends and community

d. Where they are known of and cared for

3. *Based upon common kinship relationships*: our family connections

    a. Mother and father, whether their birth parents or those who raised and nurtured the person in their infancy and youth

    b. Brothers and sisters, whether by birth or association

    c. Extended family, both in terms of formal association as well as personal connection

    d. "Adopted families:" i.e., those relationships which operate as family for the individual

4. *Based upon common friendships*: our "significant others"

    a. Immediate friends and "running partners," your "dawg"

    b. Group with which we most readily affiliate or attend, i.e., those places where we have "membership"

    c. Acquaintances who share common and/or special interests

5. *Based upon common associates*: work and play

a. Relationships at our work and place of business, school, or regular place of attendance

b. Those we see in our circle on a regular basis: grocers, gas station attendants, laundry folks, etc.

c. Connections because of recreation, ethnic, or cultural associations

C. Distinctives of the urban *oikia*

1. Every urban person has an *oikos* of which they are a part.

2. One's *oikos* connection in the city may not have anything (or very little) to do with *where the person is living*.

3. As a rule, individuals are very suspicious and distrustful of people who are not a part of their *oikos* circle.

4. In the same way, the *oikos* relationships are the most significant and impacting relationships for urbanites.

II. Why *Oikos* (Household) Evangelism Is Effective

A. *Oikos* evangelism is biblical.

1. Jesus used *oikia* to spread forth the word regarding himself.

The concept of *oikos* is a concept of connection and sharing in common.

As Christ had shared his life and his Spirit with them, they were free to share their life, money and goods with anyone who had need for them. "All the believers were one in heart and mind. No one claimed that any of [their] possessions was [their] own, but they shared everything they had" (Acts 4.32; see vv. 33–35). This movement of commonness was intimately connected to the apostles' presence and teaching, which had its roots in their life together as the Twelve and others with Jesus. The common life of Jesus with the Twelve became the common life of the apostles among the ecclesia, which became the common life of the ecclesia as household for any who had need, so "there were no needy persons among them."
~ G. W. Icenogle, *Biblical Foundations for Small Group Ministry: An Integrative Approach*. Downers Grove, IL: InterVarsity Press, 1994.

a. Luke 19.9

b. John 4.53

2. The apostles ministered in this fashion.

   a. Peter with Cornelius, Acts 10-11; cf. Acts 10.24

   b. Paul with Lydia and the Philippian jailer, Acts 16.14-35

      (1) Lydia, Acts 16.12-15

      (2) The Philippian jailer, Acts 16.29-34

3. The *oikia* became not only the place for evangelism, but the means by which new Christians were discipled and gathered into congregations, cf. the households of Priscilla and Aquila, as well as Onesiphorus at Ephesus.

   a. 1 Cor. 16.19

   b. 2 Tim. 1.16

   c. 2 Tim. 4.19

B. *Most people who come to faith in Christ* do so through an *oikos* member.

   1. Survey by Church Growth, Inc. of Monrovia, CA

a. 40,000 laypersons were polled as to how they entered into faith in Jesus Christ.

b. One basic question: "What or who was responsible for your coming to Jesus Christ and to your church?"

c. One of eight responses was possible:

   (1) A "special need" brought them to Christ and the church.

   (2) "Just walked in"

   (3) "Pastor"

   (4) "Visitation"

   (5) "Sunday School"

   (6) "Evangelistic crusade or television program"

   (7) "Church program or outreach"

   (8) "Friend or relative"

2. Survey results:

   a. Special need: 1-2%

   b. Walk-in: 2-3%

   c. Pastor: 5-6%

   d. Visitation: 1-2%

e. Sunday School: 4-5%

f. Evangelistic crusade or TV show: ½%

g. Church program: 2-3%

h. *Friend or relative: 75-90%!*

C. *Oikos* members are *receptive* to one another.

1. This kind of evangelism builds on shared history, experience, and concerns.

2. People of an *oikos* are more likely to listen to their own members than to strangers.

3. Relationships already exist, cutting short the need for the evangelist to cultivate them.

D. *Oikos* evangelism allows for *natural sharing* of the Gospel *(no cold calling)*.

1. Barriers of culture, language, relationship melt away when members of an *oikos* share with other members of their group.

2. It is the least threatening form of sharing faith.

3. It occurs through normal relational lines.

4. No cold calling is involved.

E. *Oikos* evangelism greatly increases the number of *possible contacts*.

1. *Oikos* relationships are "built in" our resident mission field.

2. All those with whom an individual is associated become possible contacts for sharing the Good News.

3. A natural evolution of faith: the "leads" are stronger than sharing with those in the midst of a culture of suspicion and mistrust.

4. *Oikos* relationships constantly re-seed a new contact base

F. *Oikos* evangelism is *efficient*: it makes follow-up more personal and natural.

1. Makes connection and affiliation with other church members easier, less strange or uncomfortable

2. Members of an *oikos* can ground their own new brothers and sisters in the faith, Prisca and Aquila, 1 Cor. 16.19.

G. *Oikos* evangelism *multiplies the workers* in the harvest field

1. It emphasizes the concept of "every person ministry," Eph. 4.11-13

2. The missionary wins the lost, but then equips the newly saved to share within their *oikos*, 2 Tim. 2.2.

3. *Oikos* evangelism takes advantage of the desire for testimony so fresh in a new believer, Mark 1.40-45.

4. Believers are to share the Gospel in the midst of their *oikos*.

III. Implications of *Oikos* for Urban Evangelism

A. Challenges

1. Some *oikia* are not open to the Gospel, and will repel the one who seeks to penetrate its ranks with it.

    a. Matt. 10.34-39

    b. Cf. Mic. 7.6

    c. Mark 13.12

    d. Luke 21.16

The idea of household management extends to stewardship and economy (from the Greek word oikos, "house") and then further to "stewardship of the world," and then it becomes a word for "the world" itself. It is used in this sense, for example, in Matthew 24.14 (and Luke 2.1, 4.5; Acts 17.6; Rom. 10.18; Heb. 1.6; Rev. 16.14).
~ Leland Ryken. *Dictionary of Biblical Imagery*. (electronic ed.). Downers Grove, IL: InterVarsity Press, 2000. p. 394.

2. If the Gospel is rejected by the leading members of an *oikos*, it may make it extremely difficult to continue to share within it.

3. Devotion to one's *oikos* may interfere with the new found allegiance of an *oikos* member to Jesus Christ, John 12.42-43.

B. Solutions

1. Whatever methods you select in sharing the Good News in your church planting neighborhood, *think oikos*!

    a. Think "economically" in every personal relationship you make and cultivate.

    b. Plan your outreaches in terms of winning the *oikos*, not just the individual.

2. Do not worry if you do not see the immediate impact of sowing seeds within the *oikia* in the neighborhoods you serve; the Gospel will spread!

3. Be willing to share the Good News even with the members of an *oikos* who, at least on the surface, possess little actual authority in its affairs.

4. *Do your homework by learning the kinship relationships*: lay a proper foundation for continued penetration within the relational web.

5. In your planning and prayer, ask God to give you the entire circle.

a. Pray for the entire group as well as for individuals.

b. Pray for boldness for members who know Christ to sow seeds within their clans.

c. Aim in your efforts for an entire *oikos*, even while working with open or curious individuals.

6. Encourage every convert to become an Andrew to members within their own *oikos*.

a. Andrew found Peter, John 1.40-42.

b. Philip found Nathanael, John 1.43-44.

7. Expect God, the Holy Spirit, to move the message of the Good News naturally through the *oikos* relationships of the converts you see.

Conclusion

» The significance of the *oikos* concept for evangelism and discipleship is plain in the apostles' outreach in the NT, and we ought to pay careful attention to the *oikia* (plural of *oikos*) making up our neighborhoods.

» An *oikos* is that web of common kinship relationships, friendships, and associations that make up a person's larger social circle.

» As we target and equip people to share the Good News within an *oikos*, we can trust God to move within these households, and hopefully, by the power of his Spirit, we can also see the Gospel spread quickly along the lines of kinship, friendship, and association.

Segue 2

Student Questions and Response

The following questions were designed to help you review the material in the second video segment. As we saw this lesson, the power of the *oikos*, once rediscovered and re-employed in urban evangelism, can produce remarkable kinds of synergy and vitality in our urban outreach strategies. By concentrating on the *oikos* as the target of our prayers, efforts, and energies, we can move along natural lines of relationship, and trust God to use those who respond within the network to become *evangelists and prophets within the network*, sharing the good news of the Kingdom with their family and friends in their webs of influence. Make sure that you comprehend the importance of this critical concept. As always, seek to be clear and concise in your answers, and support your answers with Scripture!

1. What are the roots of the concept of family network in the OT? In the NT? Review again how the NT reveals the Gospel spreading through the natural channels of the *oikos* in Acts and the rest of the NT.

2. What would be a modern definition of *oikos*? What place does place of origin, family background, and ongoing friendships play in defining the modern concept of *oikos* for city dwellers?

3. How do common *kinship relationships* and common *friendships* play into our modern ideas about *oikos* today? What about common *associates* and common *interest groups* affect the kinds of relationships that people in the city have today?

4. Why is *oikos* (or household, in the broad sense) evangelism so effective? Select one of the reasons given in the lesson and explain its significance for urban outreach? Can you think of other reasons why *oikos* evangelism might be more effective than seeking to reach people who are essentially *strangers* to us and others?

5. How do you understand the data on how most people come to faith? Is that shocking or surprising to you? What does it say about the nature of evangelism, and the kinds of strategies we must select as we seek to win our neighborhoods for Christ in the city?

6. Why is it so important that we find ways that emphasize the *natural connection* that people may have with those who are sharing the Gospel with them? What are some common ways in which we fail to emphasize this kind of connection in our evangelism strategies in the city?

7. Does an emphasis on *oikos* evangelism suggest that all outreach to *total strangers* will not be used of the Holy Spirit to bring people into the Kingdom? Explain your answer.

8. What are some of the key barriers and challenges to *oikos* evangelism? How might these barriers be effectively overcome by those seeking to do evangelism in the city?

9. List out as many possible ideas as you can to implement an *oikos* strategy of evangelism as a local church in the city. Of all of these possible ways, which ones hold promise as we explore new ways to do evangelism with *oikos* relationships in mind?

CONNECTION

Summary of Key Concepts

This lesson focuses upon the power of the *oikos* as a target for urban evangelism. This concept, which emphasizes the natural ongoing networks of relationships that urbanites have, provides us with a remarkable opportunity to re-conceive evangelism to city dwellers not as a halting presentation to total strangers, but a cultivated conversation within a network of family, friends, and associates. While the work of the evangelist will ever be necessary, we can equip men and women in the city to share the Good News with those in their web of influence.

Listed below are the critical concepts covered in this important lesson. Meditate upon these truths, and become familiar with them as you consider new strategies to win the lost in your family and community.

- In regard to outreach and methods of sharing the Good News in the city, one of the key concepts deals with *the principle of oikos*, or household evangelism. An *oikos* is a web of common kinship relationships, friendships, and associations that make up a person's larger social circle.

- Urban communities are faced with difficult challenges that must be taken into account as we strategize to engage in urban evangelism (including broken family units, economic underdevelopment, alienation and loneliness, drug abuse, violence, housing shortages, and general despair).

- The concept of *oikos* in the NT is significant, explaining not only the Church of God as the *family of God* but also as the most common term for *family unit*.

- The meaning of *oikos* is fuller than our modern day notion of family (i.e., father, mother, and children), and included blood relatives, other dependents (including slaves, employees, and "clients," among others), as well as those whom the head of the household patronized and protected. The roots of a relational network are grounded both in the Old and New Testament views of the *household*. Such networks included generational unity, kinship relationships, friendships, and associates with whom the head of the household protected and patronized.

- The outreach in the NT expanded along the lines of the *oikos*; evangelism was done in conjunction with this structure, and became the primary structure for worship, discipleship, and outreach. The *oikos* was actually considered a "church" if its members came to faith in the Lord Jesus.

- Those who live in the city today also have a *web of connection and influence* which could be considered a kind of modern day *oikos*. This includes family members, friendships, and affiliations with others based on work, living, interests, and associations.

- *Oikos* evangelism is effective, for a number of reasons. It is biblical, effective in terms of those who respond favorably to the Good News, and is based on contacts who are receptive to those within the network. Furthermore, in using those who have come to the Lord already, it both multiplies the workers who are sharing the Gospel, and emphasizes natural sharing (no cold calling) in the network. It greatly increases the number of possible positive contacts, and makes follow-up more personal.

- Evangelizing in the *oikos* does have challenges, especially when one person speaks for the entire *oikos*, the possibility of sharing can be closed if that person rejects the Lord. Nevertheless, we ought to do all we can to plan strategies which acknowledge and build upon the natural relationships that flow out of a person's *oikos*.

Throughout the NT God's people are regularly spoken of as a family, and a cluster of terms, drawn from family life, is used in discussions of the church and early Christian communities. God is "Father" (Rom. 8.15; Gal. 4.9), and those who are redeemed by Jesus Christ are God's children (Gal. 4.1–7), with Jesus Christ being the firstborn of the family (Rom. 8.29). Paul speaks in warm terms when he addresses fellow Christians as "brothers" (note, for example, Phil. 4.1;

adelphoi, lit. "brothers," includes both "brothers and sisters"). *The theme of family relationships is particularly prominent in 1 Timothy, where the church (ekklesia) is described as "the household (oikos) of God, and the pillar and bulwark of the truth" (1 Tim. 3.15; cf. Heb. 3.1–6). The purpose of this letter as a whole is to indicate "how one ought to behave in God's household." The order of the church is analogous to that of a human household. Members are to treat one another as they would the members of their own family (1 Tim. 5.1–2). They are to care for one another in need (1 Tim. 5.5, 16), while overseers are to be skillful at managing the household of God, as demonstrated by their skill with, and care for, their own immediate families (1 Tim. 3.1–7).*

~ Gerald F. Hawthorne, **Dictionary of Paul and His Letters**. (electronic ed.). Logos Library Systems. Downers Grove, IL: InterVarsity, 1997, p. 128.

Student Application and Implications

Now is the time for you to discuss with your fellow students your questions about the power of the principle of *oikos* evangelism. In regard to outreach in urban communities, this is a critical perspective, one which implemented can result in new avenues of contact with those who otherwise would be distant or closed to any appeal to the Gospel of Christ. An *oikos* is a web of common kinship relationships, friendships, and associations that make up a person's larger social circle. Truly, each of us belong to an *oikos*, and this allows you as a student to consider your own *web of connection and influence*, as well as ways that God may want you to pray for and penetrate your own *oikos* network.

Listed below are some questions designed to get you into the frame of mind to consider the implications of this for your own life and ministry. What particular questions do you have in light of the material you have just studied? Perhaps some of the questions below may spur you on to further reflection.

* How well do I comprehend the biblical and contemporary ideas associated with the notion of *oikos*? Can I see how dominant the notion of *oikos* evangelism was in the ministry of the apostles as recorded in Acts, and mentioned in the Epistles of the NT?

* Have I spent anytime tracing the patterns and structures of my own *oikos* relationships? If not, take the time to sketch out some of the main players and persons in your own *web of connections and influence*.

* As I consider this material, of all the things present, what impresses me most about the nature of *oikos* relationships, and the implications they have for

doing evangelism in the city? What am I least convinced of as I review the material?

* What are the kinds of attitudes and perspectives we will need to adopt for our evangelism strategies if we are to, in fact and in reality, begin to take the idea of *oikos* evangelism more seriously in our urban church environments?

* How soon and early ought we to begin to have children, teens, and adults begin to share the Good News with the members of their own distinct *oikos* networks? Under what conditions would it be detrimental (if any) to encourage a person to immediately go and share with the members of their *oikos* network their new found faith in Christ?

* Of all the various strategies and methods employed in urban evangelism, what three methods appear to take most seriously the reality and potential of the *oikos* network?

* Have I made a concerted effort to pray for and share the Good News with the members of my own *oikos* network? What has prevented me from doing so? What steps could I take immediately to be even more effective in sharing the life and message of the Kingdom with the members of my own *oikos* group?

CASE STUDIES

Bad Advice?

Recently, a member of the Black Muslims was dramatically converted to Christ. Encouraged by members of his new fellowship to share with family and friends about the Lord, the young disciple went and shared his decision to follow Christ with his imam (his Muslim minister), his fellow ex-Muslim colleagues, and his Muslim family. Immediately, all of these individuals took great offense at the testimony of the new Christian-converted-from-Islam. Was the advice that the new fellowship gave the young disciple "bad advice?" Should he have nurtured his relationships more before he said anything to them? Is this a case of simply persecution of Christians or bad advice in seeking to win his *oikos* network?

Amazing Grace

(Based on a true story) A young girl, the daughter of one of the most notorious drug king-pins in the community, enjoyed a wonderful week at the local Vacation Bible School in the neighborhood. On the last day, the Parent's Invitation Day, the young girl was able to persuade her drug-slinging father to attend. Using methods of strong crying, tears, and the kind of intimidation that only a young beautiful daughter can provide, she coerced her father to come, who amazingly, as a result of the simple presentation of the Gospel at the VBS program, accepted Jesus as Lord and Savior. As a result of his conversion, a major number of his associates and lieutenants also repented and came to the Lord. What does this case study reveal to us about the nature of *oikos* evangelism, especially in terms of penetrating fields and networks which are impossible to breach as *strangers*?

How Do We Change?

An urban church which recently learned about the principle of *oikos* evangelism was both excited and at a loss. While the pastoral and key lay leadership both understood and were persuaded by the teaching of *oikos*, all the methods they had used before were traditional "stranger" approaches–door to door visitation, street evangelism, block parties, and things like tract distribution and concerts in the park. You have been called in as a consultant in helping them conceive of evangelism in new, *oikos*-oriented ways. What would your strategy be to help them make the transformation to a more relational approach to urban outreach?

Let Us Join Them!

After a workshop on the power of *oikos* evangelism, a group of young people, all dressed in modern "hip-hop" baggy style, asked for a moment of the pastor's time. They were thrilled at the teaching on *oikos* evangelism, and desired to "take it to another level." "If it is true that we are open to those who are a part of our relational web," they said, "we would like permission to *intentionally penetrate* one of the local hip-hop music groups in the city. They know us, who we are, and we would like to form the kinds of relationships that would make presenting Christ to them more personal and natural. Some of us are thinking about forming a hip-hop music group, and becoming a kind of 'insider' group for evangelizing young hip-hop kids. What do you think?" What should the pastor say to these passionate young disciples about their intriguing, maybe even crazy idea?

In regard to outreach and methods of sharing the Good News in the city, one of the key concepts deals with *the principle of oikos* or household evangelism. An *oikos* is a web of common kinship relationships, friendships, and associations that make up a person's larger social circle. The concept of *oikos* in the NT is significant, explaining not only the Church of God as the *family of God* but also as the most common term for *family unit*. The biblical meaning of *oikos* was much fuller than our modern day notion of family (i.e., father, mother, and children), but included blood relatives, other dependents (including slaves, employees, and "clients," among others), as well as those whom the head of the household patronized and protected. The concept became significant in NT times, where evangelism was done in conjunction with this structure, and it became the primary structure for worship, discipleship, and outreach. The *oikos* was actually considered a "church" if its members came to faith in the Lord Jesus. For those living in the city today, this concept of a *web of connection and influence* can offer us new exciting ways to conceive of outreach in terms of family members, friendships, and affiliations with others based on work, living, interests, and associations. We ought to do all we can to plan strategies which acknowledge and build upon the natural relationships that flow out of a person's *oikos*.

Restatement of the Lesson's Thesis

If you are interested in pursuing some of the ideas of *Planting Urban Churches: Sowing*, you might want to give these books a try:

Arn, Win and Charles Arn. *The Master's Plan for Making Disciples*. 2nd Ed. Grand Rapids: Baker Books, 1998.

Green, Michael. *Evangelism in the Early Church*. Grand Rapids: Eerdmans, 1970.

McGavran, Donald and Win Arn. *How to Grow a Church*. Glendale, CA: Regal, 1973.

Resources and Bibliographies

Our ministry before the Lord is a stewardship in God's *oikos*.

*The dominance of the household concept in Paul's thought also influenced his perception of the ministry and the minister. Paul's ministry thus comes under the category of "stewardship" (**oikonomia**, 1 Cor. 9.17; Col. 1.25), that is, a task entrusted by the master to a member of the household. The one who receives this trust, the minister, is called a "steward" (**oikonomos**, 1 Cor. 4.1, 2; Titus 1.7). Such a description emphasizes the need for faithful execution of duties and accountability to the master.*

~ Gerald F. Hawthorne. **Dictionary of Paul and His Letters**. (electronic ed.). Logos Library Systems. Downers Grove, IL: InterVarsity, 1997. p. 418.

Ministry Connections

Now is the time to relate these insights to your work in ministry, especially as you can connect your own ministry to the dynamism of the *oikos* principle. Focus now on the implications of this teaching on your walk with the Lord, and specifically, in the ministry that the Lord has granted to you in your family, at your church, and on your job. In surveying all the key concepts you have covered dealing with the *oikos* principle of household evangelism, what specifically is the Holy Spirit suggesting to you about your application of them in your life and ministry? What new insight does he want you to meditate upon this week as you ponder your own web of common kinship relationships, friendships, and associations that make up your larger social circle? Is there someone to speak with or something to accomplish as a result of God's conviction in your heart? How might you help these truths come alive in the ministries and relationships you have in your own personal outreach. Search your heart and mind for the promptings of the Lord, the Spirit, and ask for his direction about any particular situation he wants you to address, respond to, and change.

Counseling and Prayer

page 313

The most natural act when we experience the dramatic power of Christ in our lives is to go and tell our brothers and friends, even as Andrew and Phillip did in the case of our Lord Jesus (cf. John 1.41-45). Seek the face of God regarding your own *oikos* web of relationships, and whether or not there is someone in that web the Lord would have you share the message of the Kingdom with. Do not seek to coerce the Lord; listen to him, be open to his leading, through the Word and your leaders, and respond as he provides occasion and opportunity. Make sure that you spend good time in prayerful intercession for other students, and encourage them to pray for you as you seek to respond to his leading (Gal. 5.25 "If we live by the Spirit, let us also walk by the Spirit").

Keep your spirit open to the Spirit of God, and allow him to teach you his lessons about this important truth.

ASSIGNMENTS

Acts 16.30-34

Scripture Memory

To prepare for class, please visit *www.tumi.org/books* to find next week's reading assignment, or ask your mentor.

Reading Assignment

Also read the following articles which are located in the Appendix. All articles are taken from *Mission Frontiers: The Bulletin of the US Center for World Mission*, Vol. 27, No. 5; September-October 2005; ISSN 0889-9436. Copyright 2005 by the U.S. Center for World Mission. Used by Permission. All Rights Reserved.

page 313 📖 5

- Decker, Frank. *When "Christian" Does Not Translate.*

- Kraft, Charles. *Pursuing Faith, Not Religion: The Liberating Quest for Contextualization.*

- Lewis, Rebecca. *Missions in the 21st Century: Working with Social Entrepreneurs?*

- McGavran, Donald. *A People Reborn: Foundational Insights on People Movements.*

- Travis, John and Anna. *Contextualization Among Hindus, Muslims, and Buddhists: A Focus on "Insider Movements."*

- Winter, Ralph D. *Editorial.*

Other Assignments

Make certain that you read carefully the textbook assignments above, as well as memorize your Scripture passage for the week. As usual, write a brief summary of your textbook reading assignment, and bring these summaries to class next week (please see the "Reading Completion Sheet" at the end of this lesson).

Now is also the time to begin to think about the particular kind of ministry project you will want to conduct. In the same way, you ought to decide what specific passage of Scripture you will use for your exegetical project. A word to the wise: *the sooner you determine your projects and the issues associated with them, the easier it will be later in the course when they become due.* So please, do not delay in determining either your ministry or exegetical project. The sooner you select, the more time you will have to prepare!

Looking Forward to the Next Lesson

Again, in this lesson we have considered the principle of *oikos* as it relates to the "E" of *Evangelism*. We saw how crucial that web of common kinship relationships, friendships, and associations that make up a person's larger social circle can be in winning urbanites to the Lord. In our next lesson we will establish the importance of following up new converts to Christ through the process of incorporating them into the local church. We will also explore the process of discipling growing believers. As we take up the role of model, mentor, and friend with these growing disciples who have been won to the Lord, we come closer to the ideal of disciple making as commanded by our Lord. Indeed, as we win, follow up, and disciple new believers in Christ, we will be able to assemble them into a functioning church. Only by planting strong, dynamic churches in the city that are filled with solidly converted and well-equipped disciples can our neighborhoods be transformed by the Gospel of Christ.

This curriculum is the result of thousands of hours of work by The Urban Ministry Institute (TUMI) and should not be reproduced without their express permission. TUMI supports all who wish to use these materials for the advance of God's Kingdom, and affordable licensing to reproduce them is available. Please confirm with your instructor that this book is properly licensed. For more information on TUMI and our licensing program, visit *www.tumi.org* and *www.tumi.org/license*.

Capstone Curriculum

Module 12: Focus on Reproduction
Reading Completion Sheet

Name _____

Date _____

For each assigned reading, write a brief summary (one or two paragraphs) of the author's main point. (For additional readings, use the back of this sheet.)

Reading 1

Title and Author: _____ Pages _____

Reading 2

Title and Author: _____ Pages _____

LESSON 3

Planting Urban Churches
Tending

page 315

Lesson Objectives

Welcome in the strong name of Jesus Christ! After your reading, study, discussion, and application of the materials in this lesson, you will be able to:

- Defend and articulate from Scripture the idea of the importance of following up new converts and discipling new believers in urban church planting.

- The act of discipleship is welcoming new believers into the Church, i.e., incorporating new believers and equipping them in the local assembly of believers, which is God's agent of the Kingdom in this world.

- Define follow-up of new believers as "incorporation into the family of God for the purpose of edification and fruitfulness, to the glory of God." This includes the notion of welcome and introduction into the body, building up in the body to the fullness of Christ, and using one's gifts to contribute to fulfilling the Great Commission, all to the glory of God.

- List the reasons why follow-up of new Christians is so essential to their spiritual well-being, including their need for protection, for new identity, for ongoing instruction and feeding, for the cultivation of new friends and life patterns, and the need for regular pastoral care.

- Articulate the dynamics of follow-up, including baptism and membership in a local assembly, worship, befriending, pastoral care, preaching and teaching, discovery and use of one's spiritual gifts, and service and sharing of one's faith.

- Explain the steps in practicing biblical follow-up: understanding the goal of discipleship as maturity, grounding the new believer in their assurance of salvation, teaching the new Christian to share their faith, and feed upon the Word of God. This also included equipping them to walk with the Lord, introducing them to other members of the body, and connecting them to a small group as the building block of their faith.

- Show how follow-up is an essential dimension of equipping believers in the *Assemble and Nurture phases* of church planting.

- Discuss carefully the role of the local church in effective discipling of new and growing Christians, especially in the sense that the Church is the place which incorporates new converts into the faith, establishes them in their walk and doctrine, and equips them for the work of the ministry.

- Inform others as to the biblical examples of discipleship (e.g., Moses and Joshua, Jesus and the Twelve, Paul and Timothy), as well as the elements involved in the apostles' investment in others' lives (through personal example, pastoral care, prayer, personal contact, sending representatives, correspondence, and delegation of authority).

- Outline the roles of the disciple-maker in the church as model, mentor, and friend.

- Understand the practical ways in which we begin to disciple other Christians in the context of the Church, i.e., through nurturing new believers, growing Christians, and potential leaders.

- Defend the notion that as we assemble believers in the church and nurture them through follow-up and discipleship, we can see growth occur which will lead to a strong, healthy, and dynamic church being planted in the city.

Teach Your Children Well

Devotion

1 Thess. 2.3-12 - For our appeal does not spring from error or impurity or any attempt to deceive, [4] but just as we have been approved by God to be entrusted with the gospel, so we speak, not to please man, but to please God who tests our hearts. [5] For we never came with words of flattery, as you know, nor with a pretext for greed— God is witness. [6] Nor did we seek glory from people, whether from you or from others, though we could have made demands as apostles of Christ. [7] But we were gentle among you, like a nursing mother taking care of her own children. [8] So, being affectionately desirous of you, we were ready to share with you not only the gospel of God but also our own selves, because you had become very dear to us. [9] For you remember, brothers, our labor and toil: we worked night and day, that we might not be a burden to any of you, while we proclaimed to you the gospel of God. [10] You are witnesses, and God also, how holy and righteous and blameless was our conduct toward you believers. [11] For you know how, like a father with his children, [12] we exhorted each one of you and encouraged you and charged you to walk in a manner worthy of God, who calls you into his own kingdom and glory.

page 318

Perhaps no other role in human life carries greater impact on the development of persons than the role of the parent. The kind of parent we had or the parenting we provide shapes a wide range of personal responses, capabilities, and perspectives. In some sense, the kinds of parents we are will dramatically affect (for good or ill) the children that we raise. This is why Paul's adoption of this imagery is so significant for understanding our role in ministry. We have not "closed the deal" after we have shared the good news of the Kingdom with the lost, and they have made a profession of faith in the Lord Jesus as Messiah and Savior. No, the work has just begun. In the same way that the most challenging and most rewarding part of parenting occurs neither at conception or birth, but in raising the child with discipline and love, so the same is true for raising godly spiritual children. Our ability to provide continuous and tender loving care to new converts will be the difference between conserving the fruit of our evangelism (to mix a metaphor), and losing it. How many people have responded to an offer of the Gospel by an enthusiastic witness who got someone to "pray the sinner's prayer" but never saw them again, and made no provision for them to continue in their Christian life? While this may be common today, it would have horrified the apostles. Our New Testament itself is evidence that the apostles were deeply concerned about the *maturity* of the new disciples, not merely the certainty of their entrance into the Kingdom. The apostles sought both *solid conversions* as well as *transformed lives of new creations in Christ*. They sought and settled for nothing less (Gal. 6.15 - "For neither circumcision counts for anything, nor uncircumcision, but a new creation.")

Perhaps no book in the New Testament gives us a full portrait of the heart of a discipler like the Thessalonian epistles. Paul's ministry there was brief, intense, and successful. His concern for their well being and growth is nakedly clear; he loved them with the very heart of a parent, willing to care for their most intimate needs and concerns, and proving it daily in practical ways of service and sacrifice. He alludes to his work among them as a "nursing mother" and as a "father cares for his children." He simply didn't go through the motions; he poured his heart and soul into them, and took pride in their growth, and pain in their error. In every way, Paul proved himself to be a spiritual parent to them, whom he took to be his very own children and kin.

Paul's use of this metaphor here illustrates a general principle which was central in his life and ministry. He used this metaphor in a number of settings in his work with growing believers and developing churches:

> *1 Cor. 4.14-15 - I do not write these things to make you ashamed, but to admonish you as my beloved children. [15] For though you have countless guides in Christ, you do not have many fathers. For I became your father in Christ Jesus through the gospel.*

> *2 Cor. 12.14-15 - Here for the third time I am ready to come to you. And I will not be a burden, for I seek not what is yours but you. For children are not obligated to save up for their parents, but parents for their children. [15] I will most gladly spend and be spent for your souls. If I love you more, am I to be loved less?*

> *1 Thess. 2.7-8 - But we were gentle among you, like a nursing mother taking care of her own children. [8] So, being affectionately desirous of you, we were ready to share with you not only the gospel of God but also our own selves, because you had become very dear to us.*

These and other texts reveal a heart of a parent.

Do you like kids? Are you like the misinformed person who "loved families but couldn't stand children!" If you desire to be used of God in the body of Christ, you must learn to love and care for little ones in the faith, and ask God to give you a parental heart, spirit, and demeanor. Sacrifice and servanthood are the staples of being a good parent, and if you yield yourself to Christ, such will be the graces the Spirit of God will need to work in your life.

The essence of apostolic ministry is to follow the example of Paul, who said to his friends in Thessalonica:

> *1 Thess. 2.11-12 - For you know how, like a father with his children, [12] we exhorted each one of you and encouraged you and charged you to walk in a manner worthy of God, who calls you into his own kingdom and glory.*

May God give us the heart of a caring mother and wisdom of a good father to raise our spiritual children well, all to the glory of God and the building up of his Church.

Nicene Creed and Prayer	After reciting and/or singing the Nicene Creed (located in the Appendix), pray the following prayer:

> *O God, you led your holy apostles to ordain ministers in every place: Grant that your Church, under the guidance of the Holy Spirit, may choose suitable persons for the ministry of Word and Sacrament, and may uphold them in their work for the extension of your kingdom; through him who is the Shepherd and Bishop of our souls, Jesus Christ our Lord, who lives and reigns with you and the Holy Spirit, one God, for ever and ever. Amen.*

~ Episcopal Church. **The Book of Common Prayer and Administrations of the Sacraments and Other Rites and Ceremonies of the Church, Together with the Psalter or Psalms of David** New York: The Church Hymnal Corporation, 1979. p. 256 |
Quiz	Put away your notes, gather up your thoughts and reflections, and take the quiz for Lesson 2, *Planting Urban Churches: Sowing*.
Scripture Memorization Review	Review with a partner, write out and/or recite the text for last class session's assigned memory verse: Acts 16.30-34.
Assignments Due	Turn in your summary of the reading assignment for last week, that is, your brief response and explanation of the main points that the authors were seeking to make in the assigned reading (Reading Completion Sheet).

Spiritual Child Abandonment

  In every place where civilized societal practices are honored, abandoning a child to their own devices and resources is considered a crime punishable by severe and prolonged prison sentences. Yet, every day many well meaning people in ministry feel no sense of shame whatsoever by sharing the good news of Christ with individuals while taking no time to ensure that they will be cared for spiritually after their acceptance of Christ as Savior. How would you finish the following sentence: "If there ever was a thing to be defined as spiritual child abandonment, it would most certainly *have to include* . . ."(.) Discuss your answers to your definitions of spiritual child abandonment.

You Don't Believe in the Power of the Holy Spirit

In a fairly stiff conversation between Christian workers who regularly went to a local prison to minister in the name of Christ, one worker accused the other of spiritual child abandonment. One brother suggested, "You go from cell to cell sharing the love of Christ, praying with men to receive the Lord, but you make no provision for their ongoing care *afterwards*. Doesn't that seem wrong to you? How can you win them but refuse to *provide for them?*" The other responded, "You are confused about the various roles of those whom God has called to do ministry. Some water, some plant, others reap, but in everything, only God gives the increase. I do not pretend that I can do everything, only my part. *You, my friend, do not believe in the power of the Holy Spirit to ground the new believer in Christ. He'll do it; he promised to do so!*" What are the major issues in this conversation, and what opinion do you have on them?

He Is Still a Baby

A new convert to Christ who has struggled with drug and alcohol abuse has been coming to church now for about three months. Unfortunately, he has had a very uneven experience in "disciplining himself for the purpose of godliness." His attendance to the service is up-and-down, and for many church events he has come smelling greatly of liquor, and is apparently under the influence of alcohol or drugs. While some desire to speak sternly and firmly to the brother about this situation, the dear brother who led him to the Lord believes that the church is simply being too hard on him. "We need to give him time to learn the Christ life," he protests. "After all, he is still only a little babe in Christ. Who knows how long it might take him to lick these problems. Let's be patient and loving." What do you think of the discipler's attitude about our new and struggling convert to the Lord?

CONTENT **Planting Urban Churches: Tending**

Segment 1: Incorporating New Disciples into the Body through Follow-Up

Rev. Dr. Don L. Davis

Summary of Segment 1

Follow-up is an essential dimension of equipping believers in the *Assemble and Nurture phases* of church planting. Following up new believers in the local church is "incorporating new converts into the family of God for the purpose of edification and fruitfulness, to the glory of God." This includes the notion of welcome and introduction into the body, building up in the body to the fullness of Christ, and using one's gifts to contribute to fulfilling the Great Commission, all to the glory of God.

Our objective for this segment, *Incorporating New Disciples into the Body through Follow-up*, is to enable you to see that:

- Everywhere in the NT the Scriptures argue the importance of the follow-up of new converts and discipling new believers in urban church planting.

- The act of follow-up includes welcoming new believers into the Church, i.e., incorporating new believers and equipping them in the local assembly of believers, which is God's agent of the Kingdom in this world.

- Following up new believers in the local church is "incorporating new converts into the family of God for the purpose of edification and fruitfulness, to the glory of God." This includes the notion of welcome and introduction into the body, building up in the body to the fullness of Christ, and using one's gifts to contribute to fulfilling the Great Commission, all to the glory of God.

- The practice of following up new Christians is essential to their spiritual well-being. New converts need immediate care and attention because of their need for protection and to understand their new identity, their need for ongoing instruction and feeding, for the cultivation of new friends and life patterns, and because of their need for immediate and regular pastoral care.

- The dynamics of follow-up include baptism and membership in a local assembly, worship, befriending, pastoral care, preaching and teaching, discovery and use of one's spiritual gifts and service, and sharing of one's faith.

- We ought to observe a number of practical steps as we practice biblical follow-up: understanding the goal of discipleship as maturity, grounding the new believer in their assurance of salvation, teaching the new Christian to share their faith, and feed upon the Word of God. This also includes equipping them to walk with the Lord, introducing them to other members of the body, and connecting them to a small group as the building block of their faith.

- Follow-up is an essential dimension of equipping believers in the *Assemble and Nurture phases* of church planting.

I. **Equipping Disciples in the Church: an Overview of the *Assemble* and *Nurture* Phases of Church Planting**

> Video Segment 1 Outline

A. Why should follow-up and discipleship occur in and through the local church?

1. The Church is the *locus of God's concern in the world*: the Church is God's means to reveal himself to the world, 1 Pet. 2.9-10.

    a. We are the people of God in the earth.

    b. God is moving through his people to declare witness to Messiah and his kingdom reign come in Jesus.

2. The Church is the *agent of the Kingdom of God* in his mission to reconcile the world to himself, 2 Cor. 5.18-21.

    a. We are ambassadors of Jesus Christ, appealing to others on God's behalf.

> *If a branch is broken from a tree, it cannot bud, if a stream is cut off from its source, it dries up . . . Nor can he who forsakes the Church of Christ attain to the rewards of Christ. He is a stranger, he is an enemy. Without the Church for your mother, you cannot have God for your Father. If it was possible to escape outside the ark of Noah, then it may be possible to escape outside of the Church.*
> ~ Cyprian the martyr/bishop, beheaded in 258 A.D. Quoted in Tony Lane, *Exploring Christian Thought*. Nashville: Thomas Nelson Publishers, 1984. p. 24.

b. We are his deputies, exercising his authority and speaking to others on his behalf and in his name.

B. We equip believers in conjunction with the local body.

1. Discipling is *in* the Church: the goal of cross-cultural ministry is to win people who join themselves to healthy local assemblies where they can grow, mature, and multiply, Col. 1.25-27.

2. Discipling is *through* the Church: the church is the best place for cross-cultural ministry to begin and thrive, since it conserves the fruit of our evangelism organically, 1 Tim. 3.15-16.

3. Discipling is *for* the Church: the goal of all ministry is the building up of the body of Christ in love, Eph. 4.9-15, of which the local assembly is one small emblem.

C. Steps to remember in bringing groups together in the *Assemble* and *Nurture* phases of urban church planting

1. The moment a person responds to the Gospel, we must connect that Christian to the church, i.e., a local assembly of believers in Messiah Jesus, Matt. 18.20.

2. Evangelize and follow up in small groups *before you assemble*: (you can't postpone caring for babies once they're born!).

    a. 1 Pet. 1.23

b. 1 Pet. 2.2-3

3. Bring your various groups together regularly for worship, fellowship, and support, Heb. 10.24-25.

4. Seek to develop a single identity as you nurture the various groups in follow-up and discipleship.

   a. Phil. 2.1-3

   b. Eph. 4.1-3

5. Use large group meetings to create a sense of overall community among the groups.

6. Seek God's mind on the right timing to bring the groups together for the public announcement of your church's formation.

7. Lay the foundation right *before you go public together*, 1 Cor. 3.9-11.

8. Never stop sharing the Gospel within the *oikia* of the group members: the Lord will add members to the body regardless of what phase we are in.

   a. Acts 2.47

   b. Acts 5.14

    c. Acts 13.48

    d. Rom. 8.30

    e. Rom. 11.5-6

II. **Equipping through Follow-Up: Incorporating and Nurturing in the Family of God**

    A. Definition: "Incorporation into the family of God for the purpose of edification and fruitfulness, to the glory of God"

        1. *Incorporation into the family of God* - introduction and welcome into the family of God, Rom. 15.5-7

            a. Making visible what has in fact become actual

            b. *Welcome as central factor* of *koinonia*
                (1) 1 John 1.1-4
                (2) John 17.3
                (3) Heb. 3.14

        2. For the purpose of *edification and fruitfulness*

            a. Edification - to build up another to the fullness of Christ, to maturity in Christ (Christlikeness) Eph. 4.11-15

b. Fruitfulness - to be used of God to raise up as many disciples as possible as quickly as we can for the sake of fulfilling the Great Commission

   (1) John 15.16

   (2) Col. 1.9-10

3. *To the glory of God* - the end of all things

   a. Matt. 5.16

   b. Eph. 3.21

   c. Phil. 2.15-16

B. Why Follow-up is necessary for new urban disciples

1. Need for protection: new converts are vulnerable to attack (e.g., the parable of the soils in Matthew 13).

   a. The devil's lies and schemes, 2 Cor. 4.4

   b. The cares of the world, 1 John 2.15-17

   c. The lack of depth and substance, Heb. 10.37-39

   d. The proneness towards error, 1 Cor. 10.12-13

2. Need to reorient their lives around their new identity in Christ: new converts require a sense of belonging and security, 2 Cor. 6.14-18.

3. Need for ongoing instruction, nurture, and feeding: new converts need to understand God's Word and will, 1 Pet. 2.2; Heb. 5.11-6.4.

4. Need for friends and cultivating new life patterns based on a kingdom perspective: new converts need friends to encourage holy living, John 13.34-35.

5. Need for regular, parental and pastoral care: new converts need godly pastors to keep watch over their souls, Heb. 13.17.

C. Dynamics of Follow-up

1. Assembling the believers into a distinct community of faith, Acts 2.42-47

2. Immediate, consistent contact after decision, 1 Thess. 3.1-6

3. Baptism and incorporation within a local assembly of believers, Heb. 10.24-25

   a. Baptism in obedience to the command of Christ, Matt. 28.19; Mark 16.15

   b. Befriending in the body: forming new relationships with the believers, Gal. 6.2

c. Worship through the sacraments and corporate worship, 1 Cor. 11.23-26

d. Feeding and care through the preaching of the Word of God, 1 Pet. 2.2

e. Pastoral care and oversight

(1) Heb. 13.7

(2) Heb. 13.17

f. Discovery and use of one's spiritual gifts, Rom. 12.4-8

g. Generosity and hospitality for the care of believers and missions, 2 Cor. 9.6-8

4. Sound biblical doctrine of Christ and his Kingdom

a. Jesus Christ, Luke 24.44-48

b. The Kingdom of God, Acts 28.23,31

c. The Nicene Creed

5. Sharing one's personal faith: *oikos* penetration, 1 Pet. 3.15-16

III. Practicing Biblical Follow-Up

A. Understand the goal of discipleship: to make disciples, not converts, Matt. 28.18-20.

B. Follow up with explanation of repentance and faith and Jesus' command for baptism as soon as possible, Acts 15.36.

C. Teach the new believer to share his or her faith immediately.

1. Mark 1.43-45

2. Ps. 107.2-3

D. Nurture them with a steady diet on the Word of God, 1 Pet. 2.2.

1. Preach and teach the Word of God in small groups and large group together, 2 Tim. 4.1-2.

2. Give a crash course on how to read and benefit from the Scriptures, 2 Tim. 2.15.

3. Get new believers a copy of the Scriptures that they can read and understand.

   a. Their own language

b. Not a paraphrase but a translation

4. Start to memorize the Word with them right away.

   a. Ps. 1.1-2

   b. Ps. 119.11

   c. Isa. 51.7

   d. Jer. 15.16

E. Equip them to walk with the Lord: explain and go through devotional times with the Lord.

   1. Ps. 42.1-2

   2. Ps. 119.164

F. Introduce them to other members of the body immediately after their decision, Rom. 15.5-7.

G. Connect them to leaders and other growing Christians in a small group, Heb. 10.24-25.

The small group as the basic building block of vital Christian community

1. Ensure participation for new believers in all four dimensions of Christian experience.

    a. Personal friendship

    b. Small group life

    c. Large group interaction

    d. Inter-group experience

2. Teaching new Christians the basics of the Christian life, Heb. 5.12ff.

3. Instruction in the disciplines of the spiritual life: worship, prayer, and the Word of God, 1 Tim. 4.7-8

4. Learning to serve others as a member of the body of Christ, the "one anothers" of the NT, Gal. 6.2; John 13.34-35

5. Communicating Christ through our words and deeds as his ambassadors, 2 Cor. 5.18-21

6. Equipping leaders who can teach others to teach others, 2 Tim. 2.2

Conclusion

> » Following up new believers in the faith is an essential dimension of the discipleship of new converts in planting urban churches.

> » Immediately after new converts have joined themselves to Christ by faith, we must incorporate them into the body of believers, grounding them in the faith, and connecting them to the life of the body that they may grow in him.

Please take as much time as you have available to answer these and other questions that the video brought out. In this segment we explored the concept of follow-up, that care we provide new believers immediately after their repentance and faith in the Lord Jesus. Following up new believers in the local church is "incorporating new converts into the family of God for the purpose of edification and fruitfulness, to the glory of God." This includes the notion of welcome and introduction into the body, building up in the body to the fullness of Christ, and using one's gifts to contribute to fulfilling the Great Commission, all to the glory of God. The practice of follow-up is critical to church planting and reproduction, and touches upon both the *Assemble* and *Nurture* phases of urban church planting. Your ability to understand this is crucial, so answer the following questions clearly and directly. Back up your answers with Scripture and good reasoning, too!

Segue 1

Student Questions and Response

page 319 3

1. What are some of the specific reasons why we need to provide new converts to Christ with immediate and loving care and protection? Of these, which do you believe is the most important reason among them?

2. Why can't we simply entrust the new believer to the Lord and the Holy Spirit, and this entrustment be sufficient for their growth and survival in Christ? What role does pastoral and spiritual care play in bringing new believers to maturity in Christ?

3. Why is it necessary to ensure that new converts are connected to a local assembly of believers as soon as possible after their commitment to Christ? Why is providing new converts with a warm welcome such an important practice in insuring their ongoing spiritual growth?

4. Explain as carefully as you can the relationship between the discipler and the Holy Spirit in helping another grow and mature in Christ.

5. What part does baptism and membership play in a new believer's follow-up? What is the relationship between a new convert's learning the Word of God and them attending sermons and studies where the Word of God is taught? Which is most important, and why?

6. Do you think it is *absolutely necessary* for a new believer to be a part of a small group of believers in order to grow? Explain your answer.

7. Can anyone disciple another, or what particular qualifications does one need in order to qualify for being a spiritual parent and friend to a new believer?

8. What is the distinction between *conversion* and *discipleship*, and how does follow-up help a person distinguish between the two?

9. Both the *Assemble* and *Nurture* stages of church planting involve much attention given to the ongoing growth of new believers. In your judgment, how soon must a new believer be brought under immediate pastoral care if they are to survive the initial attacks of the enemy? Explain your answer.

10. What are some of the practical steps involved in the practice of biblical follow-up. Why is it so important that these steps be followed *in the context of a local church*?

The High Calling of the Church in the Kingdom of God

- To love God and glorify God, Rev. 2.4; Eph. 1.5–6, 11–12, 14; 3.21; 2 Thess. 1.12

- To be a trophy of the divine grace of God, Eph. 2.7; 3.6, 10; 1 Pet. 2.9

- To make disciples of all nations through worldwide evangelization, Matt. 28.19–20; Mark 16.15; Luke 24.47; John 20.21; Acts 1.8

- To baptize new believers in Christ, and ground them in his teaching, Matt. 28.19; Phil. 4.8–9; 1 Tim. 4.6; 5.17; 2 Tim. 2.2, 24–25

- To build up believers for the sake of maturity in Christ, 1 Cor. 14.16; Eph. 4.9-16; 1 Thess. 5.11; 2 Pet. 3.18; Jude 20

- To discipline the wayward for the sake of restoring them to faith, Matt. 18

- To provide friendship, connection, fellowship for believers, Acts 2.42; 1 Cor. 1.9; 2 Cor. 8.4; 13.14; Gal. 2.9; Phil. 1.5; 2.12; 1 John 1.3, 6–7

- To care for one another in our time of need, especially the widow and the orphan, 2 Cor. 8–9; 1 Tim. 5.1–16; James 1.27

- To prepare saints for their future responsibility as co-heirs with Christ, Rom. 8.17; 2 Tim. 2.12

- To do good to all people, but especially to the household of faith, Gal. 6.10

~ Adapted from H. L. Willmington. **Willmington's Book of Bible Lists**. Wheaton, IL: Tyndale House. 1987.

Planting Urban Churches: Tending

Segment 2: Equipping the Church through Discipleship

Rev. Dr. Don L. Davis

Summary of Segment 2

The local assembly of believers is the place that God has ordained for the ongoing care and feeding of new and growing Christians. As faithful, mature believers care for new converts in the life of the local assembly of believers, these same converts will be established in every dimension of the Christian life, including their spiritual walk, their understanding and application of Christian doctrine, and their discovery and use of their gifts as they are equipped for the work of the ministry.

Our objective for this segment, *Equipping the Church through Discipleship*, is to enable you to see that:

- The local church is the context for beginning and sustaining effective discipling for new and growing Christians, especially in the sense that the local assembly of believers is the place which incorporates new converts into the faith, establishes them in their walk and doctrine, and equips them for the work of the ministry.

- The Scriptures provide a number of clear examples of God's leaders in a mentoring and modeling role. This includes notable cases such as Moses and Joshua, Elijah and Elisha, David and his "mighty men," Naomi and Ruth, Jesus and the Twelve, and Paul and Timothy.

- In the apostles' practice of discipling emerging congregations and leaders, certain key elements are seen again and again. These include their own personal example, their loving pastoral care, and faithful intercession and prayer on their behalf. We also see that they maintained ongoing personal contact with them, sent representatives to communicate to them, sent personal correspondence to them, and delegated to them both responsibility and authority as the need arose.

- The roles of the disciple-maker in the church can be summarized in the images of the discipler as a model (personal example), as a mentor (as one who coaches another to excellence), and as a friend (as one who befriends another for mutual support and care).

- All efforts toward the encouragement and training of developing disciples must be done with a commitment to and in the context of the local church. The local assembly of believers is the critical context of the church, not only for nurturing new believers to maturity, but also for identifying and equipping leaders for ministry.

- As we assemble believers in the church and nurture them through follow-up and discipleship, we can see growth occur which will lead to a strong, healthy, and dynamic church being planted in the city.

Video Segment 2 Outline

I. Equipping through Nurturing the Body: the Role of the Local Church in Effective Discipling

A. The local church brings in (incorporates) new converts in the body, Acts 2.42-27.

1. *Evangelism* takes place through the Church, Acts 2.47.

2. *Follow-up* is being incorporated into the Church, Acts 2.39.

3. *Authentic conversion* is shown by one's commitment to the body of believers.

   a. Confession before men: the testimony of faith, Rom. 10.9-10

   b. Baptism, Matt. 28.18-20

   c. The Lord's Supper with the people of God, 1 Cor. 11.23-26

B. The local church establishes new Christians in the faith: "proving the authenticity in the faith", Eph. 4.13-14.

   1. Fellowship of the Holy Spirit (in the body), 1 Cor. 12.13; Eph. 1.3; 2 Cor. 1.20; Eph. 5.18ff

   2. The Living Word of God (the Church as the pillar and ground of truth), cf. 1 Tim. 3.14-16

   3. The gifts of the Spirit, Rom. 12.4-8; 1 Cor. 12.1-27; 1 Pet. 4.10-11

   4. The prayers of the saints, James 5.16

   5. Good works: fleshing out one's love for the Lord Jesus

      a. Eph. 2.10

      b. 2 Cor. 9.8

c. 2 Tim. 2.21

d. Titus 2.14

e. Titus 3.1

C. The local church equips believers for the work of the ministry, Eph. 4.11-13.

1. God's special gifts: certain gifts are given in order to equip the saints for the work of the ministry. These are sometimes called the "fivefold gifts."

    a. Apostles: *those gifted to share the Good News and plant churches*

    b. Prophets: *those gifted to give new insights and revelations from the Lord*

    c. Evangelists: *those gifted to make the word of salvation plain to others*

    d. Pastors: *those gifted to nurture and care for the flock of God*

    e. Teachers: *those gifted to explain the meaning of Christ and his Kingdom for our lives*

2. We have differing gifts according to the special function which the Lord has given us, Rom. 12.4-8.

3. God has given special gifted individuals to the body of Christ in order that the members might be equipped for the work of the ministry, Eph. 4.6-15.

4. All the members of the body of Christ are significant and important for its growth and strength, 1 Cor. 12.12-27.

5. Whatever the special grace is that we have received from the Lord, we should use it to build up one another to God's glory, 1 Pet. 4.10-11.

6. All Christians are priests and have been given the authority and responsibility to minister to other members, bearing their burdens and so fulfilling the law of Christ, cf. 1 Pet. 2.9 with Gal. 6.2.

D. Biblical examples of discipleship

The Scriptures show that God can connect his leaders and their partners together for the sake of upbuilding, training, friendship, and equipping for ministry.

1. Moses and Joshua, Num. 27.15-20, cf. Josh. 1.1-2

2. Elijah and Elisha, 1 Kings 19; 2 Kings 2

3. David and his "mighty men", 1 Chron. 12

4. Naomi and Ruth, Ruth 1

5. Jesus and the Twelve, Mark 3.14

6. Paul and Timothy (and his band), Acts 20.4 cf. Phil. 2.20-22

E. Apostolic investment in others: elements of discipling in the Church

1. Personal example and pace-setting, 1 Cor. 11.1

2. Ongoing pastoral care and tender loving care, 1 Thess. 2.7-8

3. Intercession and prevailing prayer, Col. 1.9-10 cf. Eph. 1.15-23

4. Personal contact and association, "to be with him," Mark 3.14

5. Personal representatives, 2 Cor. 8.22

6. Personal correspondence (the Epistles), Gal. 1.1-4

7. Personal delegation and oversight of ministry, 1 Thess. 3.4-8

Paul's preferred imagery for the pastoral task is found in the parent-child relationship. To the Corinthians Paul declared: "For though you might have ten thousand guardians in Christ, you do not have many fathers. Indeed, in Christ Jesus I became your father through the gospel" (1 Cor. 4.15). Paul regarded himself as the founding father of not only the church in Corinth (1 Cor. 4.15; 2 Cor. 6.13; 12.14), but also of the churches in Philippi (Phil. 2.22) and Thessalonica (1 Thess. 2.11). Paul could also be a spiritual father to individuals, as well as to churches: during Paul's imprisonment he had become "father" to Onesimus (Philem. 10); Timothy is "my beloved son and faithful child in the Lord" (1 Cor. 4.17: similarly Phil. 2.22; 1 Tim. 1.2, 18. 2 Tim. 1.2; 2.1); Titus, too, is his "loyal child" (Titus 1.4). Indeed, Paul could even apply the metaphor of a mother to describe his relationship with his churches (1 Cor. 3.1–3; Gal. 4.19; 1 Thess. 2.7). When writing to Rome and to Colossae, however, churches he had not founded, he carefully avoided the parental—and thus the pastoral—tone.

~ Gerald F. Hawthorne. **Dictionary of Paul and His Letters** (electronic ed.). Logos Library Systems. Downers Grove, IL: InterVarsity, 1997. p. 655.

II. The Roles of the Disciple-Maker: Model, Mentor, and Friend

A. The responsibility to be a *Model* (who the discipler is)

1. "Typos" - type, pattern, example

    a. 1 Cor. 4.16

    b. Phil. 3.17

    c. 1 Thess. 2.10-14

    d. 1 Cor. 11.1

    e. 1 Thess. 1.6

    f. 1 Tim. 4.12

    g. Heb. 13.7

2. Primary misconceptions about being a model:

   a. While those who are trained by us will be like us (cf. Luke 6.40), the goal is to conform people to the image of Christ, not our own! Becoming like you as the goal, Rom. 8.29

   b. Inability to allow for difference among people (i.e., adopting a "cookie cutter mentality" of disciple-making)

   c. You cannot personally reproduce yourself in another (i.e., only Jesus makes disciples, technically).

      (1) John 15.4-5

      (2) 1 Cor. 3.7

3. Christlikeness is the goal of the Christian life.

   a. 1 Cor. 15.49

   b. Gal. 4.19

   c. Phil. 2.5

   d. 1 John 3.1-3

4. "Imitation of Christ" - is this good, bad, or ugly?

B. The responsibility to be a *Mentor* (what the discipler does)

    1. The modern example: *coach* (a teacher and counselor)

        a. 2 Tim. 3.10

        b. 1 Cor. 4.15-16

        c. Phil. 4.9

        d. Acts 20.35

    2. Primary misconceptions:

        a. Being a task master: accountability alone (pretending to be the Holy Spirit in another's life)

        b. Low expectations – non-interference as the goal

        c. Inability to balance encouragement and challenge

    3. A coach as an instructor and director: providing insight into the tasks, skills, and attitudes necessary in order to "play your position"

    4. The power of a *corner-man*: distinctions and differences

5. Excellence derived from continuous application (faithfulness): The primary standard for stewarding God's mysteries, 1 Cor. 4.1-2

C. The responsibility to *Befriend* (how the discipler relates)

1. "Yoke fellow," Phil. 4.3 - the discipler as fellow stranger and alien

2. Primary misconceptions:

   a. True friends do not confront, they only strive to understand, seeking to be indirect in their exhortation.

   b. Friends do not interfere with the personal affairs of another.

   c. Friendship precludes admonition and accountability.

3. Becoming a brother or sister, John 1.12-13

   a. Mutuality as the goal of all discipleship, i.e., *"love one another,"* John 13.34-35

   b. *Soul friendship*: walking together in mutual agreement and desire, Amos 3.3

   c. Both *giving and receiving*: the reciprocation in all healthy discipling relationships, Rom. 1.11-12

4. Nurturing a godly friendship

   a. Aristotle's three kinds of friendship:

      (1) Pleasure friends: *they only relate to you as long as you share pleasure.*

      (2) Utility friends: *they only relate to you as long as you are beneficial to them in some way.*

      (3) Character friends: *although they bring you pleasure and are beneficial to you, you relate to them because you share the same passions, desires, and commitments.*

   b. The importance of *dialogue*: open communication

   c. The importance of *honesty*: revealing one's heart

   d. The importance of *mutuality*: two-way street, Gal. 6.2-3

5. The special nature of friendship

   a. Sharpening one another

      (1) Prov. 27.17

      (2) Prov. 27.9

      (3) Isa. 35.3-4

   b. Sticks closer than a brother, Prov. 18.24

c. Loves at all times, Prov. 17.17

d. Whose wounds are faithful

(1) Prov. 27.6

(2) Ps. 141.5

III. Practical Suggestions in Equipping Believers

A. Nurture the growing believers.

1. Become a model of a faithful churchman, 1 John 2.12-14.

2. Refuse to acknowledge "Lone Ranger" ministry: submit to the authority of the leaders in your local church, Heb. 13.17.

3. Acknowledge the calling and gifting of God in the life of each person in the church (1 Cor. 12.11) "as the Holy Spirit chooses."

4. Ask the Holy Spirit to show you the gifts and place for your disciple in the body, 1 Cor. 12.4-7.

5. Encourage experimentation and participation in dimensions of the body; allow people to be "zealous for good deeds," cf. Titus 2.14.

a. Active involvement in corporate worship

b. Cell life or small group life

c. Ministry team

6. *Serve together with the disciple* in body-building ministries or activities; model what you teach, Phil. 4.9.

7. Allow the disciple to intern in a ministry or work under your supervision, oversight, and care, 2 Tim. 2.2.

8. Encourage perseverance and patience, Gal. 6.10.

B. Nurture the identified leaders.

1. Select and meet regularly with a credible leadership team, cf. Jesus' example with his disciples, Mark 3.14.

2. Pray daily and fervently for leaders and their families, Col. 1.9-10.

3. Allow the team to participate in all group celebrations and meetings, 2 Tim. 4.2.

4. Take them with you, and explain everything you're doing: assume they know nothing, Acts 16.1-5.

5. Train them to shepherd and pastor through your example, 1 Pet. 5.1-4.

Conclusion

» Effective discipling of growing Christians is a centerpiece in the planting of healthy churches in urban settings.

» The local church and the individual discipler work together to edify new converts, and help them grow to maturity in Christ.

» As we model before new believers the Christian life, mentor them in the faith, and befriend them as brothers and sisters, we can see them grow to maturity.

Segue 2

Student Questions and Response

The following questions were designed to help you review the material in the second video segment. As we observed together in this segment, the local assembly of believers is God's means of following up and discipling new believers in Christ. As faithful, mature believers in the body take personal responsibility for the care of new converts in the church, we will then be able to be establish them in the faith–in doctrine, in spiritual growth, and personal witness. Make certain that you understand these foundational concepts, answering the questions thoughtfully and carefully.

1. What role does the local church play in the follow-up and discipleship of new and growing Christians? Is it possible, under normal circumstances, to come to full maturity in Christ without the ministry of other Christians in the body? Explain your answer.

2. From a biblical point of view, what are the essentials gifts and resources that God provides in the local church for the ongoing protection, feeding, and care of new believers?

3. According to Ephesians 4, what are those special individually gifted persons given to the body for the work of equipping the saints for the work of the ministry? Are these gifted people provided *within* every local church or *to the Church in general*? Explain your answer.

4. Give an example from the Scriptures of a relationship where God connected his leaders with partners for the sake of upbuilding, training, friendship, and equipping for ministry. What principles of discipleship do we learn from this example?

5. What are the elements the apostles employed in their ongoing investment in leaders and with new congregations they were discipling? Of these methods, which are appropriate today for us as we equip new converts to live the Christian life?

6. What is involved and what are the responsibilities in the role of the discipler as model, mentor, and friend? How do these roles interact as we care for growing Christians?

7. In what ways must Christ always remain the goal of any and all efforts to disciple another? What are some of the potential problems that could occur in a discipling relationship if we shift our focus away from Christ and maturity in him?

8. Why is one's own churchmanship so important to discipling others? Can or should we even attempt to disciple another if we refuse to participate in a local assembly under the authority of legitimate pastoral authority? Explain.

9. In planting a church, what is the role of discipling leaders? Are there differences in training emerging Christian leaders for the exercise of authority in the body, and training Christians to live the Christian life? Explain your answer. (You may want to refer to the chapters in the NT that focus on leadership discipleship, e.g., Acts 20, 1 Tim. 3; Titus 1; 1 Pet. 5; Eph. 4, etc.).

CONNECTION

Summary of Key Concepts

This lesson focuses upon the concept of follow-up and discipleship in church planting in the city. The acts of follow-up and discipleship welcome new believers into the Church and ground them in the faith respectively. Nothing ensures the viability of disciples in the body more than the deliberate incorporating of new believers in the local assembly of believers, which is God's agent of the Kingdom in this world. The concepts below summarize the key insights this lesson was designed to offer on these important spiritual ministries. Carefully meditate on them as they fill out the notion of welcoming new believers into the body, building up in the body to the fullness of Christ, and using one's gifts to contribute to fulfilling the Great Commission, all to the glory of God.

- Everywhere in the NT the Scriptures argue the importance of the follow-up of new converts and discipling new believers in urban church planting.

- The act of follow-up includes welcoming new believers into the church, i.e., incorporating new believers and equipping them in the local assembly of believers, which is God's agent of the Kingdom in this world.

- Following up new believers in the local church is "incorporating new converts into the family of God for the purpose of edification and fruitfulness, to the glory of God." This includes the notion of welcome and introduction into the body, building up in the body to the fullness of Christ, and using one's gifts to contribute to fulfilling the Great Commission, all to the glory of God.

- The practice of follow-up of new Christians is essential to their spiritual well-being. New converts need immediate care and attention because of their need for protection and to understand their new identity, their need for ongoing instruction and feeding, for the cultivation of new friends and life patterns, and because of their need for immediate and regular pastoral care.

- The dynamics of follow-up include baptism and membership in a local assembly, worship, befriending, pastoral care, preaching and teaching, discovery and use of one's spiritual gifts, and service and sharing of one's faith.

- We ought to observe a number of practical steps as we practice biblical follow-up: understanding the goal of discipleship as maturity, grounding the new believer in their assurance of salvation, teaching the new Christian to share their faith, and feed upon the Word of God. This also includes equipping them to walk with the Lord, introducing them to other members of the body, and connecting them to a small group as the building block of their faith.

- Follow-up is an essential dimension of equipping believers in the Assemble and Nurture phases of church planting.

- The local church is the context for beginning and sustaining effective discipling for new and growing Christians, especially in the sense that the local assembly of believers is the place which incorporates new converts into the faith, establishes them in their walk and doctrine, and equips them for the work of the ministry.

- The Scriptures provide a number of clear examples of God's leaders in a mentoring and modeling role. This includes notable cases such as Moses and Joshua, Elijah and Elisha, David and his "mighty men," Naomi and Ruth, Jesus and the Twelve, and Paul and Timothy.

- In the apostles' practice of discipling emerging congregations and leaders, certain key elements are seen again and again. These include their own personal example, their loving pastoral care, and faithful intercession and prayer on their behalf. We also see that they maintained ongoing personal contact with them, sent representatives to communicate to them, sent personal correspondence to them, and delegated to them both responsibility and authority as the need arose.

- The roles of the disciple-maker in the church can be summarized in the images of the discipler as a model (personal example), as a mentor (as one who coaches another to excellence), and as a friend (as one who befriends another for mutual support and care).

- All efforts toward the encouragement and training of developing disciples must be done with a commitment to and in the context of the local church. The local assembly of believers is the critical context of the church, not only for nurturing new believers to maturity, but also for identifying and equipping leaders for ministry.

- As we assemble believers in the church and nurture them through follow-up and discipleship, we can see growth occur which will lead to a strong, healthy, and dynamic church being planted in the city.

Student Application and Implications

Now is the time for you to discuss with your fellow students in depth questions about follow-up and discipleship. Your own ministry for Christ will undoubtedly intersect with these important practices. That is, you will have plenty of opportunity in your work to follow up new Christians and welcome them to the family, as well as help immature believers get on the path to maturity. As you have reflected on these truths, perhaps certain issues and themes have come to mind related to your own life and ministry.

In light of your own situation today, what would you say are the issues you need to clarify and resolve as you pursue this kind of work in the body? What issues have come to light as you have studied and analyzed these concepts? The questions below are designed to work with your own questions in this more personal exploration of these practices.

* Have you ever been followed up in the body of Christ, in other words, were you welcomed and introduced properly into the faith in the context of a local church? Who befriended you when you first came to Christ? Were you baptized immediately and did you join the church? Why or why not?

* Who discipled you in the faith? Did a person or group take personal interest in your own development and assist you to grow in your own spiritual walk and personal witness? If you weren't discipled, how would you say you grew in your Christian life–describe the kind of walk you have had since you came to Jesus.

* What effect do you think your own follow-up and discipleship has had on your view of these ideas? In other words, can you see how your own experience of being followed up and discipled has either positively or negatively affected your view of them?

* Does the leadership in the church where you currently attend and serve emphasize the need for follow-up and discipleship? What methods and opportunities for this does it provide for those who desire to grow? Does it actually offer courses in helping members follow up and disciple others?

* In your current responsibility at the church, who is responsible for your training and development? How often do you meet with them about your own growth? What do you need to ask your mentors for that would help you continue to grow in Christ and in ministry?

* In what ways might you be able to volunteer your time and service to disciple others, either in your own church setting, or to help with a new ministry or church plant you know of?

* Has the Holy Spirit ever given you the sense that he would like to you disciple in a more formal capacity, either as a leader, a deacon or elder, or even as a pastor? How have you responded to these leadings? What does he seem to be saying now about this role for you in your life?

* What specific areas in your life today require your attention in order to get to a place to offer more of your life and time to follow up and disciple others?

The Shepherding Movements

Over the last years, one discipling movement has attracted a lot of attention because of its insistence on the need for new believers to be shepherded and led in the context of small groups. In many cases, such groups have helped many new believers to grow and mature in Christ; in other cases many have suffered due to overbearing, authoritarian leaders who have essentially robbed believers of their freedom. Some groups have actually forced believers not to marry, to avoid certain kinds of relationships and practices, and even disallowed believers from associating with or listening to certain leaders and Christian organizations. The possibility of abuse is always present when discipleship is emphasized. What are the ways in which we can protect ourselves and others from "discipleship gone out of control?" How do we defend ourselves from authoritarian leaders and legalistic schemes of accountability?

page 320 *4*

Follow-Up and Discipleship, Jehovah's Witness Style

Perhaps no religious group in the West reveals the power of follow-up and discipleship better than the Jehovah's Witnesses. With the organization that rivals a Fortune 1000 company, the Witnesses keep careful records of the responses that inquirers and seekers have to their message. They are careful to avoid "those who want to argue" from "those seeking the truth." Furthermore, those who seem interested in their teaching are "followed up" with religious discipline, and when they do respond, the new "convert" immediately receives a person or couple whose sole responsibility is to incorporate the new Jehovah's Witness into the "organizational culture" they embody. Why do you believe the Jehovah's Witnesses are so effective at "follow-up" and "discipleship" in their own organizational environment, and so many Bible-believing churches are notoriously poor at it? What lessons can we learn from them regarding the need for careful, organized follow-up on "those seeking the truth" of Christ that we share the Gospel with?

Were They Ever Saved?

One question that ultimately gets raised in circles that do not tend to emphasize follow-up and discipleship is this: *what is the fate of those who make a profession of faith, even come to the church, but do not stay in the church?* On one side, some suggest that all true believers will not only profess faith, but they will also persevere in faith as believers in Christ. Others on the other side suggest that the reason why these new professors are not persevering is that they have never been adequately followed up and discipled. They claim that if we were to follow the example of Jesus and the apostles and actually equip the saints for ministry, we would not see such a fall off after profession, but many professing Christians would remain true to their profession, and follow Christ in the church. What do you think of these arguments?

Whose Curriculum Do We Follow?

In all books on follow-up and discipleship you will find a broad range of suggestions on what *themes to cover* with the new convert, and *what order to cover them*. Some want to concentrate on basic Bible doctrine, while others want to concentrate on the actual Bible itself, perhaps a Gospel or an Epistle. If you were suddenly placed in a position to oversee the training and equipping of those following up and discipling new converts in your church or church plant, what would your curriculum be. Write out a list of the top five themes you would suggest for those being trained to disciple others, and be prepared to give a defense for your outline.

Restatement of the Lesson's Thesis

Everywhere in the NT the Scriptures cite the importance of follow-up and discipling in church planting. The acts of follow-up and discipleship, which are essential dimensions of equipping believers in the *Assemble and Nurture phases* of church planting, involve welcoming new believers into the Church, i.e., incorporating new believers and equipping them in the local assembly of believers, which is God's agent of the Kingdom in this world. Following up new believers in the local church is "incorporating new converts into the family of God for the purpose of edification and fruitfulness, to the glory of God." Discipleship includes equipping new and growing Christians to walk with the Lord, connecting them to the body, and discovering their gifts for ministry in service to Christ. The local church is the context for both follow-up and discipleship, and both seek the edification and fruitfulness of new and growing Christians in the church. As we win the lost, assemble new believers in the body and nurture them through follow-up and discipleship, we can see growth occur which will lead to a strong, healthy, and dynamic churches being planted in the city.

Resources and Bibliographies

If you are interested in pursuing some of the ideas of *Planting Urban Churches: Tending*, you might want to give these books a try:

Eims, Leroy. *The Lost Art of Disciple Making*. Grand Rapids: Zondervan Publishing House, 1978.

Moore, Waylon B. *Multiplying Disciples: The New Testament Method of Church Growth*. Colorado Springs, CO: Navpress, 1981.

------. *New Testament Follow-up for Pastors and Laymen*. Grand Rapids: Eerdmans, 1963.

Ortiz, Juan Carlos. *Disciple*. Orlando: Creation House, 1995.

Phillips, Keith. *The Making of A Disciple*. Old Tappan, New Jersey: Fleming H. Revell Company, 1981.

Ministry Connections

Now think carefully about how and in what specific ways you can relate these truths concerning follow-up and discipleship both to your own life and/or to your ministry through your church. Regardless of the role you currently play in your church, the need to follow up new converts and disciple growing Christians will be ever present. Your response to opportunities that exist in your church and ministry are numerous, and you will need to ask God, the Holy Spirit, for specific leading and direction as to where you can best serve the church in these ways.

Think specifically now of your own life and ministry calling. How God might want you to change or alter your ministry approach based on these truths is largely dependent on your ability to hear what the Holy Spirit is saying to you about where you are, where your pastoral leadership is, where the members of your church are, and what specifically God is calling you to do right now, if anything, about these truths. Do not feel the need to react to these ideas; rather, spend time in both prayer and meditation before the Lord regarding your own ministries of follow-up and discipling. Moreover, you may already be involved in ministries such as this, whether with individuals or with groups, and the Lord wants you to continue in that work. What is important here is your ability to listen to the Lord, and respond to his specific leading regarding your ministry of discipleship in your church and ministry.

Above all, then, please seek the Lord's face as you ask him for his leading on how you can connect these truths in a practical way to your service for him. Come back next week ready to share your insights with the other learners in your class if the Lord so leads you.

| Counseling and Prayer | Not only ought we to seek the Lord's face for his direction in our lives and ministries, we ought to ask others to remember us in prayer as well. It could be that as you have been studying this material regarding discipleship that the Holy Spirit has surfaced specific needs you have that call for the fervent prayer of others on your behalf. The promise of Jesus in answer to prayer is clear and without equivocation. Hear his word in Matthew 7.7-11:

> *Ask, and it will be given to you; seek, and you will find; knock, and it will be opened to you. [8] For everyone who asks receives, and the one who seeks finds, and to the one who knocks it will be opened. [9] Or which one of you, if his son asks him for bread, will give him a stone? [10] Or if he asks for a fish, will give him a serpent? [11] If you then, who are evil, know how to give good gifts to your children, how much more will your Father who is in heaven give good things to those who ask him!*

The Lord's willingness to bless us and answer prayer on our behalf should encourage you to seek real prayer support in the development of your ministry, not only in this lesson but in all the various ministries in which you serve. Do not hesitate to ask your instructor or find a partner in prayer who can share the burden and lift up your requests to God. Of course, also remember the ministry of your church leaders and especially your pastor to lift these issues up to God on your behalf. Be open to God and allow him to lead you as he determines.

ASSIGNMENTS

Scripture Memory

2 Timothy 2.1-2

Reading Assignment

To prepare for class, please visit *www.tumi.org/books* to find next week's reading assignment, or ask your mentor.

Other Assignments

page 320 📖 *5*

Make certain you set aside ample time to carefully read the upcoming textbook assignment, as well as respond to the material by filling out your worksheet containing your summary of the reading material for the week. Also, by this time in your study you should have selected the text for your exegetical project, and have turned in your proposal for your ministry project. If you have not, please do so as soon as possible.

Looking Forward to the Next Lesson

This week we examined the critical role that the follow-up of new converts plays in planting urban churches. After believers have joined themselves to Christ by faith, we must incorporate them into the body of believers, grounding them in the faith, and connecting them to the life of the body that they may grow in him. We also analyzed the importance of effective discipling to urban church planting, seeing the central role played both by the Christian community and the individual discipler. In our next and final lesson we will introduce the final "E" of urban church planting, *Empowerment*. We will turn our attention to the final letter in our PLANT acrostic, which stands for *Transition*. All that we do in preparing, launching, assembling, and nurturing these new congregations is for the purpose of change, to *transition the church to independence and maturity*. Our desire is to see healthy, reproducing churches in the city that become agents of change and freedom in their communities, in Jesus name. This is only be possible if the Spirit raises up qualified leaders whom God can use to enable these new churches to thrive and reproduce. In the next lesson we will explore our role in working together with God to see such a generation of leaders raised up in the city.

Capstone Curriculum

Module 12: Focus on Reproduction
Reading Completion Sheet

Name _____

Date _____

For each assigned reading, write a brief summary (one or two paragraphs) of the author's main point. (For additional readings, use the back of this sheet.)

Reading 1

Title and Author: _____ Pages _____

Reading 2

Title and Author: _____ Pages _____

Planting Urban Churches
Reaping

page 321

Lesson Objectives

Welcome in the strong name of Jesus Christ! After your reading, study, discussion, and application of the materials in this lesson, you will be able to:

- Articulate the concept of *Empowerment*, as it relates in the urban church planting process. This process seeks to help the emerging church become sufficient to work with other congregations as leadership authority is given over to the church in order that it may become a self-governing, self-supporting, and self-reproducing church.

- Support biblically and logically the notion that raising up godly leaders who can shepherd and protect the church is the single greatest responsibility of effective urban church planting. Without godly gifted leaders taking responsibility for the well being of the newly formed church, the likelihood that it will survive, let alone thrive, are nil to none.

- Give evidence of the kinds of investments that are necessary in order for the leadership team of a church to have the authority, character, competence and membership support necessary to ensure a dynamic healthy church.

- List out some of the major challenges involved in empowering an emerging church for maturity and reproduction. These include the issue of authority, avoiding dependence while ensuring friendship and connection, and encouraging the church to not merely survive but reproduce itself for Christ.

- Outline the four central aspects of godly church leadership: the godly leader must be *commissioned*, i.e., a person of distinct recognized call; the godly leader must be a person of *character*, i.e., a person of proven experience; the godly leader must be a person of *competence:* a person of gifting and skill; finally, the godly leader must be a person of *community:* a person who lives to serve and sacrifice on behalf of others.

- Provide an overview, a snapshot, a blueprint of the three concepts and seven criteria related to empowerment which ensure the kind of church that effective urban church planters seek to empower and reproduce. These concepts include striving to ensure the church's independence, ensuring godly association with other churches, and encouraging ongoing reproduction in service and mission.

- Outline the seven criteria which define an empowered urban church. A newly planted urban church is empowered for reproduction when 1) a faithful group of converted, gathered, and maturing disciples of Jesus are in assembly; 2) it has selected its own pastors and leaders; 3) it has redefined the relationship it has with missionaries and workers who help to found it; 4) it encourages unique, burden-driven, gift-oriented ministries from its members; 5) it generates its own resources and income for operations, ministry and missions; 6) it faithfully stewards its resources and facilities, and 7) it is focused on reproducing itself, in service to the Lord and advance of the Kingdom in mission.

- Be able to recognize what a focus on reproduction will demand: pouring into the leaders who share the vision, sacrificing on behalf of the vision God gave, and doing your part in fulfilling the Great Commission, starting where we live and from there, to the ends of the earth.

God Will Lay the Cloak On

Devotion

1 Kings 19.14-21 - He said, "I have been very jealous for the Lord, the God of hosts. For the people of Israel have forsaken your covenant, thrown down your altars, and killed your prophets with the sword, and I, even I only, am left, and they seek my life, to take it away." And the Lord said to him, "Go, return on your way to the wilderness of Damascus. And when you arrive, you shall anoint Hazael to be king over Syria. [16] And Jehu the son of Nimshi you shall anoint to be king over Israel, and Elisha the son of Shaphat of Abel-meholah you shall anoint to be prophet in your place. [17] And the one who escapes from the sword of Hazael shall Jehu put to death, and the one who escapes from the sword of Jehu shall Elisha put to death. [18] Yet I will leave seven thousand in Israel, all the knees that have not bowed to Baal, and every mouth that has not kissed him." [19] So he departed from there and found Elisha the son of Shaphat, who was plowing with twelve yoke of oxen in front of him, and he was with the twelfth. Elijah passed by him and cast his cloak upon him. [20] And he left the oxen and ran after Elijah and said, "Let me kiss my father and my mother, and then I will follow you." And he said to him, "Go back again, for what have I done to you?" [21] And he returned from following him and took the yoke of oxen and sacrificed them and boiled their flesh with the yokes of the oxen and gave it to the people, and they ate. Then he arose and went after Elijah and assisted him.

Times of transition can be hard or easy, depending on the circumstances and the challenges contained in the situation. The transition from Elijah's prophetic ministry to Elisha was neither easy nor trouble free. Elijah, after a remarkable victory for the Lord on Mt. Carmel over the prophets of Baal, found himself depressed and dejected. His ministry had not had the kind of impact he had wished; he had even speculated that "I have been very jealous for the Lord, the God of hosts. For the people of Israel have forsaken your covenant, thrown down your altars, and killed your prophets with the sword, and I, even I only, am left, and they seek my life, to take it away." He felt alone, defeated, and pursued. Not a great place to be in when you're asked to define your ministry.

God is very careful to remind Elijah that the work of the ministry is his; God has never surrendered the final responsibility for change and transformation to his messenger and minister. We are *used by the Lord*; we are not, however, *the Lord himself*. God gave Elijah instructions about the "next step of ministry" he had for him, and assured Elijah that even in the face of his "unsuccessful work," the Lord had reserved 7,000 worshipers who refused to bow the knee to nor kiss the idol of Baal but remained faithful to the covenant of Yahweh.

It was in this setting and at this time that the transition of leadership occurred for Elijah. In verse 19 we see how Elijah departed from that place, and *found Elisha the son of Shaphat*, who was plowing with twelve yoke of oxen in a field. The text shows that Elijah passed by Elisha, and when he passed him, he cast his cloak upon him. Elisha knew the implications of this act, and asked for leave to settle family matters. Elijah's response reveals that leadership in the Lord's army is all volunteer. Their exchange reveals that leadership is a set-apart calling that involves a confirmed call, and a willingness to act of that call, no matter what. Elisha does not disappoint, for from that very time on, he acted on this call and became one of the greatest prophets in all of Jewish history.

A key lesson we learn here is plain: God is the one who calls men and women to ministry, and is it he who empowers them by his Spirit to fulfill that ministry. The appointing, the promoting, the leading, and the outfitting for the work is his, and the glory, therefore, will also be his. In one sense, placing the cloak on Elisha is *God himself, through the prophet Elijah, laying the cloak on him*. When God desires to work among his people for his own sovereign purpose and sake, he selects a person, prepares them for the call, and then leads them into his will, in his own way and for his own purposes, in his own manner.

We would do well in ministry to remember who it is we serve before we overmuch worry about *what we are doing*. The Lord Jesus is *Lord* of the harvest; he will raise up men and women to represent his interests and advance his Kingdom anywhere and among anyone whom he chooses. He alone *lays the cloak on*. Psalm 75.6-7 - For not from the east or from the west and not from the wilderness comes lifting up, [7] but it is God who executes judgment, putting down one and lifting up another.

After reciting and/or singing the Nicene Creed (located in the Appendix), pray the following prayer:

> *Eternal Lord God whose servants, the ministers of your Church encounter many difficulties and temptations in the course of their work: Sustain them in their vocation replenish them with the truth of the gospel and keep them faithful in prayer: Grant that in the issues of our day they may lead with courage and wisdom and guide them by your Spirit in their ministry to the diverse needs of men; through Jesus Christ our Lord.*

~ The Church of the Province of South Africa. **Minister's Book for Use With the Holy Eucharist and Morning and Evening Prayer**. Braamfontein: Publishing Department of the Church of the Province of South Africa. pp. 110-111

Nicene Creed and Prayer

Put away your notes, gather up your thoughts and reflections, and take the quiz for Lesson 3, *Planting Urban Churches: Tending*.

Quiz

Review with a partner, write out and/or recite the text for last class session's assigned memory verse: 2 Timothy 2.1-2.

Scripture Memorization Review

Turn in your summary of the reading assignment for last week, that is, your brief response and explanation of the main points that the authors were seeking to make in the assigned reading (Reading Completion Sheet).

Assignments Due

What Truly Qualifies

Today in many Christian church settings, the primary criterion for Christian leadership is academic and professional preparation. In other words, unless you have a seminary degree or similar kind of academic and professional credential, many congregations would not even place you in the running, if in fact you had submitted your name for the pastoral leadership position. Some churches go further yet, demanding seminary or some kind of equivalent credential to even participate in music, youth, children, and other kinds of church ministries. What do you think truly qualifies a man or woman for exercising leadership in the Church of God? Be specific.

Hard to Be a Pastor

The pastoral ministry is in disarray in some places. Many ministers are leaving their traditions in droves, being absorbed in "secular life." Some denominations are desperate for new pastoral candidates; their seminaries numbers are shrinking, and they are having to resort to all kinds of new, innovative ways of sharing pastors with congregations, allowing pastors to become itinerant, shepherding a number of congregations. Some areas are truly hard hit, and many denominational leaders lament with the current systems of producing leaders, which are slow, expensive, and insufficient. Why do you think it is becoming so difficult to find qualified pastors for many of the existing churches today? What might this suggest about the need to raise up a new generation of leaders, using different strategies to train and fund them?

Those Aren't Really Churches

In a conversation on the nature of church and the pastorate, one professor made a rather shocking claim about urban churches. He commented that many urban churches were not truly churches in any traditional way; they were a mixture of folk religion, Christian belief, and social family networks, and could barely be called "Christian" because they have not contributed like other churches to the theological and ministry structures of the historic Church. With not a hint of emotion or judgmentalism, the professor went on to say that if we use the traditional criteria for church that has been recognized in most denominations throughout church history, these are either barely churches, and some aren't really churches at all. What would be your definition of a *true church?* What is your reaction to the professor's bold (if not somewhat ill-informed) claim that many urban churches were not really *churches at all?*

Planting Urban Churches: Reaping

Segment 1: Transitioning Leaders Toward Independence

Rev. Dr. Don L. Davis

Empowerment is the final stage of effective urban church planting (cf. *Evangelism, Equipping,* and *Empowerment).* This last phase focuses on the final step of the PLANT acrostic, or *transition toward independence and maturity.* Above all things, we must strive to raise up a generation of leaders for the congregation who will go on to take full responsibility for the care and feeding of the members, and ensure its ongoing growth and mission. Effective urban church planters must seek to *invest as much time and energy as possible into qualified leaders,* those who are commissioned by God, proven in character, competent to serve, and willing to sacrifice on behalf of the community.

Our objective for this segment, *Transitioning Leaders Toward Independence,* is to enable you to see that:

- The final "E' of effective urban church planting refers to the concept of *Empowerment*, that process which seeks to help the emerging church become sufficient to work with other congregations as leadership authority is given over to the church in order that it may become a self-governing, self-supporting, and self-reproducing church.

- Raising up godly leaders who faithfully and responsibly shepherd and protect the church is the single greatest responsibility of effective urban church planting. Without godly gifted leaders taking responsibility for the well being of the newly formed church, the likelihood that it will survive, let alone thrive, are nil to none.

- In order to ensure a dynamic, healthy urban church, the church planter must do all that he or she can to invest into a leadership team who will have the authority, character, competence and membership support necessary to cause it to grow and mature in Christ.

Summary of Segment 1

- In order to readily and rightly empower emerging urban churches, important obstacles must be overcome and challenges must be met to ensure that they both mature and reproduce. These include the issue of authority, avoiding dependence while ensuring friendship and connection, and encouraging the church to not merely survive but reproduce itself for Christ.

- Equipping competent leaders for the emerging church is the greatest task of the church plant team. Godly church leadership can be understood through four interrelated aspects: the godly leader must be *commissioned,* i.e., a person of distinct recognized call; the godly leader must be a person of *character,* i.e., a person of proven experience; the godly leader must be a person of *competence:* a person of gifting and skill; finally, the godly leader must be a person of *community:* a person who lives to serve and sacrifice on behalf of others.

Video Segment 1 Outline

I. Empowerment: Transitioning Leaders Toward Independence

A. Purposes to pursue

To transfer leadership of the growing church over to its own leaders and members, in order that they may become a self-governing, self-supporting, and self-reproducing church

1. The focus is upon *appointing and equipping leaders who can take over responsibility for the church.*

    a. Acts 14.23

    b. Acts 20.32

    c. Titus 1.5

2. The stage in church planting is the "T" of the PLANT acrostic, and stands for "transition."

3. The result will be *churches with solid men and women in place who can continue the work of evangelism, discipling, and church planting in the city.*

   a. 2 Tim. 2.2

   b. 1 Thess. 3.12-13

B. Plans to implement

To invest as much as possible into the leadership team of the church in order that they may have the commissioning (authority), character, competence, and community (membership support) necessary to ensure a healthy, dynamic church

1. The need is for order and discipline in the equipping of leaders.

   a. Titus 1.5

   b. 1 Cor. 14.40

   c. Col. 2.5

2. The need is for godly elders and leaders who will shepherd the flock of God, ensuring ongoing growth and reproduction for the Kingdom.

   a. Acts 20.24-28

      b. 1 Pet. 5.1-4

3. The need is for wisdom and insight in knowing just when the Holy Spirit wants the transfer of leadership to occur.

C. Perspectives to adopt

To be aware of the unique challenges, difficulties, and opportunities which are connected to the Empowerment phase of urban church planting

1. Transition should not be the end of relationship or connection to the independent church, but the *transfer of authority* over to its leaders and its members, Acts 14.23.

2. Empowerment is about *giving power over to*; to empower an urban church we must see that some kind of authority, power, resources, or goods have been turned over to them for their ongoing management and stewardship.

3. The principle of "avoiding dependence" should not be translated as "be as stingy as possible;" we must *provide* for our children *without spoiling them*, 2 Cor. 12.14.

4. No pastor or church can function as an isolated, disconnected community: the "selfs" never meant (not do they mean) that a church is independent of other fellowships in the community.

5. The goal of transition is reproduction, not survival: all that takes place in the church plant should be engineered with the goal of "putting reproduction into the DNA" of the emerging fellowship.

6. There is no perfect moment of transfer: transition denotes *change* and all the parties concerned will probably have problems with it (in one way or another).

II. Commission: a Person of Distinct Call

A. The leader of God's church must acknowledge and embrace God's call on their lives to lead in the household of God.

2 Tim. 1.13-14 - "Follow the pattern of the sound words that you have heard from me, in the faith and love that are in Christ Jesus. [14] By the Holy Spirit who dwells within us, guard the good deposit entrusted to you."

B. Key Scripture

1. Leadership in the church is a gift conferred with the blessing of legitimate authority, 1 Tim. 4.14.

2. God gives his apostolic church planters authority to appoint elders and set up leaders in the church.

    a. Titus 1.5

    b. Acts 14.23

    c. 2 Tim. 2.2

3. Through the laying on of hands and by confirmation of the Holy Spirit, leaders are granted authority to represent Christ in the church, 2 Tim. 1.6-14.

C. Critical concept: on the Authority of God

　　1. The leader of the church acts on God's recognized call and authority, Matt. 28.18-20; Titus 2.11-15.

　　2. This authority is acknowledged by the saints, Acts 6.1-6.

D. Central elements of godly call and commission

　　1. God has issued the call and the leader has responded.

　　2. Confirmation has been given by members of the body itself.

　　3. The leader has a deep sense of personal conviction of the call, based on their conscience and the Holy Scriptures.

　　4. They demonstrate a personal burden for a particular task or people.

　　5. Confirmation by leaders, officially granted by the laying on of hands

E. Satanic strategy to abort: *to make the call muddy or premature*

　　1. A muddy call: the leader is not certain of the call and evidences this uncertainty in all they do, 1 Cor. 14.7-8.

　　2. A premature call: laying on of hands too soon before a potential leader is ready or has heard the call of God

a. Acts 6.6

b. 1 Tim. 5.22

F. Key steps in recognizing the call in a potential leader of the church

1. Identify God's call

2. Discover your burden

3. Be confirmed both by the members and by present leadership

G. Results: deep confidence toward God arising from God's call, 2 Tim. 1.5-8

III. Character: a Person of Proven Experience

A. Definition: reflects the character of Christ in their personal convictions, conduct, and lifestyle

Titus 1.5-9 - This is why I left you in Crete, so that you might put what remained into order, and appoint elders in every town as I directed you— [6] if anyone is above reproach, the husband of one wife, and his children are believers and not open to the charge of debauchery or insubordination. [7] For an overseer, as God's steward, must be above reproach. He must not be arrogant or quick-tempered or a drunkard or violent or greedy for gain, [8] but hospitable, a lover of good, self-controlled, upright, holy, and disciplined. [9] He must hold firm to the trustworthy word as taught, so that he may be able to give instruction in sound doctrine and also to rebuke those who contradict it.

B. Key Scriptures

1. They must have the reputation and experience of being faithful and wise managers, Luke 12.42.

2. They must be trustworthy, 1 Cor. 4.1-2.

3. They must be persons of sterling character and reputation, 1 Tim. 3.1-7.

4. They must steward their gift of leadership with sober commitment and heart, 1 Pet. 4.10.

C. Critical concept: in the humility of Christ

1. God's leader demonstrates the mind and lifestyle of Christ in his or her actions and relationships, Phil. 2.5-11.

2. God's leader is faithful over God's house even as Christ was faithful, Heb. 3.1-2.

D. Central elements of a leader of character

1. Passion for Christlikeness, Phil. 3.4-16

2. Radical lifestyle for the Kingdom, Acts 20.24

3. Serious pursuit of holiness, Heb. 12.14

4. Discipline in the personal life, 1 Tim. 4.7-8

5. Fulfills role-relationships as bond-slave of Jesus Christ, administrating all affairs of the church as a faithful steward, Phil. 2.5-11; 1 Cor. 4.1-2

6. Provides an attractive model for others in their conduct, speech, and lifestyle (the fruit of the Spirit), Heb. 13.7

E. Satanic strategy to abort: substitute ministry activity and/or hard work and industry for godliness and Christlikeness

1. Substituting place or prominence for character and godliness

2. Excusing shallowness by appealing to sincerity

F. Key steps to building character in potential leaders

1. Provide an example, 1 Cor. 11.1.

2. Teach potential leaders how to abide in Christ, John 15.4-5.

3. Discipline for godliness, 1 Tim. 4.7-8.

4. Pursue holiness in all things, 1 Pet. 1.14-16.

G. Results: powerful Christlike example provided for others to follow, Phil. 3.17

IV. **Competence: a Person of Depth and Skill**

A. Definition: Respond in the power of the Spirit with excellence in carrying out their appointed tasks and ministry

   Acts 20.32 - And now I commend you to God and to the word of his grace, which is able to build you up and to give you the inheritance among all those who are sanctified.

B. Key Scriptures:

   1. Facility and obedience to the words of Jesus is the most important resource in liberating those under our leadership, John 8.31-32.

   2. Depth of knowledge should be linked to a heart full of goodness and an ability to instruct (counsel) others into the ways of Jesus and his Kingdom, Rom. 15.14.

   3. The gifts of the Holy Spirit should be present in the leader's life and ministry, Eph. 4.11-13.

   4. The ability to rightly divide and accurately handle God's Holy Scriptures is essential for godly leadership.

      a. 2 Tim. 2.15

b. 2 Tim. 3.16-17

C. Critical concept: by the power of the Spirit: God's leader operates in the gifting and anointing of the Holy Spirit.

1. The Word of the Lord is sufficient for all that the man or woman of God needs to lead, as he directs, 2 Tim. 3.16-17; Isa. 55.8-11; Ps. 1.1-3.

2. The gifts of the Holy Spirit in the life of the leader provide unction and wisdom to deal with the various needs that he or she will face, 1 Pet. 4.10-11; Rom. 12.3-8; 1 Cor. 12.1-30; Eph. 4.11-16.

D. Central elements of a leader outfitted for the task

1. Endowments and gifts from the Spirit, 1 Pet. 4.10-11

2. Sound discipling from an able mentor, 2 Tim. 2.2

3. Skill in the spiritual disciplines, Heb. 5.11-14

4. Ability to teach and preach the Word of God, 1 Tim. 5.17-18

5. Capable to evangelize, follow up and disciple new converts, Rom. 1.16; Mark 8.38; 1 Cor. 2.2

6. Strategic in the use of resources and people to accomplish God's task

E. Satanic strategy to abort: function on natural gifting and personal ingenuity rather than on the Spirit's leading and gifting, Zech. 4.6

F. Key steps to empowering a potential leader's competencies

1. Discover the Spirit's gifts, Eph. 4.11-12

2. Receive excellent training from an able mentor, 2 Tim. 2.2

3. Master the Word of God, 2 Tim. 3.16-17

G. Results: dynamic working of the Holy Spirit through those who may appear "ignorant and unlearned," cf. Acts 4.13

V. Community: a Person for Others

A. Definition: Regards multiplying disciples in the body of Christ as the primary role of ministry

John 21.15-17 - When they had finished breakfast, Jesus said to Simon Peter, "Simon, son of John, do you love me more than these?" He said to him, "Yes, Lord; you know that I love you." He said to him, "Feed my lambs." [16] He said to him a second time, "Simon, son of John, do you love me?" He said to him, "Yes, Lord; you know that I love you." He said to him, "Tend my sheep." [17] He said to him the third time, "Simon, son of John, do you love me?" Peter was grieved because he said to him the third time, "Do you love me?" and he said to him, "Lord, you know everything; you know that I love you." Jesus said to him, "Feed my sheep."

B. Key Scriptures:

1. Pours out their life as one who is charged to guard, protect, and feed the flock of God, ensuring its growth, nurture, and blessing, Acts 20.28; 1 Pet. 5.1-4; John 21.15-17

2. Equips the members of the body in such a way that each member is empowered to share the good news of the Kingdom in their own *oikos* context, Eph. 4.9-15

C. Critical concept: for the growth of the Church

1. God's leader uses all of his or her resources to equip and empower the body of Christ for her goal and task.

2. God's leader seeks to empower the members of the body in order that they may fulfill their calling together as a body.

    a. As a community called to display God's excellencies, 1 Pet. 2.9

    b. As a temple called to be a holy temple for God's presence, Eph. 2.19ff

    c. As a body that works to demonstrate God's acts in the world, Rom. 12.4-8

    d. As a family that reveals the very life and love of the God who called them into existence, 1 John 3.1-2; John 1.12-13

D. Central elements of a leader with a shepherd's heart

1. Genuine love for and desire to serve God's people, John 21.17; 1 Thess. 2.7-10

2. Disciples faithful individuals, 2 Tim. 2.2

3. Ensures incorporation and growth in small groups, Heb. 10.24-25

4. Pastors (shepherds) and equips believers in the congregation, 1 Pet. 5.1-4

5. Nurtures associations, networks among Christians and churches for the sake of the unity of the Church, Eph. 4.1-3; Phil. 1.27-28

6. Advances new movements among God's people locally, Rom. 15.18-21

E. Satanic strategy to abort: exalts tasks and activities above equipping the saints and developing Christian community

1. Turning the leadership of the church into a purely administrative position

2. Preaching themselves and their own burden and life rather than selfless sacrifice on behalf of the body, 2 Cor. 4.2-6

F. Key steps to ensuring a leader for the community

1. Recruit leaders who love the people of God, John 21.15-17.

2. Commission elders and church in transition to independence.

3. Select elders formally through congregational and/or appointed means.

4. Formally commission elders and the church to independence.

5. Formally adopt constitution and bylaws and approve move to incorporate.

6. Focus on reproduction: strive to equip every member for ministry, not keeping things afloat.

G. Results: multiplying disciples in the Church, Eph. 4.9-15

Conclusion

» Empowerment refers to the transition of the church's affairs and direction to leaders who can provide solid Christian leadership and oversight of the church as we transfer authority into their hands.

» In order to empower the church and transition towards its independence, we must *invest as much as we possibly can into a leadership team of the church in order that they may have the commissioning (authority), character, competence, and community (membership support) necessary to ensure a healthy, dynamic church.*

Segue 1

Student Questions and Response

page 322 📖 *2*

Please explore now some of the ideas presented in the last video segment. *Empowerment* deals with the final stage of effective urban church planting, *Evangelism* and *Equipping* being the first two stages. Also, *Empowerment* highlights the final step of the PLANT acrostic, or *transition toward independence and maturity*. This focus on transfer of leadership is central to the success of church planting; enabling urban disciples of Christ to follow the leading of the Holy Spirit through the leaders and members he has provided to them. Keep these important concepts in mind as you grapple with the following questions. Support your answers with Scripture.

1. Why is the concept of *Empowerment* such a central notion for effective *urban church planting*? In what sense can we say that a church is *not empowered* if it neither has its own leadership nor the ability to be a self-governing, self-supporting, and self-reproducing church?

2. What is the relationship between raising up godly leaders who lead the congregation and the likelihood of the church's survival and reproduction? Who is ultimately responsible for raising up leaders for the Church? (cf. Acts 20.28 - Pay careful attention to yourselves and to all the flock, in which the Holy Spirit has made you overseers, to care for the Church of God, which he obtained with his own blood.)

3. True or False. "Without godly gifted leaders taking responsibility for the well being of the newly formed church, the likelihood that it will survive, let alone thrive, are nil to none." Explain your answer.

4. Why is it important that the church planter and the church plant team devote a large amount of its energy and resources in raising up a leadership team who will have the authority, character, competence and membership support necessary to cause it to grow and mature in Christ? What are "time and resource wasters" which might sidetrack a team from this primary responsibility?

5. List some of the key obstacles that must be overcome in order to empower urban churches for maturity and reproduction. Of these challenges, which do you suspect is the greatest or most fundamental challenge that must be given priority over the others? Explain your answer.

6. What is the difference between helping an urban church avoid dependence, on the one hand, and yet, the need for the church planters to avoid

stinginess and hoarding on the other? How can you best decide if an activity or event is breeding dependence in the urban church plant?

7. What are some clear and helpful ways to discern whether or not a prospective leader is *commissioned,* i.e., a person of distinct recognized call? How can we determine whether the prospective leader is a person of *character,* i.e., a person of proven experience? How can we detect if they are a person of *competence:* a person of gifting and skill? What about their identity as a person of *community:* a person who lives to serve and sacrifice on behalf of others?

8. If no leaders emerge, given these criteria, what is the church planter to assume, if anything at all?

What Does a Church Planter Look Like?

The task of church planting requires people who are uniquely gifted. Since you are reading these words, you may be asking, "Am I a church planter?"

A planter's **S.H.A.P.E.** includes:

Spiritual gifts: Gifts of ministry bestowed by the Holy Spirit

Heart or passion: A burden to establish an outreach toward a specific people group, in a particular location, or through a specific type of ministry

Abilities: Entrepreneurial talents useful in planting (or perhaps in generating income in a bi-vocational church plant)

Personality type: Analysis of personality types often appearing in church planters

Experiences: Tools for describing experiences to help the planter understand when, where, and how to plant a church

~ Ed Stetzer. **Planting New Churches in a Postmodern Age.** Nashville: Broadman and Holman Publishers, 2003. p. 78.

Planting Urban Churches: Reaping

Segment 2: A Blueprint for an Urban Church that Focuses on Reproduction

Rev. Dr. Don L. Davis

Summary of Segment 2

All effective church planting in the city, including all that we do in preparing, launching, assembling, and nurturing believers there, culminates in transitioning the church for the purpose of it becoming salt and light in Christ's name to the community. Empowered urban churches are those who have been enabled to become independent, who start to associate with other churches for the purpose of fellowship and service, and who reproduce themselves through kingdom-oriented witness.

Our objective for this segment, *A Blueprint for an Urban Church that Focuses on Reproduction*, is to enable you to see that:

- Three concepts highlight the character of a process that proves to be empowering to an emerging urban church. An urban church is being empowered for ministry in Christ if we are enabling the church to run its own affairs and so transition to independence, ensuring that the church is connected to other assemblies in godly association, and being encouraged through its giving, service, and mission to reproduce itself, advancing the Kingdom of God in the ways that God leads.

- An empowered urban church can be identified according to seven interrelated criteria, all of which together provide a clear portrait of a church that will reproduce.

    "A newly planted urban church is empowered for reproduction when..."

    1) a faithful group of converted, gathered, and maturing disciples of Jesus function together in worship and fellowship

    2) it is governed by its own pastors and leaders under its own processes

    3) it no longer functions in dependence upon the missionaries and workers who help to found it

    4) it encourages and spawns unique, burden-driven, gift-oriented ministries carried out by its members

5) it generates its own resources and income for operations, ministry and missions

6) it faithfully stewards its resources and facilities with kingdom priorities in mind, and

7) it is focused on reproducing itself, in service to the Lord and advance of the Kingdom in mission.

- Focusing on reproduction demands a plan to pour into the leaders who share the vision, a commitment to sacrifice on behalf of the vision God gave, and an investment to do your part in fulfilling the Great Commission, starting where we live and from there, to the ends of the earth.

I. **Empowerment: Transitioning toward Independence, Association, and Reproduction**

Video Segment 2 Outline

A. Independence: *transfer of authority to the leaders and its members*, Acts 14.23

1. A healthy church can govern its own affairs under the Lord, 1 Cor. 12.1ff.

2. A healthy church can meet the needs of its members and leaders, Gal. 6.2.

3. A healthy church can reproduce itself through evangelism, discipleship, and planting new churches, 1 Thess. 1.5-10.

B. Association: *healthy relationship and connection with other growing congregations and leaders*, 2 Cor. 8.1-5

1. A healthy church is independent but it is never isolated, 1 Cor. 4.14-16.

2. A healthy church is connected to the other leaders and congregations in its own locale, 1 Thess. 2.14.

3. A healthy church has a burden to participate in the Great Commission globally, Eph. 4.4-6; Col. 3.11; Gal. 3.28.

C. Reproduction: *a passion to multiply workers and reproduce churches in order to make a significant contribution to the fulfillment of the Great Commission*, 1 Thess. 1.4-8

1. A healthy church is stable and secure in its leadership and membership, 1 Tim. 5.15-17.

2. A healthy church is reproducing itself within its own culture, evangelizing, discipling, and planting other churches, 2 Cor. 9.2.

3. A healthy church is supporting the Great Commission advancement around the world by praying, giving, sending, 2 Cor. 8.1ff.

    a. *An active prayer ministry* for missions, Matt. 9.35-38

    b. *A generous support of missions* in the world, 2 Cor. 9.6-7; 2 Cor. 8.9

    c. *A steady stream of sending workers* into the field, Phil. 2.19-30

II. The Magnificent Seven: the Blueprint for a Church That Is Focused on Reproduction

A. Criteria One: a Faithful Group of Converted, Gathered, Maturing Disciples of Jesus, Eph. 4.11-16

1. Solid conversions to Jesus Christ as Lord and Savior

2. Self-identity as a separate Christian assembly with its own passionate spirituality, inspiring worship, and presence in the community

3. Possesses clear sense of membership, ownership, belonging; able to bring new members in easily through strong orientation and loving relationships

4. Clear sense of welcoming membership, disciplining members, restoring them

5. Incorporating people smoothly into the life of the body (i.e., small group life, friendships, large group fellowship, etc.)

B. Criteria Two: Selection of Its Own Pastors and Leaders, 1 Pet. 5.1-4

1. Creation of a charter/by-laws/constitution/covenant delineating role of pastor(s) and relationship to body

2. Installation of pastors and leaders endorsed by leadership and confirmed by the members

3. Granted authority to pastor, shepherd, and provide oversight to the flock

4. Accountable to the church's membership for their life and ministry

5. No outside hindrances or interference on what the leaders and members believe God desires for them

C. Criteria Three: Newly Defined Relationship with Missionaries Who Helped Found the Church, Acts 20.24-28

1. No longer children only, but *partners and colleagues*

2. Leaders exercise authority for the direction of the body without appeal to the missionaries

3. Responsibility for direction and operation lie with the leaders and members alone

4. Missionaries change their role in the church; become friends, colleagues, co-workers.

D. Criteria Four: Distinctive and Unique Burden-driven, Gift-oriented Ministries of the Church, 1 Pet. 4.9-11

1. Pastoral staff equips members for the work of the ministry

2. Members identify their gifts in the Spirit, and employ them practically in the life of the church in worship, leadership, fellowship, teaching, and ministry

3. Clear mission and vision of the church's purpose and goals to mature and grow in number as God leads

4. Members operate with freedom and the blessing of the leaders, given room to experiment in order to find new ways to do justice, love mercy, and walk humbly with their God

5. Reproducing new assemblies built into the DNA of our church (i.e., to fund and support other efforts of church planting around our city and beyond)

E. Criteria Five: Generating Own Resources and Income for Operations, Ministry, and Missions, 2 Cor. 8.6-11

1. Leaders and members look to God alone as source of supply to implement their vision

2. Members support the vision of the church through regular, generous, and sacrificial giving to the church

3. A commitment to remain financially free (liberated from debt and dependence on outside support)

4. Active, abundant, and generous programs to address needs of members

5. Commitment to demonstrate justice and mercy within the community

6. Contributing generously to evangelism and missions, at home and abroad

F. Criteria Six: Faithful Stewardship of Church Resources and Facilities

Matt. 25.21 - His master said to him, "Well done, good and faithful servant. You have been faithful over a little; I will set you over much. Enter into the joy of your master."

2 Cor. 2.17 - For we are not, like so many, peddlers of God's word, but as men of sincerity, as commissioned by God, in the sight of God we speak in Christ.

2 Cor. 4.2 - But we have renounced disgraceful, underhanded ways. We refuse to practice cunning or to tamper with God's word, but by the open statement of the truth we would commend ourselves to everyone's conscience in the sight of God.

1. People of integrity managing the monies and properties of the body

2. Simple, transparent structures to administer the church business

3. Careful, up-to-date inventory of the church's resources

4. Clear record keeping of the church's funds and finances, purchases, and allocations available to all leaders and members

5. Responsible purchase and upkeep of the church's equipment and facilities

G. Criteria Seven: a Focus on Reproduction, Phil. 2.14-16

1. A commitment to make planting other churches a part of the church's identity

2. A deep passion to associate with groups of leaders and churches that share its burdens

3. A determination to make praying, giving, and going the life blood of the church's identity

4. Sending members to engage in missions projects around the nation and globe

5. A determination to give sacrificially, and to be faithful till the end

III. Final Word

A. A focus on reproduction will demand *pouring yourselves into leaders who share your vision*, 2 Tim. 1.6-14.

B. A focus on reproduction will require *a willingness to sacrifice on behalf of the vision that God has given*, Acts 20.24.

C. A focus on reproduction will result in *you doing your part in fulfilling the Great Commission in your urban neighborhood, and from there, across the nation and world!* Mark 16.15-18.

Conclusion

» The kind of community that is empowered is one that is striving for its own independence, associating with other churches in fellowship and service, and ministering in Jesus' name to the community.

» God desires that we plant the kind of churches in the city that will not only survive, but also thrive and reproduce themselves as they seek to be an outpost and agent of the Kingdom of God in the city.

» The Lord will lead you as you in obedience to his Spirit go into your community to plant the Church of Jesus Christ, depending upon the leading of his Spirit and his Word to accomplish this important task.

Segue 2
Student Questions and Response

The following questions were designed to help you review the material in the second video segment. We saw in this segment how all effective urban church planting culminates in a process that transfers leadership into the hands of the church, i.e., that *transitions the church for the purpose of it becoming salt and light in Christ's name to the community*. We have not empowered a church if it has not grown to the point where its leaders and members are set free to govern the affairs of the church themselves, able to form healthy relationships with other like-minded fellowships, and then begin to reproduce themselves in tangible projects of giving, service, ministry, and mission for Christ in the community and beyond. Understanding the role of empowerment and the necessary transition that must occur in an emerging church is central to do cross-cultural church planting. Answer the following questions, keeping in mind these important insights covered in the last segment.

1. What are the three concepts that describe a process that proves to be empowering for an emerging urban church? Why is it important that the leaders and members of an emerging church run their own affairs and grow toward independence in order to be empowered? Why is associating with other assemblies key to real empowerment? Why can't a church be called empowered if it has not begun to give, serve, minister, and bear witness to the Kingdom?

2. What are the seven criteria which give us a blueprint of a healthy emerging church?

3. Why can't a church be called viable if it fails to faithfully assemble a committed group of converted, gathered, and maturing disciples of Jesus regularly? Why is the gathering of the faithful a sign of a healthy church?

4. Can a church reproduce itself if it is not governed by its own pastors and leaders, ruling under their own protocols and processes? Explain your answer.

5. Why is it necessary for the emerging church to redefine its relationship with the missionaries, church planters, and workers who helped to found it? What are the range of possibilities that the new church can outline for these workers?

6. Why must an effective church be defined in terms of its ability to encourage and sustain credible burden-driven, gift-oriented ministries carried out by its own members?

7. Can a church be empowered that is financially dependent on resources from the outside? In what sense must a church be able to generate its own resources and income for it own ministry operations, ministry, and faithfully steward those resources and facilities with kingdom priorities in mind?

8. Why must commitment to missions, both home and abroad, always be included as a criteria for a healthy, viable church?

9. Of all the attitudes, resources, and gifts needed to plant effective urban churches, what do you believe are the most important? Defend your answer with Scripture.

Summary of Key Concepts

This lesson focuses upon the *Empowerment* phase of effective church planting, and covers the final letter "T" in the PLANT acrostic: Prepare, Launch, Assemble, Nurture, *Transition*. The heart and soul of these processes and activities concern our ability to raise up a qualified core of commissioned leaders of proven character who possess the competence to lead the community which God has called them to. This transfer of authority and leadership is for the purpose of empowering the church, i.e., enabling them to grow toward independence, associate with other churches for fellowship and service, and reproduce themselves in kingdom-oriented witness and ministry. The concepts below outline the major insights and principles covered in the lesson.

- The final "E" of effective urban church planting refers to the concept of *Empowerment*, that process which seeks to help the emerging church become sufficient to work with other congregations as leadership authority is given over to the church in order that it may become a self-governing, self-supporting, and self-reproducing church.

- Raising up godly leaders who faithfully and responsibly shepherd and protect the church is the single greatest responsibility of effective urban church planters. Without these gifted leaders, urban churches will be subject to division, heresy, and stagnation.

- In order to ensure a dynamic, healthy urban church, the church planter must do all that he or she can in order to invest into a leadership team who will have the authority, character, competence and membership support necessary to cause it to grow and mature in Christ.

- Effective *Empowerment* demands that we overcome the ever-present challenges to transferring authority to the leaders and members. These include the issue of authority, avoiding dependence while ensuring friendship and connection, and encouraging the church to not merely survive but reproduce itself for Christ.

- The leaders who can effectively lead emerging urban churches must be *commissioned*, i.e., persons of a distinctly recognized call, of *character*, i.e., persons of proven experience; of *competence*, i.e., persons of gifting and skill, and persons of *community*, i.e., persons committed to serve and sacrifice on behalf of the members of the body.

- An urban church is being empowered for ministry in Christ if we are enabling the church to run its own affairs and so transition to independence, ensuring that the church is connected to other assemblies in godly association, and being encouraged through its giving, service, and mission to reproduce itself, advancing the Kingdom of God in the ways that God leads.

- A newly planted urban church is empowered for reproduction when a faithful group of converted, gathered, and maturing disciples of Jesus function together in worship and fellowship, and is governed by its own pastors and leaders under its own processes. Such a fellowship no longer functions in dependence upon the missionaries and workers who help to found it, and it encourages and spawns unique, burden-driven, gift-oriented ministries carried out by its members. An empowered church generates its own resources and income for operations, ministry and mission, and faithfully stewards its resources and facilities with kingdom priorities in mind. Finally, an empowered church is focused on reproducing itself, in service to the Lord and advance of the Kingdom in mission.

* Focusing on reproduction demands a plan to pour into the leaders who share the vision, a commitment to sacrifice on behalf of the vision God gave, and an investment to do your part in fulfilling the Great Commission, starting where we live and from there, to the ends of the earth.

Student Application and Implications

Now is the time for you to discuss with your fellow students your questions about the importance of *Empowerment* in transitioning a church plant to its own independent fellowship. This notion of empowerment resonates with what the Scriptures teach about maturity, which, while not being in total independence, highlights the issue of being able to teach others and cause them to grow. Look at two examples of this idea of growing to the point of no longer being a child, but being a teacher as well:

Heb. 5.11-14 - About this we have much to say, and it is hard to explain, since you have become dull of hearing. [12] For though by this time you ought to be teachers, you need someone to teach you again the basic principles of the oracles of God. You need milk, not solid food, [13] for everyone who lives on milk is unskilled in the word of righteousness, since he is a child. [14] But solid food is for the mature, for those who have their powers of discernment trained by constant practice to distinguish good from evil.

Eph. 4.11-16 - And he gave the apostles, the prophets, the evangelists, the pastors and teachers, [12] to equip the saints for the work of ministry, for building up the body of Christ, [13] until we all attain to the unity of the faith and of the knowledge of the Son of God, to mature manhood, to the measure of the stature of the fullness of Christ, [14] so that we may no longer be children, tossed to and fro by the waves and carried about by every wind of doctrine, by human cunning, by craftiness in deceitful schemes. [15] Rather, speaking the truth in love, we are to grow up in every way into him who is the head, into Christ, [16] from whom the whole body, joined and held together by every joint with which it is equipped, when each part is working properly, makes the body grow so that it builds itself up in love.

These texts make plain that God intends for us to no longer be children, but grow to the point of equipping others. And, what is true for us as individuals, can also be related to churches. God wants churches to grow!

Now that you have had a chance to think about empowerment and maturity, what kinds of issues and themes come to mind for you? Are you clear about the importance of empowerment, and the central role that the transition process plays in the overall church planting effort? Some of the questions below may highlight others questions along this line as well.

* Is *Empowerment* as much attitude as it is a practice or action? Explain.

* If we refuse to allow churches to govern their own affairs, handle their own finances, and determine their own ministry direction, how can we say that we are empowering them?

* How do issues like race, class, and culture shape and play into these issues of empowerment, transfer of leadership, and growing toward independence?

* Can an urban church be in a position of depending on the resources and personnel of a suburban church and it not result in an unhealthy, dependent relationship on the wealthier church? How so?

* What if an urban church plant, despite all of its bests efforts, simply can't find anyone or any group willing to take responsibility to shepherd and lead it? What options are available to us if that occurs?

* Must we always suspect that every church plant in the city will succeed? Justify your answer with an appeal to the apostles' experience in church planting.

* How would you know that God would want you to be involved in empowering urban churches for ministry? What kind of persons would make the best candidates to empower city people for ministry?

* Can a person be called in from the outside to an urban church and that be an empowering decision? What about a person from a different color or culture? Must you speak the language of the people in order to lead an empowered church?

* What is the likelihood that an urban church will last if it fails to connect with a larger association of churches which provides it with friendship and support?

What Are Church Planting Movements?

page 323 📖 3

Before we chase after Church Planting Movements, we need to adopt a working definition to be sure we will recognize them when we see them. A Church Planting Movement is *a rapid multiplication of indigenous churches planting churches that sweeps through a people group or population segment*. . . .

First, a Church Planting Movement *reproduces rapidly*. Within a very short time, newly planted churches are already starting new churches that follow the same pattern of rapid reproduction.

"How rapid is rapid?" you may ask. Perhaps the best answer is, "Faster than you think possible." Though the rate varies from place to place, Church Planting Movements always outstrip the population growth rate as they race toward reaching the entire people group. . . .

The second key word in our definition of Church Planting Movements is *multiplication*. Church Planting Movements do not simply add new churches. Instead, they multiply. Surveys of Church Planting Movements indicate that virtually every church is engaged in starting multiple new churches. Church Planting Movements multiply churches and believers like Jesus multiplied the loaves and fishes.

Perhaps this is why Church Planting Movements are devoid of goals to start ten or twenty additional churches in a country or city. Instead, these churches are satisfied with nothing less than a vision to reach their entire people group or city—and eventually the whole world! As each church realizes that it has the capacity and responsibility to reproduce itself, the numbers start compounding exponentially.

The third word is *indigenous*. Indigenous literally means generated from within, as opposed to started by outsiders. In Church Planting Movements, the first church or churches may be started by outsiders, but very quickly the momentum shifts from the outsiders to the insiders. Consequently, within a short time, the new believers coming to Christ in Church Planting Movements may not even know that a foreigner was ever involved in the work. In their eyes the movement looks, acts, and feels homegrown.

The fourth part of our definition is *churches planting churches*. Though church planters may start the first churches, at some point the churches themselves get into the act. When churches begin planting churches, a tipping point is reached and a movement is launched.

A tipping point occurs when new church starts reach a critical mass and, like falling dominoes, cascade into an out of control movement flowing from church to church to church. Many near-Church Planting Movements fall short at this critical point, as church planters struggle to control the reproducing churches. But when the momentum of reproducing churches outstrips the ability of the planters to control it, a movement is underway.

Finally, Church Planting Movements occur within people groups or interrelated population segments. Because Church Planting Movements involve the communication of the Gospel message, they naturally occur within shared language and ethnic boundaries. However, they rarely stop there. As the Gospel works its changing power in the lives of these new believers, it compels them to take the message of hope to other people groups.

~ David Garrison. **Church Planting Movements: How God is Redeeming a Lost World.** Midlothian, VA: WIGTake Resources, 2004. pp. 21-23.

CASE STUDIES

Not Quite Ready

(Based on a true story) A multi-racial urban church of about 75 members, with about $40,000 in the bank, its own by-laws and 501(c)(3) authorization, and a solid leadership core of elders, felt God's leading to join a evangelical denomination of largely Anglo, upper middle class believers. In negotiations with the denomination's district leadership, it was made known to them that they were not quite ready yet. They had no ongoing track record that they could sustain a mortgage, no proof of expansive growth, and their constitution was far more elder oriented than congregational in government, which was the denomination's vision of church governance. By most standards, this church was stronger than most urban churches will ever be. Based on this case study alone, discuss the likelihood of urban churches finding a home in one of the major White evangelical denominations today. Should urban churches form their own associations? Are there denominations more conducive to urban church issues than the major evangelical White ones?

Never-Ending Stream

An urban church plant has become dependent on the resources, personnel, and monies from outside suburban denominations in its district. The pastor, who is a gifted, loving minister but "not from the neighborhood," sees no real problem in this relationship. On the one hand, monies, services, and volunteer help stream in from the outside to sustain the little urban church, whose membership is small and not able to pay their pastor's and staff's salary. On the other hand, the urban church is highlighted in every newsletter and bulletin article on the denomination's "urban outreach," and the identity of the congregation has become a place which allows suburban believers of the denomination to come and "experience the city" with their friends in the church. A small but vocal minority of urban Christians want to break away and go "cold turkey" from the suburban resources. Others feel this is unnecessary and counter-productive, since most of the ministry of the church would end, as they know it, since virtually all of it is staffed and funded from the outside. How would you counsel these members to resolve these issues?

He's Not the Right Guy

An urban church plant is about to "take wings and fly;" after nearly four years of investment, the little congregation has grown to the point of becoming its own independent congregation in association with a Pentecostal denomination. Everything has gone remarkably well, except for a brewing conflict between the current leadership team (made up of 95% people from the community) and the head church planter, a person from outside, but who is godly, committed, and pastoral. The leadership team has gathered around a couple they want to ordain to be pastors of the church, but the church planter has serious questions, both about their financial integrity and doctrinal orthodoxy. The church planter knows of some rather shady dealings the couple has had financially in the past, and he is disturbed at their view of the Trinity, a kind of modalistic view that isn't real clear about the deity of Christ. He has sought to introduce these issues to the leadership team, only to be rebuffed as an "outsider," and a "foot dragger." Everyone in the church plant loves the couple and believes they will make a great pastoral couple. What would you advise the pastor to do, in light of his current situation, and the momentum growing to make the couple the pastoral family of the new church?

Restatement of the Lesson's Thesis

The *Empowerment* phase of effective church planting is the last of the three, with *Evangelism and Equipping* being the first two. This phase also covers the final letter "T" in the PLANT acrostic: Prepare, Launch, Assemble, Nurture, *Transition*. The heart and soul of these processes and activities concern our ability to raise up a qualified core of commissioned leaders of proven character who possess the competence to lead the community which God has called them to. Raising up godly leaders who faithfully and responsibly shepherd and protect the Church is the single greatest responsibility of effective urban church planters. Without gifted leaders, urban churches will be subject to division, heresy, and stagnation. The nature of empowerment involves our ability to enable urban churches to grow toward independence, to associate with other churches for fellowship and service, and to reproduce themselves in kingdom-oriented witness and ministry. Our overall goal is that the churches may become a self-governing, self-supporting, and self-reproducing church.

The leaders who can effectively lead emerging urban churches must be *commissioned*, i.e., persons of a distinctly recognized call, of *character*, i.e., persons of proven experience; of *competence*, i.e., persons of gifting and skill, and persons of *community*, i.e., persons committed to serve and sacrifice on behalf of the members of the body. A newly planted urban church is empowered for reproduction when a faithful group of converted, gathered, and maturing disciples of Jesus function together in worship and fellowship, and is governed by its own pastors and leaders under its own processes. Such a fellowship no longer functions in dependence upon the missionaries and workers who help to found it, and it encourages and spawns unique, burden-driven, gift-oriented ministries carried out by its members. An empowered church generates its own resources and income for operations, ministry and mission, and faithfully stewards its resources and facilities with kingdom priorities in mind. Finally, an empowered church is focused on reproducing itself, in service to the Lord and advance of the Kingdom in mission.

Resources and Bibliographies

If you are interested in pursuing some of the ideas of *Planting Urban Churches: Reaping*, you might want to give these books a try:

Feeney, James H. *Church Planting by the Team Method*. Anchorage: Abbott Loop Christian Center, 1988.

Garrison, David. *Church Planting Movements: How God is Redeeming a Lost World*. Midlothian, VA: WIGTake Resources, 2004.

Logan, Robert E. And Steven L. Ogne. *Churches Planting Churches*. Carol Stream, IL: ChurchSmart Resources, 1995.

------. *The Church Planter's Toolkit*. Carol Stream, IL: ChurchSmart Resources, 1991. An audiocassette album.

Malphurs, Aubrey. *Planting Growing Churches for the 21st Century*. Grand Rapids: Baker Book House, 1992.

Schwarz, Christian A. *Natural Church Development*. Carol Stream, IL: ChurchSmart Resources, 1996.

Stetzer, Ed. *Planting New Churches in a Postmodern Age*. Nashville: Broadman and Holman Publishers, 2003.

Wagner, C. Peter. *Church Planting for a Great Harvest*. Ventura, CA: Regal Books, 1990.

World Impact, Inc. *School for Urban Cross-cultural Church Planting Manual*. Wichita, KS: World Impact Press, 2003.

Ministry Connections

In the coming days you will be responsible to apply the insights you have learned from this course of study in a practicum that you and your mentor agree to. The ramifications of effective urban church planting for your life and ministry in the city are numerous and rich: think of all the ways that this teaching can influence your devotional life, your prayers, your response to your church, your attitude at work, and on and on and on. Your ability to articulate your learning to others in a way that is clear, concise, and compelling is a large part of representing our Lord in ministry. What is significant is that you seek to correlate this teaching with your life, work, and ministry. The ministry project is designed for this, and in the next days you will have the opportunity to share these insights in real-life, actual ministry environments. Make certain that you prepare carefully for your ministry project, and ask for the Holy Spirit's leading and direction as you address your insights before your chosen audience and venue. God can use your learning to encourage and challenge others to follow Christ more intimately and intensely!

Counseling and Prayer

We have now come to the end of our study of effective urban church planting. Survey the material, not only in this lesson but in the previous lessons as well. Are there any outstanding issues, situations, or opportunities that you still need the guidance and leading of the Holy Spirit for? Are there important aspects of your studies in this lesson that you require further instruction, dialogue, and insight? Are there any specific issues or people has God laid upon your heart that demand your further and more fervent supplication and prayer? Allow the Lord Jesus to speak his will to your heart, and then take the necessary time to receive the kind of counsel and prayer you need to do what the Spirit has shown you.

ASSIGNMENTS

Scripture Memory

No assignment due.

Reading Assignment

No assignment due.

Other Assignments

page 323 📖 4

Your ministry project and your exegetical project should now be outlined, determined, and accepted by your instructor. Make sure that you plan ahead, so you will not be late in turning in your assignments.

Final Exam Notice

The final will be a take home exam, and will include questions taken from the first three quizzes, new questions on material drawn from this lesson, and essay questions which will ask for your short answer responses to key integrating questions. Also, you should plan on reciting or writing out the verses memorized for the course on the exam. When you have completed your exam, please notify your mentor and make certain that they get your copy.

Please note: Your module grade cannot be determined if you do not take the final exam and turn in all outstanding assignments to your mentor (ministry project, exegetical project, and final exam).

The Last Word about this Module

The Lord Jesus Christ has given his people the commission to go and make disciples among all peoples of the earth (Matt. 28.18-20). Anchored in his authority and empowered by his Holy Spirit, we are called to evangelize the lost, equip disciples to obey his commands, and empower the Church to be agents of the Kingdom across the globe. We are given the high calling to go into communities and plant churches that will represent his interests and authorities in their own communities as outposts of the Kingdom of God.

In this module we have carefully outlined that process from beginning to end using the PLANT acrostic. As we *Evangelize* a community we *Prepare* as a team to go and share the Good News in a specific the field, and *Launch* our initiatives into the field as the Lord leads. We *Equip* those believers who respond favorably to the Gospel, *Assembling* them together in Christian community and *Nurturing* them through follow-up and discipleship. Finally, we *Empower* the new congregation to represent Christ as his Church as we *Transition* and transfer the leadership from the hands of the missionaries to those leaders charged with the responsibility to protect and care for the church, and ensure its ongoing growth and reproduction.

In this lesson we examined the role of investing in godly leaders who can provide solid Christian leadership and oversight of the church as we prepare to transfer authority into their hands. In order to empower the church and transition towards its independence, we must *invest as much as we possibly can into a leadership team of the church in order that they may have the commissioning* (authority), *character, competence, and community* (membership support) *necessary to ensure a healthy, dynamic* church. We looked at the kind of churches which God can use to serve as congregations where the broken, despised, and hurting can find refuge, where the Word of God is preached and lived, and where the hope of Christ's return is celebrated and expressed in obedience and love.

Our sincere prayer for you in your studies of these truths is that the Holy Spirit, the Fire and Light given to us by the Lord to do his work, will lead and bless you as you go in obedience to Christ's command to plant churches throughout the cities of America and world. May the Lord bless you and keep you as you give your all for his best, seeking in every way to fulfill the Great Commission in the city where you are.

Amen and amen!

Appendices

187	Appendix 1: **The Nicene Creed** *(with Scripture memory passages)*
188	Appendix 2: **We Believe: Confession of the Nicene Creed (Common Meter)**
189	Appendix 3: **The Story of God: Our Sacred Roots**
190	Appendix 4: **The Theology of Christus Victor**
191	Appendix 5: **Christus Victor: An Integrated Vision for the Christian Life**
192	Appendix 6: **Old Testament Witness to Christ and His Kingdom**
193	Appendix 7: **Summary Outline of the Scriptures**
195	Appendix 8: **From Before to Beyond Time**
197	Appendix 9: **There Is a River**
198	Appendix 10: **A Schematic for a Theology of the Kingdom and the Church**
199	Appendix 11: **Living in the Already and the Not Yet Kingdom**
200	Appendix 12: **Jesus of Nazareth: The Presence of the Future**
201	Appendix 13: **Traditions**
209	Appendix 14: **Paul's Partnership Theology**
210	Appendix 15: **Selecting a Credible Criteria for Independence**
213	Appendix 16: **Spiritual Gifts Specifically Mentioned in the New Testament**
215	Appendix 17: **Paul's Team Members**
217	Appendix 18: **Nurturing Authentic Christian Leadership**
218	Appendix 19: **The Role of Women in Ministry**
222	Appendix 20: **Discerning the Call: The Profile of a Cross-Cultural Urban Church Planter**
223	Appendix 21: **How to PLANT a Church**
230	Appendix 22: **Defining the Leaders and Members of a Church Plant Team**
231	Appendix 23: **Equipping the Church Plant Team Member**
232	Appendix 24: **The Communal Context of Authentic Christian Leadership**
233	Appendix 25: **Church Planting Models**

Page	Entry
235	Appendix 26: **From Deep Ignorance to Credible Witness**
236	Appendix 27: **Different Traditions of African American Response**
239	Appendix 28: **Targeting Unreached Groups in Churched Neighborhoods**
240	Appendix 29: **Dealing with Old Ways**
241	Appendix 30: **Overview Plant to Birth Models**
242	Appendix 31: **Overview of Church Plant Planning Phases**
243	Appendix 32: **Investment, Empowerment, and Assessment**
244	Appendix 33: **Five Views of the Relationship between Christ and Culture**
245	Appendix 34: **That We May Be One**
255	Appendix 35: **Advancing the Kingdom in the City**
257	Appendix 36: **Creating Coherent Urban Church Planting Movements**
258	Appendix 37: **The Oikos Factor: Spheres of Relationship and Influence**
259	Appendix 38: **The Complexity of Difference: Race, Culture, Class**
260	Appendix 39: **Culture, Not Color: Interaction of Class, Culture, and Race**
261	Appendix 40: **Authentic Freedom in Jesus Christ**
262	Appendix 41: **Apostolicity**
263	Appendix 42: **Apostolic Band: Cultivating Outreach for Dynamic Harvest**
264	Appendix 43: **The Church Plant Team: Forming an Apostolic Band**
265	Appendix 44: **Translating the Story of God**
266	Appendix 45: **Three Levels of Ministry Investment**
267	Appendix 46: **World Impact's Vision: Toward a Biblical Strategy to Impact the Inner City**
268	Appendix 47: **Ralph D. Winter Editorial**
272	Appendix 48: **When "Christian" Does Not Translate**
274	Appendix 49: **Pursuing Faith, Not Religion: The Liberating Quest for Contextualization**
278	Appendix 50: **Contextualization Among Hindus, Muslims, and Buddhists**
284	Appendix 51: **A People Reborn: Foundational Insights on People Movements**
288	Appendix 52: **Missions in the 21st Century: Working with Social Entrepreneurs?**
290	Appendix 53: **Documenting Your Work**

APPENDIX 1
The Nicene Creed

Memory Verses ⇩

Rev. 4.11 (ESV) *Worthy are you, our Lord and God, to receive glory and honor and power, for you created all things, and by your will they existed and were created.*

John 1.1 (ESV) *In the beginning was the Word, and the Word was with God, and the Word was God.*

1 Cor.15.3-5 (ESV) *For what I received I passed on to you as of first importance: that Christ died for our sins according to the Scriptures, that he was buried, that he was raised on the third day according to the Scriptures, and that he appeared to Peter, and then to the Twelve.*

Rom. 8.11 (ESV) *If the Spirit of him who raised Jesus from the dead dwells in you, he who raised Christ Jesus from the dead will also give life to your mortal bodies through his Spirit who dwells in you.*

1 Pet. 2.9 (ESV) *But you are a chosen race, a royal priesthood, a holy nation, a people for his own possession, that you may proclaim the excellencies of him who called you out of darkness into his marvelous light.*

1 Thess. 4.16-17 (ESV) *For the Lord himself will descend from heaven with a cry of command, with the voice of an archangel, and with the sound of the trumpet of God. And the dead in Christ will rise first. Then we who are alive, who are left, will be caught up together with them in the clouds to meet the Lord in the air, and so we will always be with the Lord.*

We believe in one God,   *(Deut. 6.4-5; Mark 12.29; 1 Cor. 8.6)*
    the Father Almighty,   *(Gen. 17.1; Dan. 4.35; Matt. 6.9; Eph. 4.6; Rev. 1.8)*
    Maker of heaven and earth   *(Gen 1.1; Isa. 40.28; Rev. 10.6)*
    and of all things visible and invisible.   *(Ps. 148; Rom. 11.36; Rev. 4.11)*

We believe in one Lord Jesus Christ, the only Begotten Son of God,
    begotten of the Father before all ages,
    God from God, Light from Light, True God from True God,
    begotten not created,
    of the same essence as the Father,   *(John 1.1-2; 3.18; 8.58; 14.9-10; 20.28; Col. 1.15, 17; Heb. 1.3-6)*
    through whom all things were made.   *(John 1.3; Col. 1.16)*

Who for us men and for our salvation came down from heaven
    and was incarnate by the Holy Spirit and the virgin Mary
    and became human.   *(Matt. 1.20-23; John 1.14; 6.38; Luke 19.10)*
    Who for us too, was crucified under Pontius Pilate,
    suffered, and was buried.   *(Matt. 27.1-2; Mark 15.24-39, 43-47; Acts 13.29; Rom. 5.8; Heb. 2.10; 13.12)*
    The third day he rose again
    according to the Scriptures,   *(Mark 16.5-7; Luke 24.6-8; Acts 1.3; Rom. 6.9; 10.9; 2 Tim. 2.8)*
    ascended into heaven,
    and is seated at the right hand of the Father.   *(Mark 16.19; Eph. 1.19-20)*
    He will come again in glory
    to judge the living and the dead,
    and his Kingdom will have no end.
      (Isa. 9.7; Matt. 24.30; John 5.22; Acts 1.11; 17.31; Rom. 14.9; 2 Cor. 5.10; 2 Tim. 4.1)

We believe in the Holy Spirit, the Lord and life-giver,
    (Gen. 1.1-2; Job 33.4; Ps. 104.30; 139.7-8; Luke 4.18-19; John 3.5-6; Acts 1.1-2; 1 Cor. 2.11; Rev. 3.22)
    who proceeds from the Father and the Son,   *(John 14.16-18, 26; 15.26; 20.22)*
    who together with the Father and Son
    is worshiped and glorified,   *(Isa. 6.3; Matt. 28.19; 2 Cor. 13.14; Rev. 4.8)*
    who spoke by the prophets.   *(Num. 11.29; Mic. 3.8; Acts 2.17-18; 2 Pet. 1.21)*

We believe in one holy, catholic, and apostolic Church.
    (Matt. 16.18; Eph. 5.25-28; 1 Cor. 1.2; 10.17; 1 Tim. 3.15; Rev. 7.9)

We acknowledge one baptism for the forgiveness of sin,   *(Acts 22.16; 1 Pet. 3.21; Eph. 4.4-5)*
    And we look for the resurrection of the dead
    And the life of the age to come.   *(Isa. 11.6-10; Mic. 4.1-7; Luke 18.29-30; Rev. 21.1-5; 21.22-22.5)*

Amen.

APPENDIX 2

We Believe: Confession of the Nicene Creed (Common Meter*)

Rev. Dr. Don L. Davis, 2007. All Rights Reserved.

* This song is adapted from the Nicene Creed, and set to Common Meter (8.6.8.6.), meaning it can be sung to tunes of the same meter, such as: *O, for a Thousand Tongues to Sing; Alas, and Did My Savior Bleed?; Amazing Grace; All Hail the Power of Jesus' Name; There Is a Fountain; Joy to the World*

The Father God Almighty rules, Maker of earth and heav'n.
Yes, all things seen and those unseen, by him were made, and given!

We hold to one Lord Jesus Christ, God's one and only Son,
Begotten, not created, too, he and our Lord are one!

Begotten from the Father, same, in essence, God and Light;
Through him all things were made by God, in him were given life.

Who for us all, for salvation, came down from heav'n to earth,
Was incarnate by the Spirit's pow'r, and the Virgin Mary's birth.

Who for us too, was crucified, by Pontius Pilate's hand,
Suffered, was buried in the tomb, on third day rose again.

According to the Sacred text all this was meant to be.
Ascended to heav'n, to God's right hand, now seated high in glory.

He'll come again in glory to judge all those alive and dead.
His Kingdom rule shall never end, for he will reign as Head.

We worship God, the Holy Spirit, our Lord, Life-giver known,
With Fath'r and Son is glorified, Who by the prophets spoke.

And we believe in one true Church, God's people for all time,
Cath'lic in scope, and built upon the apostolic line.

Acknowledging one baptism, for forgiv'ness of our sin,
We look for Resurrection day–the dead shall live again.

We look for those unending days, life of the Age to come,
When Christ's great Reign shall come to earth, and God's will shall be done!

APPENDIX 3
The Story of God: Our Sacred Roots
Rev. Dr. Don L. Davis

The Alpha and the Omega	Christus Victor	Come, Holy Spirit	Your Word Is Truth	The Great Confession	His Life in Us	Living in the Way	Reborn to Serve
The LORD God is the source, sustainer, and end of all things in the heavens and earth. All things were formed and exist by his will and for his eternal glory, the triune God, Father, Son, and Holy Spirit. Rom. 11.36.							
THE TRIUNE GOD'S UNFOLDING DRAMA — God's Self-Revelation in Creation, Israel, and Christ				THE CHURCH'S PARTICIPATION IN GOD'S UNFOLDING DRAMA — Fidelity to the Apostolic Witness to Christ and His Kingdom			
The Objective Foundation: The Sovereign Love of God — God's Narration of His Saving Work in Christ				The Subjective Practice: Salvation by Grace through Faith — The Redeemed's Joyous Response to God's Saving Work in Christ			
The Author of the Story	*The Champion of the Story*	*The Interpreter of the Story*	*The Testimony of the Story*	*The People of the Story*	*Re-enactment of the Story*	*Embodiment of the Story*	*Continuation of the Story*
The Father as Director	Jesus as Lead Actor	The Spirit as Narrator	Scripture as Script	As Saints, Confessors	As Worshipers, Ministers	As Followers, Sojourners	As Servants, Ambassadors
Christian Worldview	Communal Identity	Spiritual Experience	Biblical Authority	Orthodox Theology	Priestly Worship	Congregational Discipleship	Kingdom Witness
Theistic and Trinitarian Vision	Christ-centered Foundation	Spirit-Indwelt and -Filled Community	Canonical and Apostolic Witness	Ancient Creedal Affirmation of Faith	Weekly Gathering in Christian Assembly	Corporate, Ongoing Spiritual Formation	Active Agents of the Reign of God
Sovereign Willing	Messianic Representing	Divine Comforting	Inspired Testifying	Truthful Retelling	Joyful Excelling	Faithful Indwelling	Hopeful Compelling
Creator — True Maker of the Cosmos	Recapitulation — Typos and Fulfillment of the Covenant	Life-Giver — Regeneration and Adoption	Divine Inspiration — God-breathed Word	The Confession of Faith — Union with Christ	Song and Celebration — Historical Recitation	Pastoral Oversight — Shepherding the Flock	Explicit Unity — Love for the Saints
Owner — Sovereign Disposer of Creation	Revealer — Incarnation of the Word	Teacher — Illuminator of the Truth	Sacred History — Historical Record	Baptism into Christ — Communion of Saints	Homilies and Teachings — Prophetic Proclamation	Shared Spirituality — Common Journey through the Spiritual Disciplines	Radical Hospitality — Evidence of God's Kingdom Reign
Ruler — Blessed Controller of All Things	Redeemer — Reconciler of All Things	Helper — Endowment and the Power	Biblical Theology — Divine Commentary	The Rule of Faith — Apostles' Creed and Nicene Creed	The Lord's Supper — Dramatic Re-enactment	Embodiment — Anamnesis and Prolepsis through the Church Year	Extravagant Generosity — Good Works
Covenant Keeper — Faithful Promisor	Restorer — Christ, the Victor over the powers of evil	Guide — Divine Presence and Shekinah	Spiritual Food — Sustenance for the Journey	The Vincentian Canon — Ubiquity, antiquity, universality	Eschatological Foreshadowing — The Already/Not Yet	Effective Discipling — Spiritual Formation in the Believing Assembly	Evangelical Witness — Making Disciples of All People Groups

APPENDIX 4

The Theology of Christus Victor
A Christ-Centered Biblical Motif for Integrating and Renewing the Urban Church

Rev. Dr. Don L. Davis

	The Promised Messiah	The Word Made Flesh	The Son of Man	The Suffering Servant	The Lamb of God	The Victorious Conqueror	The Reigning Lord in Heaven	The Bridegroom and Coming King
Biblical Framework	Israel's hope of Yahweh's anointed who would redeem his people	In the person of Jesus of Nazareth, the Lord has come to the world	As the promised king and divine Son of Man, Jesus reveals the Father's glory and salvation to the world	As Inaugurator of the Kingdom of God, Jesus demonstrates God's reign present through his words, wonders, and works	As both High Priest and Paschal Lamb, Jesus offers himself to God on our behalf as a sacrifice for sin	In his resurrection from the dead and ascension to God's right hand, Jesus is proclaimed as Victor over the power of sin and death	Now reigning at God's right hand till his enemies are made his footstool, Jesus pours out his benefits on his body	Soon the risen and ascended Lord will return to gather his Bride, the Church, and consummate his work
Scripture References	Isa. 9.6-7 Jer. 23.5-6 Isa. 11.1-10	John 1.14-18 Matt. 1.20-23 Phil. 2.6-8	Matt. 2.1-11 Num. 24.17 Luke 1.78-79	Mark 1.14-15 Matt. 12.25-30 Luke 17.20-21	2 Cor. 5.18-21 Isa. 52-53 John 1.29	Eph. 1.16-23 Phil. 2.5-11 Col. 1.15-20	1 Cor. 15.25 Eph. 4.15-16 Acts. 2.32-36	Rom. 14.7-9 Rev. 5.9-13 1 Thess. 4.13-18
Jesus' History	The pre-incarnate, only begotten Son of God in glory	His conception by the Spirit, and birth to Mary	His manifestation to the Magi and to the world	His teaching, exorcisms, miracles, and mighty works among the people	His suffering, crucifixion, death, and burial	His resurrection, with appearances to his witnesses, and his ascension to the Father	The sending of the Holy Spirit and his gifts, and Christ's session in heaven at the Father's right hand	His soon return from heaven to earth as Lord and Christ: the Second Coming
Description	The biblical promise for the seed of Abraham, the prophet like Moses, the son of David	In the Incarnation, God has come to us; Jesus reveals to humankind the Father's glory in fullness	In Jesus, God has shown his salvation to the entire world, including the Gentiles	In Jesus, the promised Kingdom of God has come visibly to earth, demonstrating his binding of Satan and rescinding the Curse	As God's perfect Lamb, Jesus offers himself up to God as a sin offering on behalf of the entire world	In his resurrection and ascension, Jesus destroyed death, disarmed Satan, and rescinded the Curse	Jesus is installed at the Father's right hand as Head of the Church, Firstborn from the dead, and supreme Lord in heaven	As we labor in his harvest field in the world, so we await Christ's return, the fulfillment of his promise
Church Year	Advent	Christmas	Season after Epiphany Baptism and Transfiguration	Lent	Holy Week Passion	Eastertide Easter, Ascension Day, Pentecost	Season after Pentecost Trinity Sunday	Season after Pentecost All Saints Day, Reign of Christ the King
	The Coming of Christ	*The Birth of Christ*	*The Manifestation of Christ*	*The Ministry of Christ*	*The Suffering and Death of Christ*	*The Resurrection and Ascension of Christ*	*The Heavenly Session of Christ*	*The Reign of Christ*
Spiritual Formation	As we await his Coming, let us proclaim and affirm the hope of Christ	O Word made flesh, let us every heart prepare him room to dwell	Divine Son of Man, show the nations your salvation and glory	In the person of Christ, the power of the reign of God has come to earth and to the Church	May those who share the Lord's death be resurrected with him	Let us participate by faith in the victory of Christ over the power of sin, Satan, and death	Come, indwell us, Holy Spirit, and empower us to advance Christ's Kingdom in the world	We live and work in expectation of his soon return, seeking to please him in all things

APPENDIX 5
Christus Victor
An Integrated Vision for the Christian Life
Rev. Dr. Don L. Davis

For the Church
- The Church is the primary extension of Jesus in the world
- Ransomed treasure of the victorious, risen Christ
- *Laos:* The people of God
- God's new creation: presence of the future
- Locus and agent of the Already/Not Yet Kingdom

For Theology and Doctrine
- The authoritative Word of Christ's victory: the Apostolic Tradition: the Holy Scriptures
- Theology as commentary on the grand narrative of God
- *Christus Victor* as core theological framework for meaning in the world
- The Nicene Creed: the Story of God's triumphant grace

For Spirituality
- The Holy Spirit's presence and power in the midst of God's people
- Sharing in the disciplines of the Spirit
- Gatherings, lectionary, liturgy, and our observances in the Church Year
- Living the life of the risen Christ in the rhythm of our ordinary lives

For Gifts
- God's gracious endowments and benefits from *Christus Victor*
- Pastoral offices to the Church
- The Holy Spirit's sovereign dispensing of the gifts
- Stewardship: divine, diverse gifts for the common good

Christus Victor
Destroyer of Evil and Death
Restorer of Creation
Victor o'er Hades and Sin
Crusher of Satan

For Worship
- People of the Resurrection: unending celebration of the people of God
- Remembering, participating in the Christ event in our worship
- Listen and respond to the Word
- Transformed at the Table, the Lord's Supper
- The presence of the Father through the Son in the Spirit

For Evangelism and Mission
- Evangelism as unashamed declaration and demonstration of *Christus Victor* to the world
- The Gospel as Good News of kingdom pledge
- We proclaim God's Kingdom come in the person of Jesus of Nazareth
- The Great Commission: go to all people groups making disciples of Christ and his Kingdom
- Proclaiming Christ as Lord and Messiah

For Justice and Compassion
- The gracious and generous expressions of Jesus through the Church
- The Church displays the very life of the Kingdom
- The Church demonstrates the very life of the Kingdom of heaven right here and now
- Having freely received, we freely give (no sense of merit or pride)
- Justice as tangible evidence of the Kingdom come

APPENDIX 6
Old Testament Witness to Christ and His Kingdom

Rev. Dr. Don L. Davis

Christ Is Seen in the OT's:	Covenant Promise and Fulfillment	Moral Law	Christophanies	Typology	Tabernacle, Festival, and Levitical Priesthood	Messianic Prophecy	Salvation Promises
Passage	Gen. 12.1-3	Matt. 5.17-18	John 1.18	1 Cor. 15.45	Heb. 8.1-6	Mic. 5.2	Isa. 9.6-7
Example	The Promised Seed of the Abrahamic covenant	The Law given on Mount Sinai	Commander of the Lord's army	Jonah and the great fish	Melchizedek, as both High Priest and King	The Lord's Suffering Servant	Righteous Branch of David
Christ As	Seed of the woman	The Prophet of God	God's present Revelation	Antitype of God's drama	Our eternal High Priest	The coming Son of Man	Israel's Redeemer and King
Where Illustrated	Galatians	Matthew	John	Matthew	Hebrews	Luke and Acts	John and Revelation
Exegetical Goal	To see Christ as heart of God's sacred drama	To see Christ as fulfillment of the Law	To see Christ as God's revealer	To see Christ as antitype of divine typos	To see Christ in the Temple *cultus*	To see Christ as true Messiah	To see Christ as coming King
How Seen in the NT	As fulfillment of God's sacred oath	As *telos* of the Law	As full, final, and superior revelation	As substance behind the historical shadows	As reality behind the rules and roles	As the Kingdom made present	As the One who will rule on David's throne
Our Response in Worship	God's veracity and faithfulness	God's perfect righteousness	God's presence among us	God's inspired Scripture	God's ontology: his realm as primary and determinative	God's anointed servant and mediator	God's resolve to restore his kingdom authority
How God Is Vindicated	God does not lie: he's true to his word	Jesus fulfills all righteousness	God's fulness is revealed to us in Jesus of Nazareth	The Spirit spoke by the prophets	The Lord has provided a mediator for humankind	Every jot and tittle written of him will occur	Evil will be put down, creation restored, under his reign

APPENDIX 7
Summary Outline of the Scriptures
Rev. Dr. Don L. Davis

1. GENESIS - Beginnings
   a. Adam
   b. Noah
   c. Abraham
   d. Isaac
   e. Jacob
   f. Joseph

2. EXODUS - Redemption, (out of)
   a. Slavery
   b. Deliverance
   c. Law
   d. Tabernacle

3. LEVITICUS - Worship and Fellowship
   a. Offerings, sacrifices
   b. Priests
   c. Feasts, festivals

4. NUMBERS - Service and Walk
   a. Organized
   b. Wanderings

5. DEUTERONOMY - Obedience
   a. Moses reviews history and law
   b. Civil and social laws
   c. Palestinian Covenant
   d. Moses' blessing and death

6. JOSHUA - Redemption (into)
   a. Conquer the land
   b. Divide up the land
   c. Joshua's farewell

7. JUDGES - God's Deliverance
   a. Disobedience and judgment
   b. Israel's twelve judges
   c. Lawless conditions

8. RUTH - Love
   a. Ruth chooses
   b. Ruth works
   c. Ruth waits
   d. Ruth rewarded

9. 1 SAMUEL - Kings, Priestly Perspective
   a. Eli
   b. Samuel
   c. Saul
   d. David

10. 2 SAMUEL - David
    a. King of Judah
         (9 years - Hebron)
    b. King of all Israel
         (33 years - Jerusalem)

11. 1 KINGS - Solomon's Glory, Kingdom's Decline
    a. Solomon's glory
    b. Kingdom's decline
    c. Elijah the prophet

12. 2 KINGS - Divided Kingdom
    a. Elisha
    b. Israel (N. Kingdom falls)
    c. Judah (S. Kingdom falls)

13. 1 CHRONICLES - David's Temple Arrangements
    a. Genealogies
    b. End of Saul's reign
    c. Reign of David
    d. Temple preparations

14. 2 CHRONICLES - Temple and Worship Abandoned
    a. Solomon
    b. Kings of Judah

15. EZRA - The Minority (Remnant)
    a. First return from exile - Zerubbabel
    b. Second return from exile - Ezra (priest)

16. NEHEMIAH - Rebuilding by Faith
    a. Rebuild walls
    b. Revival
    c. Religious reform

17. ESTHER - Female Savior
    a. Esther
    b. Haman
    c. Mordecai
    d. Deliverance: Feast of Purim

18. JOB - Why the Righteous Suffer
    a. Godly Job
    b. Satan's attack
    c. Four philosophical friends
    d. God lives

19. PSALMS - Prayer and Praise
    a. Prayers of David
    b. Godly suffer; deliverance
    c. God deals with Israel
    d. Suffering of God's people - end with the Lord's reign
    e. The Word of God (Messiah's suffering and glorious return)

20. PROVERBS - Wisdom
    a. Wisdom versus folly
    b. Solomon
    c. Solomon - Hezekiah
    d. Agur
    e. Lemuel

21. ECCLESIASTES - Vanity
    a. Experimentation
    b. Observation
    c. Consideration

22. SONG OF SOLOMON - Love Story

23. ISAIAH - The Justice (Judgment) and Grace (Comfort) of God
    a. Prophecies of punishment
    b. History
    c. Prophecies of blessing

24. JEREMIAH - Judah's Sin Leads to Babylonian Captivity
    a. Jeremiah's call; empowered
    b. Judah condemned; predicted Babylonian captivity
    c. Restoration promised
    d. Prophesied judgment inflicted
    e. Prophesies against Gentiles
    f. Summary of Judah's captivity

25. LAMENTATIONS - Lament over Jerusalem
    a. Affliction of Jerusalem
    b. Destroyed because of sin
    c. The prophet's suffering
    d. Present desolation versus past splendor
    e. Appeal to God for mercy

26. EZEKIEL - Israel's Captivity and Restoration
    a. Judgment on Judah and Jerusalem
    b. Judgment on Gentile nations
    c. Israel restored; Jerusalem's future glory

27. DANIEL - The Time of the Gentiles
    a. History; Nebuchadnezzar, Belshazzar, Daniel
    b. Prophecy

28. HOSEA - Unfaithfulness
    a. Unfaithfulness
    b. Punishment
    c. Restoration

29. JOEL - The Day of the Lord
    a. Locust plague
    b. Events of the future day of the Lord
    c. Order of the future day of the Lord

30. AMOS - God Judges Sin
    a. Neighbors judged
    b. Israel judged
    c. Visions of future judgment
    d. Israel's past judgment blessings

31. OBADIAH - Edom's Destruction
    a. Destruction prophesied
    b. Reasons for destruction
    c. Israel's future blessing

32. JONAH - Gentile Salvation
    a. Jonah disobeys
    b. Other suffer
    c. Jonah punished
    d. Jonah obeys; thousands saved
    e. Jonah displeased, no love for souls

33. MICAH - Israel's Sins, Judgment, and Restoration
    a. Sin and judgment
    b. Grace and future restoration
    c. Appeal and petition

34. NAHUM - Nineveh Condemned
    a. God hates sin
    b. Nineveh's doom prophesied
    c. Reasons for doom

35. HABAKKUK - The Just Shall Live by Faith
    a. Complaint of Judah's unjudged sin
    b. Chaldeans will punish
    c. Complaint of Chaldeans' wickedness
    d. Punishment promised
    e. Prayer for revival; faith in God

36. ZEPHANIAH - Babylonian Invasion Prefigures the Day of the Lord
    a. Judgment on Judah foreshadows the Great Day of the Lord
    b. Judgment on Jerusalem and neighbors foreshadows final judgment of all nations
    c. Israel restored after judgments

37. HAGGAI - Rebuild the Temple
    a. Negligence
    b. Courage
    c. Separation
    d. Judgment

38. ZECHARIAH - Two Comings of Christ
    a. Zechariah's vision
    b. Bethel's question; Jehovah's answer
    c. Nation's downfall and salvation

39. MALACHI - Neglect
    a. The priest's sins
    b. The people's sins
    c. The faithful few

Summary Outline of the Scriptures (continued)

1. MATTHEW - Jesus the King
   a. The Person of the King
   b. The Preparation of the King
   c. The Propaganda of the King
   d. The Program of the King
   e. The Passion of the King
   f. The Power of the King

2. MARK - Jesus the Servant
   a. John introduces the Servant
   b. God the Father identifies the Servant
   c. The temptation initiates the Servant
   d. Work and word of the Servant
   e. Death, burial, resurrection

3. LUKE - Jesus Christ the Perfect Man
   a. Birth and family of the Perfect Man
   b. Testing of the Perfect Man; hometown
   c. Ministry of the Perfect Man
   d. Betrayal, trial, and death of the Perfect Man
   e. Resurrection of the Perfect Man

4. JOHN - Jesus Christ is God
   a. Prologue - the Incarnation
   b. Introduction
   c. Witness of Jesus to his Apostles
   d. Passion - witness to the world
   e. Epilogue

5. ACTS - The Holy Spirit Working in the Church
   a. The Lord Jesus at work by the Holy Spirit through the Apostles at Jerusalem
   b. In Judea and Samaria
   c. To the uttermost parts of the Earth

6. ROMANS - The Righteousness of God
   a. Salutation
   b. Sin and salvation
   c. Sanctification
   d. Struggle
   e. Spirit-filled living
   f. Security of salvation
   g. Segregation
   h. Sacrifice and service
   i. Separation and salutation

7. 1 CORINTHIANS - The Lordship of Christ
   a. Salutation and thanksgiving
   b. Conditions in the Corinthian body
   c. Concerning the Gospel
   d. Concerning collections

8. 2 CORINTHIANS - The Ministry in the Church
   a. The comfort of God
   b. Collection for the poor
   c. Calling of the Apostle Paul

9. GALATIANS - Justification by Faith
   a. Introduction
   b. Personal - Authority of the Apostle and glory of the Gospel
   c. Doctrinal - Justification by faith
   d. Practical - Sanctification by the Holy Spirit
   e. Autographed conclusion and exhortation

10. EPHESIANS - The Church of Jesus Christ
    a. Doctrinal - the heavenly calling of the Church
       A Body
       A Temple
       A Mystery
    b. Practical - The earthly conduct of the Church
       A New Man
       A Bride
       An Army

11. PHILIPPIANS - Joy in the Christian Life
    a. Philosophy for Christian living
    b. Pattern for Christian living
    c. Prize for Christian living
    d. Power for Christian living

12. COLOSSIANS - Christ the Fullness of God
    a. Doctrinal - In Christ believers are made full
    b. Practical - Christ's life poured out in believers, and through them

13. 1 THESSALONIANS - The Second Coming of Christ:
    a. Is an inspiring hope
    b. Is a working hope
    c. Is a purifying hope
    d. Is a comforting hope
    e. Is a rousing, stimulating hope

14. 2 THESSALONIANS - The Second Coming of Christ
    a. Persecution of believers now; judgment of unbelievers hereafter (at coming of Christ)
    b. Program of the world in connection with the coming of Christ
    c. Practical issues associated with the coming of Christ

15. 1 TIMOTHY - Government and Order in the Local Church
    a. The faith of the Church
    b. Public prayer and women's place in the Church
    c. Officers in the Church
    d. Apostasy in the Church
    e. Duties of the officer of the Church

16. 2 TIMOTHY - Loyalty in the Days of Apostasy
    a. Afflictions of the Gospel
    b. Active in service
    c. Apostasy coming; authority of the Scriptures
    d. Allegiance to the Lord

17. TITUS - The Ideal New Testament Church
    a. The Church is an organization
    b. The Church is to teach and preach the Word of God
    c. The Church is to perform good works

18. PHILEMON - Reveal Christ's Love and Teach Brotherly Love
    a. Genial greeting to Philemon and family
    b. Good reputation of Philemon
    c. Gracious plea for Onesimus
    d. Guiltless illustration of Imputation
    e. General and personal requests

19. HEBREWS - The Superiority of Christ
    a. Doctrinal - Christ is better than the Old Testament economy
    b. Practical - Christ brings better benefits and duties

20. JAMES - Ethics of Christianity
    a. Faith tested
    b. Difficulty of controlling the tongue
    c. Warning against worldliness
    d. Admonitions in view of the Lord's coming

21. 1 PETER - Christian Hope in the Time of Persecution and Trial
    a. Suffering and security of believers
    b. Suffering and the Scriptures
    c. Suffering and the sufferings of Christ
    d. Suffering and the Second Coming of Christ

22. 2 PETER - Warning Against False Teachers
    a. Addition of Christian graces gives assurance
    b. Authority of the Scriptures
    c. Apostasy brought in by false testimony
    d. Attitude toward Return of Christ: test for apostasy
    e. Agenda of God in the world
    f. Admonition to believers

23. 1 JOHN - The Family of God
    a. God is Light
    b. God is Love
    c. God is Life

24. 2 JOHN - Warning against Receiving Deceivers
    a. Walk in truth
    b. Love one another
    c. Receive not deceivers
    d. Find joy in fellowship

25. 3 JOHN - Admonition to Receive True Believers
    a. Gaius, brother in the Church
    b. Diotrephes
    c. Demetrius

26. JUDE - Contending for the Faith
    a. Occasion of the epistle
    b. Occurrences of apostasy
    c. Occupation of believers in the days of apostasy

27. REVELATION - The Unveiling of Christ Glorified
    a. The person of Christ in glory
    b. The possession of Jesus Christ - the Church in the World
    c. The program of Jesus Christ - the scene in Heaven
    d. The seven seals
    e. The seven trumpets
    f. Important persons in the last days
    g. The seven vials
    h. The fall of Babylon
    i. The eternal state

APPENDIX 8

From Before to Beyond Time:
The Plan of God and Human History

*Adapted from: Suzanne de Dietrich. **God's Unfolding Purpose**. Philadelphia: Westminster Press, 1976.*

I. Before Time (Eternity Past) 1 Cor. 2.7
   A. The Eternal Triune God
   B. God's Eternal Purpose
   C. The Mystery of Iniquity
   D. The Principalities and Powers

II. Beginning of Time (Creation and Fall) Gen. 1.1
   A. Creative Word
   B. Humanity
   C. Fall
   D. Reign of Death and First Signs of Grace

III. Unfolding of Time (God's Plan Revealed Through Israel) Gal. 3.8
   A. Promise (Patriarchs)
   B. Exodus and Covenant at Sinai
   C. Promised Land
   D. The City, the Temple, and the Throne (Prophet, Priest, and King)
   E. Exile
   F. Remnant

IV. Fullness of Time (Incarnation of the Messiah) Gal. 4.4-5
   A. The King Comes to His Kingdom
   B. The Present Reality of His Reign
   C. The Secret of the Kingdom: the Already and the Not Yet
   D. The Crucified King
   E. The Risen Lord

V. The Last Times (The Descent of the Holy Spirit) Acts 2.16-18
   A. Between the Times: the Church as Foretaste of the Kingdom
   B. The Church as Agent of the Kingdom
   C. The Conflict Between the Kingdoms of Darkness and Light

VI. The Fulfillment of Time (The Second Coming) Matt. 13.40-43
   A. The Return of Christ
   B. Judgment
   C. The Consummation of His Kingdom

VII. Beyond Time (Eternity Future) 1 Cor. 15.24-28
   A. Kingdom Handed Over to God the Father
   B. God as All in All

From Before to Beyond Time
Scriptures for Major Outline Points

I. Before Time (Eternity Past)

1 Cor. 2.7 (ESV) - But we impart a secret and hidden wisdom of God, *which God decreed before the ages* for our glory (cf. Titus 1.2).

II. Beginning of Time (Creation and Fall)

Gen. 1.1 (ESV) - *In the beginning*, God created the heavens and the earth.

III. Unfolding of Time (God's Plan Revealed Through Israel)

Gal. 3.8 (ESV) - And the Scripture, foreseeing that God would justify the Gentiles by faith, *preached the Gospel beforehand to Abraham*, saying, "In you shall all the nations be blessed" (cf. Rom. 9.4-5).

IV. Fullness of Time (The Incarnation of the Messiah)

Gal. 4.4-5 (ESV) - *But when the fullness of time had come*, God sent forth his Son, born of woman, born under the law, to redeem those who were under the law, so that we might receive adoption as sons.

V. The Last Times (The Descent of the Holy Spirit)

Acts 2.16-18 (ESV) - But this is what was uttered through the prophet Joel: "'*And in the last days it shall be*,' God declares, 'that I will pour out my Spirit on all flesh, and your sons and your daughters shall prophesy, and your young men shall see visions, and your old men shall dream dreams; even on my male servants and female servants in those days I will pour out my Spirit, and they shall prophesy.'"

VI. The Fulfillment of Time (The Second Coming)

Matt. 13.40-43 (ESV) - Just as the weeds are gathered and burned with fire, *so will it be at the close of the age*. The Son of Man will send his angels, and they will gather out of his kingdom all causes of sin and all lawbreakers, and throw them into the fiery furnace. In that place there will be weeping and gnashing of teeth. Then the righteous will shine like the sun in the Kingdom of their Father. He who has ears, let him hear.

VII. Beyond Time (Eternity Future)

1 Cor. 15.24-28 (ESV) - Then comes the end, when he delivers the Kingdom to God the Father after destroying every rule and every authority and power. For he must reign until he has put all his enemies under his feet. The last enemy to be destroyed is death. For "God has put all things in subjection under his feet." But when it says, "all things are put in subjection," it is plain that he is excepted who put all things in subjection under him. When all things are subjected to him, then the Son himself will also be subjected to him who put all things in subjection under him, that God may be all in all.

APPENDIX 9

"There Is a River"

Identifying the Streams of a Revitalized Authentic Christian Community in the City[1]

Rev. Dr. Don L. Davis • *Psalm 46.4 (ESV) - There is a river whose streams make glad the city of God, the holy habitation of the Most High.*

Tributaries of Authentic Historic Biblical Faith			
Recognized Biblical Identity	*Revived Urban Spirituality*	*Reaffirmed Historical Connectivity*	*Refocused Kingdom Authority*
The Church Is **One**	The Church Is **Holy**	The Church Is **Catholic**	The Church Is **Apostolic**
A Call to Biblical Fidelity Recognizing the Scriptures as the anchor and foundation of the Christian faith and practice	A Call to the Freedom, Power, and Fullness of the Holy Spirit Walking in the holiness, power, gifting, and liberty of the Holy Spirit in the body of Christ	A Call to Historic Roots and Continuity Confessing the common historical identity and continuity of authentic Christian faith	A Call to the Apostolic Faith Affirming the apostolic tradition as the authoritative ground of the Christian hope
A Call to Messianic Kingdom Identity Rediscovering the story of the promised Messiah and his Kingdom in Jesus of Nazareth	A Call to Live as Sojourners and Aliens as the People of God Defining authentic Christian discipleship as faithful membership among God's people	A Call to Affirm and Express the Global Communion of Saints Expressing cooperation and collaboration with all other believers, both local and global	A Call to Representative Authority Submitting joyfully to God's gifted servants in the Church as undershepherds of true faith
A Call to Creedal Affinity Embracing the Nicene Creed as the shared rule of faith of historic orthodoxy	A Call to Liturgical, Sacramental, and Catechetical Vitality Experiencing God's presence in the context of the Word, sacrament, and instruction	A Call to Radical Hospitality and Good Works Expressing kingdom love to all, and especially to those of the household of faith	A Call to Prophetic and Holistic Witness Proclaiming Christ and his Kingdom in word and deed to our neighbors and all peoples

---

[1] This schema is an adaptation and is based on the insights of the **Chicago Call** statement of May 1977, where various leading evangelical scholars and practitioners met to discuss the relationship of modern evangelicalism to the historic Christian faith.

APPENDIX 10
A Schematic for a Theology of the Kingdom and the Church
The Urban Ministry Institute

The Reign of the One, True, Sovereign, and Triune God, the LORD God, Yahweh, God the Father, Son, and Holy Spirit

The Father	The Son	The Spirit
Love - 1 John 4.8 Maker of heaven and earth and of all things visible and invisible	Faith - Heb. 12.2 Prophet, Priest, and King	Hope - Rom. 15.13 Lord of the Church
Creation All that exists through the creative action of God.	**Kingdom** The Reign of God expressed in the rule of his Son Jesus the Messiah.	**Church** The one, holy, apostolic community which functions as a witness to (Acts 28.31) and a foretaste of (Col. 1.12; James 1.18; 1 Pet. 2.9; Rev. 1.6) the Kingdom of God.
The eternal God, sovereign in power, infinite in wisdom, perfect in holiness, and steadfast in love, is the source and goal of all things.	**Freedom** *(Slavery)* Jesus answered them, "Truly, truly, I say to you, everyone who commits sin is a slave to sin. The slave does not remain in the house forever; the son remains forever. So if the Son sets you free, you will be free indeed." - John 8.34-36 (ESV)	*The Church is an Apostolic Community Where the Word is Rightly Preached. Therefore it is a Community of:* **Calling** - For freedom Christ has set us free; stand firm therefore, and do not submit again to a yoke of slavery. - Gal. 5.1 (ESV) (cf. Rom. 8.28-30; 1 Cor. 1.26-31; Eph. 1.18; 2 Thess. 2.13-14; Jude 1.1) **Faith** - ". . . for unless you believe that I am he you will die in your sins". . . . So Jesus said to the Jews who had believed in him, "If you abide in my word, you are truly my disciples, and you will know the truth, and the truth will set you free." - John 8.24b, 31-32 (ESV) (cf. Ps. 119.45; Rom. 1.17, 5.1-2; Eph. 2.8-9; 2 Tim. 1.13-14; Heb. 2.14-15; James 1.25) **Witness** - The Spirit of the Lord is upon me, because he has anointed me to proclaim good news to the poor. He has sent me to proclaim liberty to the captives and recovering of sight to the blind, to set at liberty those who are oppressed, to proclaim the year of the Lord's favor. - Luke 4.18-19 (ESV) (cf. Lev. 25.10, Prov. 31.8, Matt. 4.17; 28.18-20; Mark 13.10, Acts 1.8; 8.4, 12; 13.1-3; 25.20; 28.30-31)
Rom. 8.18-21 →		
O, the depth of the riches and wisdom and knowledge of God! How unsearchable are his judgments, and how inscrutable his ways! For who has known the mind of the Lord, or who has been his counselor? Or who has ever given a gift to him, that he might be repaid?" For from him and through him and to him are all things. To him be glory forever! Amen! - Rom. 11.33-36 (ESV) (cf. 1 Cor. 15.23-28; Rev.)	**Wholeness** *(Sickness)* But he was wounded for our transgressions; he was crushed for our iniquities; upon him was the chastisement that brought us peace, and with his stripes we are healed. - Isa. 53.5 (ESV)	*The Church is One Community Where the Sacraments are Rightly Administered. Therefore it is a Community of:* **Worship** - You shall serve the Lord your God, and he will bless your bread and your water, and I will take sickness away from among you. - Exod. 23.25 (ESV) (cf. Ps. 147.1-3; Heb. 12.28; Col. 3.16; Rev. 15.3-4; 19.5) **Covenant** - And the Holy Spirit also bears witness to us; for after the saying, "This is the covenant that I will make with them after those days, declares the Lord: I will put my laws on their hearts, and write them on their minds," then he adds, "I will remember their sins and their lawless deeds no more." - Heb. 10.15-17 (ESV) (cf. Isa. 54.10-17, Ezek. 34.25-31; 37.26-27, Mal. 2.4-5; Luke 22.20; 2 Cor. 3.6, Col. 3.15; Heb. 8.7-13; 12.22-24; 13.20-21) **Presence** - In him you also are being built together into a dwelling place for God by his Spirit. - Eph. 2.22 (ESV) (cf. Exod. 40.34-38, Ezek. 48.35, Matt. 18.18-20)
Rev. 21.1-5 →		
	Justice *(Selfishness)* Behold, my servant whom I have chosen, my beloved with whom my soul is well pleased. I will put my Spirit upon him, and he will proclaim justice to the Gentiles. He will not quarrel or cry aloud, nor will anyone hear his voice in the streets; a bruised reed he will not break, and a smoldering wick he will not quench, until he brings justice to victory. - Matt. 12.18-20 (ESV)	*The Church is a Holy Community Where Discipline is Rightly Ordered. Therefore it is a Community of:* **Reconciliation** - For he himself is our peace, who has made us both one and has broken down in his flesh the dividing wall of hostility by abolishing the law of commandments and ordinances, that he might create in himself one new man in place of the two, so making peace, and might reconcile us both to God in one body through the cross, thereby killing the hostility. And he came and preached peace to you who were far off and peace to those who were near. For through him we both have access in one Spirit to the Father. - Eph. 2.14-18 (ESV) (cf. Exod. 23.4-9; Lev. 19.34; Deut. 10.18-19; Ezek. 22.29; Mic. 6.8; 2 Cor. 5.16-21) **Suffering** - Since therefore Christ suffered in the flesh, arm yourselves with the same way of thinking, for whoever has suffered in the flesh has ceased from sin, so as to live for the rest of the time in the flesh no longer for human passions but for the will of God. - 1 Pet. 4.1-2 (ESV) (cf. Luke 6.22; 10.3; Rom. 8.17; 2 Tim. 2.3; 3.12; 1 Pet. 2.20-24; Heb. 5.8; 13.11-14) **Service** - But Jesus called them to him and said, "You know that the rulers of the Gentiles lord it over them, and their great ones exercise authority over them. It shall not be so among you. But whoever would be great among you must be your servant, and whoever would be first among you must be your slave even as the Son of Man came not to be served but to serve, and to give his life as a ransom for many." - Matt. 20.25-28 (ESV) (cf. 1 John 4.16-18; Gal. 2.10)
Isa. 11.6-9 →		

APPENDIX 11
Living in the Already and the Not Yet Kingdom
Rev. Dr. Don L. Davis

The Spirit: The pledge of the inheritance **(arrabon)**
The Church: The foretaste **(aparche)** of the Kingdom
"In Christ": The rich life **(en Christos)** we share as citizens of the Kingdom

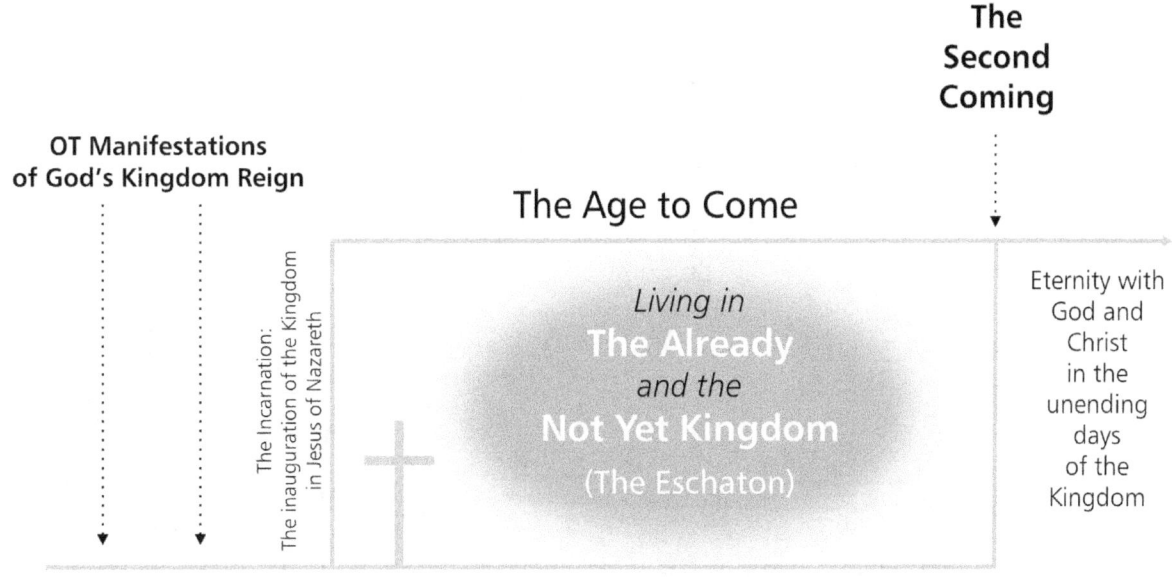

Internal enemy: The flesh (*sarx*) and the sin nature
External enemy: The world (*kosmos*) the systems of greed, lust, and pride
Infernal enemy: The devil (*kakos*) the animating spirit of falsehood and fear

Jewish View of Time

This Present Age | The Age to Come

The Coming of Messiah
The restoration of Israel
The end of Gentile oppression
The return of the earth to Edenic glory
Universal knowledge of the Lord

APPENDIX 12
Jesus of Nazareth: The Presence of the Future
Rev. Dr. Don L. Davis

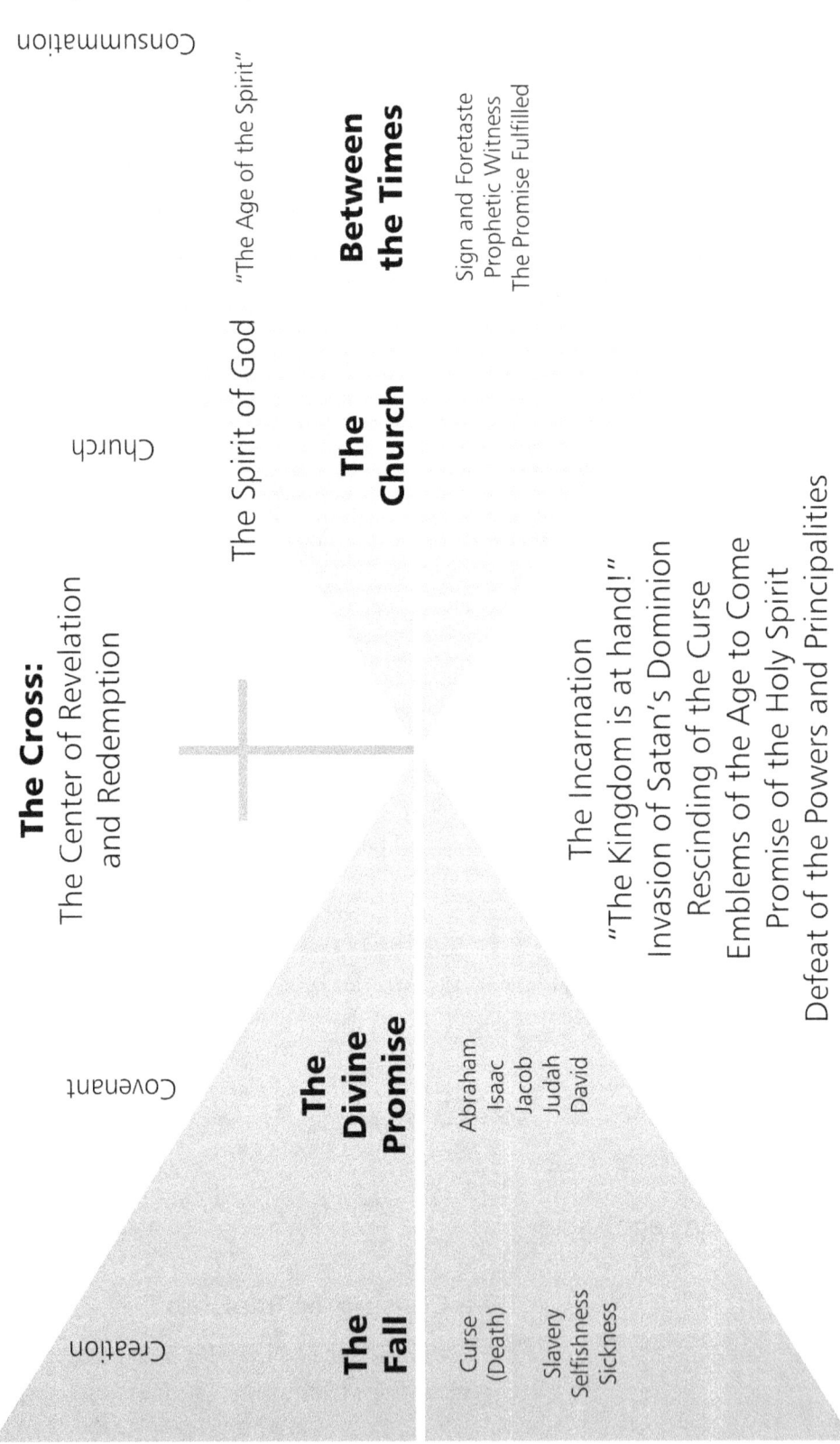

APPENDIX 13

Traditions
(Paradosis)
Dr. Don L. Davis and Rev. Terry G. Cornett

Strong's Definition

Paradosis. Transmission, i.e. (concretely) a precept; specifically, the Jewish traditionary law

Vine's Explanation

denotes "a tradition," and hence, by metonymy, (a) "the teachings of the rabbis," . . . (b) "apostolic teaching," . . . of instructions concerning the gatherings of believers, of Christian doctrine in general . . . of instructions concerning everyday conduct.

1. **The concept of tradition in Scripture is essentially positive.**

    Jer. 6.16 (ESV) - Thus says the Lord: "Stand by the roads, and look, and ask for the ancient paths, where the good way is; and walk in it, and find rest for your souls. But they said, 'We will not walk in it'" (cf. Exod. 3.15; Judg. 2.17; 1 Kings 8.57-58; Ps. 78.1-6).

    2 Chron. 35.25 (ESV) - Jeremiah also uttered a lament for Josiah; and all the singing men and singing women have spoken of Josiah in their laments to this day. They made these a rule in Israel; behold, they are written in the Laments (cf. Gen. 32.32; Judg. 11.38-40).

    Jer. 35.14-19 (ESV) - The command that Jonadab the son of Rechab gave to his sons, to drink no wine, has been kept, and they drink none to this day, for they have obeyed their father's command. I have spoken to you persistently, but you have not listened to me. I have sent to you all my servants the prophets, sending them persistently, saying, 'Turn now every one of you from his evil way, and amend your deeds, and do not go after other gods to serve them, and then you shall dwell in the land that I gave to you and your fathers.' But you did not incline your ear or listen to me. The sons of Jonadab the son of Rechab have kept the command that their father gave them, but this people has not obeyed me. Therefore, thus says the

Traditions (continued)

Lord, the God of hosts, the God of Israel: Behold, I am bringing upon Judah and all the inhabitants of Jerusalem all the disaster that I have pronounced against them, because I have spoken to them and they have not listened, I have called to them and they have not answered." But to the house of the Rechabites Jeremiah said, "Thus says the Lord of hosts, the God of Israel: Because you have obeyed the command of Jonadab your father and kept all his precepts and done all that he commanded you, therefore thus says the Lord of hosts, the God of Israel: Jonadab the son of Rechab shall never lack a man to stand before me."

2. **Godly tradition is a wonderful thing, but not all tradition is godly.**

   Any individual tradition must be judged by its faithfulness to the Word of God and its usefulness in helping people maintain obedience to Christ's example and teaching.[1] In the Gospels, Jesus frequently rebukes the Pharisees for establishing traditions that nullify rather than uphold God's commands.

   Mark 7.8 (ESV) - You leave the commandment of God and hold to the tradition of men" (cf. Matt. 15.2-6; Mark 7.13).

   Col. 2.8 (ESV) - See to it that no one takes you captive by philosophy and empty deceit, according to human tradition, according to the elemental spirits of the world, and not according to Christ.

3. **Without the fullness of the Holy Spirit, and the constant edification provided to us by the Word of God, tradition will inevitably lead to dead formalism.**

   Those who are spiritual are filled with the Holy Spirit, whose power and leading alone provides individuals and congregations a sense of freedom and vitality in all they practice and believe. However, when the practices and teachings of any given tradition are no longer infused by the power of the Holy Spirit and the Word of God, tradition loses its effectiveness, and may actually become counterproductive to our discipleship in Jesus Christ.

   Eph. 5.18 (ESV) - And do not get drunk with wine, for that is debauchery, but be filled with the Spirit.

---

[1] *"All Protestants insist that these traditions must ever be tested against Scripture and can never possess an independent apostolic authority over or alongside of Scripture." (J. Van Engen, "Tradition,"* **Evangelical Dictionary of Theology**, *Walter Elwell, Gen. ed.) We would add that Scripture is itself the "authoritative tradition" by which all other traditions are judged. See "Appendix A, The Founders of Tradition: Three Levels of Christian Authority," p. 4.*

Traditions (continued)

Gal. 5.22-25 (ESV) - But the fruit of the Spirit is love, joy, peace, patience, kindness, goodness, faithfulness, gentleness, self-control; against such things there is no law. And those who belong to Christ Jesus have crucified the flesh with its passions and desires. If we live by the Spirit, let us also walk by the Spirit.

2 Cor. 3.5-6 (ESV) - Not that we are sufficient in ourselves to claim anything as coming from us, but our sufficiency is from God, who has made us competent to be ministers of a new covenant, not of the letter but of the Spirit. For the letter kills, but the Spirit gives life.

4. **Fidelity to the Apostolic Tradition (teaching and modeling) is the essence of Christian maturity.**

    2 Tim. 2.2 (ESV) - and what you have heard from me in the presence of many witnesses entrust to faithful men who will be able to teach others also.

    1 Cor. 11.1-2 (ESV) - Be imitators of me, as I am of Christ. Now I commend you because you remember me in everything and maintain the traditions even as I delivered them to you (cf.1 Cor. 4.16-17, 2 Tim. 1.13-14, 2 Thess. 3.7-9, Phil. 4.9).

    1 Cor. 15.3-8 (ESV) - For I delivered to you as of first importance what I also received: that Christ died for our sins in accordance with the Scriptures, that he was buried, that he was raised on the third day in accordance with the Scriptures, and that he appeared to Cephas, then to the twelve. Then he appeared to more than five hundred brothers at one time, most of whom are still alive, though some have fallen asleep. Then he appeared to James, then to all the apostles. Last of all, as to one untimely born, he appeared also to me.

5. **The Apostle Paul often includes an appeal to the tradition for support in doctrinal practices.**

    1 Cor. 11.16 (ESV) - If anyone is inclined to be contentious, we have no such practice, nor do the churches of God (cf. 1 Cor. 1.2, 7.17, 15.3).

Traditions (continued)

> 1 Cor. 14.33-34 (ESV) - For God is not a God of confusion but of peace. As in all the churches of the saints, the women should keep silent in the churches. For they are not permitted to speak, but should be in submission, as the Law also says.

6. **When a congregation uses received tradition to remain faithful to the "Word of God," they are commended by the apostles.**

   > 1 Cor. 11.2 (ESV) - Now I commend you because you remember me in everything and maintain the traditions even as I delivered them to you.

   > 2 Thess. 2.15 (ESV) - So then, brothers, stand firm and hold to the traditions that you were taught by us, either by our spoken word or by our letter.

   > 2 Thess. 3.6 (ESV) - Now we command you, brothers, in the name of our Lord Jesus Christ, that you keep away from any brother who is walking in idleness and not in accord with the tradition that you received from us.

Appendix A

The Founders of Tradition: Three Levels of Christian Authority

Exod. 3.15 (ESV) - God also said to Moses, "Say this to the people of Israel, 'The Lord, the God of your fathers, the God of Abraham, the God of Isaac, and the God of Jacob, has sent me to you.' This is my name forever, and thus I am to be remembered throughout all generations."

1. **The Authoritative Tradition: the Apostles and the Prophets (The Holy Scriptures)**

   Eph. 2.19-21 (ESV) - So then you are no longer strangers and aliens, but you are fellow citizens with the saints and members of the household of God, built on the foundation of the apostles and prophets, Christ Jesus himself being the cornerstone, in whom the whole structure, being joined together, grows into a holy temple in the Lord.

   ~ The Apostle Paul

Traditions (continued)

Those who gave eyewitness testimony to the revelation and saving acts of Yahweh, first in Israel, and ultimately in Jesus Christ the Messiah. This testimony is binding for all people, at all times, and in all places. It is the authoritative tradition by which all subsequent tradition is judged.

2. The Great Tradition: the Ecumenical Councils and their Creeds[2]

What has been believed everywhere, always, and by all.

~ Vincent of Lerins

The Great Tradition is the core dogma (doctrine) of the Church. It represents the teaching of the Church as it has understood the Authoritative Tradition (the Holy Scriptures), and summarizes those essential truths that Christians of all ages have confessed and believed. To these doctrinal statements the whole Church, (Catholic, Orthodox, and Protestant)[3] gives its assent. The worship and theology of the Church reflects this core dogma, which finds its summation and fulfillment in the person and work of Jesus Christ. From earliest times, Christians have expressed their devotion to God in its Church calendar, a yearly pattern of worship which summarizes and reenacts the events of Christ's life.

3. Specific Church Traditions: the Founders of Denominations and Orders

The Presbyterian Church (U.S.A.) has approximately 2.5 million members, 11,200 congregations and 21,000 ordained ministers. Presbyterians trace their history to the 16th century and the Protestant Reformation. Our heritage, and much of what we believe, began with the French lawyer John Calvin (1509-1564), whose writings crystallized much of the Reformed thinking that came before him.

~ The Presbyterian Church, U.S.A.

Christians have expressed their faith in Jesus Christ in various ways through specific movements and traditions which embrace and express the Authoritative Tradition and the Great Tradition in unique ways. For instance,

---

[2] See Appendix B, "Defining the Great Tradition."

[3] Even the more radical wing of the Protestant reformation (Anabaptists) who were the most reluctant to embrace the creeds as dogmatic instruments of faith, did not disagree with the essential content found in them. "They assumed the Apostolic Creed–they called it 'The Faith,' *Der Glaube*, as did most people." See John Howard Yoder, **Preface to Theology: Christology and Theological Method.** Grand Rapids: Brazos Press, 2002. pp. 222-223.

Traditions (continued)

Catholic movements have arisen around people like Benedict, Francis, or Dominic, and among Protestants people like Martin Luther, John Calvin, Ulrich Zwingli, and John Wesley. Women have founded vital movements of Christian faith (e.g., Aimee Semple McPherson of the Foursquare Church), as well as minorities (e.g., Richard Allen of the African Methodist Episcopal Church or Charles H. Mason of the Church of God in Christ, who also helped to spawn the Assemblies of God), all which attempted to express the Authoritative Tradition and the Great Tradition in a specific way consistent with their time and expression.

The emergence of vital, dynamic movements of the faith at different times and among different peoples reveal the fresh working of the Holy Spirit throughout history. Thus, inside Catholicism, new communities have arisen such as the Benedictines, Franciscans, and Dominicans; and outside Catholicism, new denominations have emerged (Lutherans, Presbyterians, Methodists, Church of God in Christ, etc.). Each of these specific traditions have "founders," key leaders whose energy and vision helped to establish a unique expression of Christian faith and practice. Of course, to be legitimate, these movements must adhere to and faithfully express both the Authoritative Tradition and the Great Tradition. Members of these specific traditions embrace their own unique practices and patterns of spirituality, but these unique features are not necessarily binding on the Church at large. They represent the unique expressions of that community's understanding of and faithfulness to the Authoritative and Great Traditions.

Specific traditions seek to express and live out this faithfulness to the Authoritative and Great Traditions through their worship, teaching, and service. They seek to make the Gospel clear within new cultures or sub-cultures, speaking and modeling the hope of Christ into new situations shaped by their own set of questions posed in light of their own unique circumstances. These movements, therefore, seek to contextualize the Authoritative tradition in a way that faithfully and effectively leads new groups of people to faith in Jesus Christ, and incorporates those who believe into the community of faith that obeys his teachings and gives witness of him to others.

Traditions (continued)

Appendix B

Defining the "Great Tradition"

The Great Tradition (sometimes called the "classical Christian tradition") is defined by Robert E. Webber as follows:

> *[It is] the broad outline of Christian belief and practice developed from the Scriptures between the time of Christ and the middle of the fifth century*
>
> ~ Webber. **The Majestic Tapestry**.
> Nashville: Thomas Nelson Publishers, 1986. p. 10.

This tradition is widely affirmed by Protestant theologians both ancient and modern.

> *Thus those ancient Councils of Nicea, Constantinople, the first of Ephesus, Chalcedon, and the like, which were held for refuting errors, we willingly embrace, and reverence as sacred, in so far as relates to doctrines of faith, for they contain nothing but the pure and genuine interpretation of Scripture, which the holy Fathers with spiritual prudence adopted to crush the enemies of religion who had then arisen.*
>
> ~ John Calvin. **Institutes**. IV, ix. 8.

> *. . . most of what is enduringly valuable in contemporary biblical exegesis was discovered by the fifth century.*
>
> ~ Thomas C. Oden. **The Word of Life**.
> San Francisco: HarperSanFrancisco, 1989. p. xi

> *The first four Councils are by far the most important, as they settled the orthodox faith on the Trinity and the Incarnation.*
>
> ~ Philip Schaff. **The Creeds of Christendom**. Vol. 1.
> Grand Rapids: Baker Book House, 1996. p. 44.

Our reference to the Ecumenical Councils and Creeds is, therefore, focused on those Councils which retain a widespread agreement in the Church among Catholics, Orthodox, and Protestants. While Catholic and Orthodox share common agreement on the first seven councils, Protestants tend to affirm and use primarily the first four. Therefore, those councils which continue to be shared by the whole Church are completed with the Council of Chalcedon in 451.

Traditions (continued)

It is worth noting that each of these four Ecumenical Councils took place in a pre-European cultural context and that none of them were held in Europe. They were councils of the whole Church and they reflected a time in which Christianity was primarily an eastern religion in it's geographic core. By modern reckoning, their participants were African, Asian, and European. The councils reflected a church that ". . . has roots in cultures far distant from Europe and preceded the development of modern European identity, and [of which] some of its greatest minds have been African" (Oden, *The Living God*, San Francisco: HarperSanFrancisco, 1987, p. 9).

Perhaps the most important achievement of the Councils was the creation of what is now commonly called the Nicene Creed. It serves as a summary statement of the Christian faith that can be agreed on by Catholic, Orthodox, and Protestant Christians.

The first four Ecumenical Councils are summarized in the following chart:

Name/Date/Location	Purpose
First Ecumenical Council 325 A.D. Nicea, Asia Minor	Defending against: *Arianism* Question answered: *Was Jesus God?* Action: *Developed the initial form of the Nicene Creed to serve as a summary of the Christian faith*
Second Ecumenical Council 381 A.D. Constantinople, Asia Minor	Defending against: *Macedonianism* Question answered: *Is the Holy Spirit a personal and equal part of the Godhead?* Action: *Completed the Nicene Creed by expanding the article dealing with the Holy Spirit*
Third Ecumenical Council 431 A.D. Ephesus, Asia Minor	Defending against: *Nestorianism* Question answered: *Is Jesus Christ both God and man in one person?* Action: *Defined Christ as the Incarnate Word of God and affirmed his mother Mary as* **theotokos** *(God-bearer)*
Fourth Ecumenical Council 451 A.D. Chalcedon, Asia Minor	Defending against: *Monophysitism* Question answered: *How can Jesus be both God and man?* Action: *Explained the relationship between Jesus' two natures (human and Divine)*

APPENDIX 14
Paul's Partnership Theology
Our Union with Christ and Partnership in Kingdom Ministry

Adapted from Brian J. Dodd. **Empowered Church Leadership**. *Downers Grove: InterVarsity Press, 2003.*

The Apostolic fondness for Greek terms compounded with the prefix syn (with or co-)

English Translation of the Greek Term	Scripture References
Co-worker (*Synergos*)	Rom 16.3, 7, 9, 21; 2 Cor. 8.23; Phil. 2.25; 4.3; Col. 4.7, 10, 11, 14; Philem. 1, 24
Co-prisoner (*Synaichmalotos*)	Col. 4.10; Philem. 23
Co-slave (*Syndoulous*)	Col. 1.7; 4.7
Co-soldier (*Systratiotes*)	Phil. 2.25; Philem. 2
Co-laborer (*Synathleo*)	Phil. 4.2-3

APPENDIX 15

Selecting a Credible Criteria for Independence
Navigating Toward a Healthy Transition
Don L. Davis

In order to establish a smooth transition from a missionary-led community to an indigenous, independent church community, we must identify and agree upon a clear criteria which would help us know when the transition is complete. In other words, everything depends on all of the key players' ability (i.e., missionaries, elders, and church community) to be crystal clear regarding our assumptions about what the transition involves and what we are seeking to accomplish. If, for any reason, we are unclear as to our expectations and directions together, we can easily misunderstand one another, and prolong the process, or even make the transition period unnecessarily painful.

The following categories are given as a guide, a criteria which may help you as leaders critically assess whether you have covered all necessary areas of transition. The list is suggestive, not exhaustive, and is not meant to be a final summary, but a tickler to help you think carefully through all of the issues necessary to make your period of transition an open and supportive one.

1. **A Faithful Group of Converted, Gathered, Maturing Disciples of Jesus**

    a. Solid conversions to Jesus Christ as Lord and Savior

    b. Self-identity as a separate Christian assembly with its own passionate spirituality, inspiring worship, and presence in the community

    c. Possess a clear sense of membership, ownership, belonging; able to bring new members in easily through strong orientation and loving relationships

    d. Clear sense of entering membership, disciplining members, restoring them

    e. Incorporating people smoothly into the life of the body (i.e., small group life, friendships, large group fellowship, etc.)

2. **Identified, Commissioned, and Released Indigenous Leaders**

    a. Selected by and for the body publicly and prayerfully

    b. Determiners of the church's direction and operation

    c. Accountable to the church's membership for their life and ministry

Selecting a Credible Criteria for Independence (continued)

d. The body exercising wisdom as it determines which leaders to fund (i.e., how many it can afford to fund fully or partially), while at the same time relying on lay leaders and members to meet its needs as God leads

e. Acknowledged separately from missionary leadership as authority of the body

3. **Selection of its Own Pastor and Pastoral Staff**

    a. Creation of a charter/by-laws/constitution/covenant delineating role of pastor(s) and relationship to body

    b. Installation of a pastor duly ratified by membership and endorsed by leadership

    c. Formal recognition of pastor's authority and responsibility

    d. Affirmation of community's support and submission to pastoral leadership

4. **Limited and Decreasing Oversight, Participation, and Direction**

    a. Missionaries have surrendered all significant positions and authority

    b. Clear understanding of the role of the missionaries presently serving our body

    c. Distinct lines between missionaries and indigenous leaders in decision-making and direction setting of the church

    d. Encouragement for missionaries to seek God's leading regarding new communities to target for new outreaches of the Gospel

5. **Distinctive and Unique Burden-Driven, Gift-Oriented Ministries of the Church**

    a. Clear mission and vision of the church's purpose and goals to mature and grow in number as God leads

    b. Reproducing new assemblies built into the DNA of our church (i.e., to fund and support other efforts of church planting around our city and beyond)

    c. Open doorways for members to explore ministry opportunities that coincide with the body's vision to mobilize its members to minister in their community.

Selecting a Credible Criteria for Independence (continued)

    d. Ongoing equipping of the body members by the pastoral staff to enable members to do the work of the ministry

    e. Regular programming for worship, teaching, fellowship, and mission funded and directed by the church's personnel and members

6. Generating Non-Missionary Ministry Resources and Operating Income

    a. Deep conviction within the congregation that they will look to God alone as the source of supply to implement their vision

    b. Development of a plan to make the congregation financially free and independent of outside missionary support

    c. Clear guidelines under which support and aid can be given to the body

    d. Identifying independent sources for ongoing access to cash resources that would help support the effort

7. Acquisition and Stewardship of the Church's Equipment, Resources, and Facilities

    a. Functional, user-friendly structures created to administer the church's business and stewardship

    b. Careful, ongoing inventory of the church's resources

    c. Clear record keeping of the church's funds and finances, purchases, and allocations

    d. Responsible purchase and upkeep of the church's equipment and facilities

8. Development of its Own New Friends, Siblings, Volunteers, and Partners

    a. Recognition from other Christian communities, inside and outside community

    b. New relationships with outside churches or other organizations who would continue to support the effort with work groups and short term help

    c. New affiliation with church denominations or groups whose vision resonates with the church

    d. Associations to increase the effectiveness of the church's outreach and mission

APPENDIX 16
Spiritual Gifts Specifically Mentioned in the New Testament
Rev. Terry G. Cornett

Administration	1 Cor. 12.28	The ability to bring order to Church life.
Apostleship	1 Cor. 12.28; Eph. 4.11	The ability to establish new churches among the unreached, nurture them to maturity, and exercise the authority and wisdom necessary to see them permanently established and able to reproduce; and/or A gift unique to the founding of the Church age which included the reception of special revelation and uniquely binding leadership authority
Discernment	1 Cor. 12.10	The ability to serve the Church through a Spirit-given ability to distinguish between God's truth (his presence, working, and doctrine) and fleshly error or satanic counterfeits
Evangelism	Eph. 4.11	The passion and the ability to effectively proclaim the Gospel so that people understand it
Exhortation	Rom. 12.8	The ability to give encouragement or rebuke that helps others obey Christ
Faith	1 Cor. 12.9	The ability to build up the Church through a unique ability to see the unrealized purposes of God and unwaveringly trust God to accomplish them
Giving	Rom. 12.8	The ability to build up a church through taking delight in the consistent, generous sharing of spiritual and physical resources
Healing	1 Cor. 12.9; 12.28	The ability to exercise faith that results in restoring people to physical, emotional, and spiritual health
Interpretation	1 Cor. 12.10	The ability to explain the meaning of an ecstatic utterance so that the Church is edified
Knowledge	1 Cor. 12.8	The ability to understand scriptural truth, through the illumination of the Holy Spirit, and speak it out to edify the body; and/or The supernatural revelation of the existence, or nature, of a person or thing which would not be known through natural means

Spiritual Gifts Specifically Mentioned in the New Testament (continued)

Leadership	Rom. 12.8	Spiritually inspired courage, wisdom, zeal, and hard work which motivate and guide others so that they can effectively participate in building the Church
Mercy	Rom. 12.8	Sympathy of heart which enables a person to empathize with and cheerfully serve those who are sick, hurting, or discouraged
Ministering (or Service, or Helping, or Hospitality)	Rom. 12.7; 1 Pet. 4.9	The ability to joyfully perform any task which benefits others and meets their practical and material needs (especially on behalf of the poor or afflicted)
Miracles	1 Cor. 12.10; 12.28	The ability to confront evil and do good in ways that make visible the awesome power and presence of God
Pastoring	Eph. 4.11	The desire and ability to guide, protect, and equip the members of a congregation for ministry
Prophecy	1 Cor. 12.28; Rom. 12.6	The ability to receive and proclaim openly a revealed message from God which prepares the Church for obedience to him and to the Scriptures
Teaching	1 Cor. 12.28; Rom. 12.7; Eph. 4.11	The ability to explain the meaning of the Word of God and its application through careful instruction
Tongues	1 Cor. 12.10; 12.28	Ecstatic utterance by which a person speaks to God (or others) under the direction of the Holy Spirit
Wisdom	1 Cor. 12.8	Spirit-revealed insight that allows a person to speak godly instruction for solving problems; and/or Spirit-revealed insight that allows a person to explain the central mysteries of the Christian faith

APPENDIX 17
Paul's Team Members
Don L. Davis

Achaicus, A Corinthian who visited Paul at Philippi, 1 Cor. 16.17.

Archippus, Colossian disciple whom Paul exhorted to fulfill his ministry, Col. 4.17; Philem. 2.

Aquila, Jewish disciple Paul found at Corinth, Acts 18.2, 18, 26; Rom. 16.3; 1 Cor. 16.19; 2 Tim. 4.19.

Aristarchus, With Paul on 3rd journey, Acts 19.29; 20.4; 27.2; Col. 4.10; Philem. 24.

Artemas, Companion of Paul at Nicopolis, Titus 3.12.

Barnabas, A Levite, cousin of John Mark, and companion with Paul in several of his journeys, cf. Acts 4.36, 9.27; 11.22, 25, 30; 12.25; chs. 13, 14, and 15; 1 Cor. 9.6; Gal. 2.1, 9, 13; Col. 4.13.

Carpus, Disciple of Troas, 2 Tim. 4.13.

Claudia, Female disciple of Rome, 2 Tim. 4.21.

Clement, Fellow-laborer at Phillipi, Phil. 4.3.

Crescens, A disciple at Rome, 2 Tim. 4.10.

Demas, A laborer of Paul at Rome, Col. 4.14; Philem. 24; 2 Tim. 4.10.

Epaphras, Fellow laborer and prisoner, Col. 1.7, 4.12; Philem. 23.

Epaphroditus, Messenger between Paul and the churches, Phil. 2.25, 4.18.

Eubulus, Disciple of Rome, 2 Tim. 4.21.

Euodia, Christian woman of Philippi, Phil. 4.2

Fortunatus, Part of the Corinthian team, 1 Cor. 16.17.

Gaius, 1) A Macedonian companion, Acts 19.29; 2) A disciple/companion in Derbe, Acts 20.4.

Jesus (Justus), A Jewish disciple at Colossae, Col. 4.11.

John Mark, Companion of Paul and cousin of Barnabas, Acts 12.12, 15; 15.37, 39; Col. 4.10; 2 Tim. 4.11; Philem. 24.

Linus, A Roman Companion of Paul, 2 Tim. 4.21.

Luke, Physician and fellow-traveler with Paul, Col. 4.14; 2 Tim. 4.11; Philem. 24.

Paul's Team Members (continued)

Onesimus, Native of Colossae and slave of Philemon who served Paul, Col. 4.9; Philem. 10.

Hermogenes, A team member who abandoned Paul in prison, 2 Tim. 1.15.

Phygellus, One with Hermogenes turned from Paul in Asia, 2 Tim. 1.15.

Priscilla (Prisca), Wife of Aquila of Pontus and fellow-worker in the Gospel, Acts 18.2, 18, 26; Rom. 16.3; 1 Cor. 16.19.

Pudens, A Roman companion of Paul, 2 Tim. 4.21.

Secundus, Companion of Paul on his way from Greece to Syria, Acts 20.4.

Silas, Disciple, fellow laborer, and prisoner with Paul, Acts 15.22, 27, 32, 34, 40; 16.19, 25, 29; 17.4, 10, etc.

Sopater, Accompanied Paul to Syria, Acts 20.4.

Sosipater, Kinsman of Paul, Rom. 16.21.

Silvanus, Probably same as Silas, 2 Cor. 1.19; 1 Thess. 1.1; 2 Thess. 1.1.

Sosthenes, Chief Ruler of the Synagogue of Corinth, laborer with Paul there, Acts 18.17.

Stephanus, One of the first believers of Achaia and visitor to Paul, 1 Cor. 1.16; 16.15; 16.17.

Syntyche, One of Paul's female "fellow workers" in Philippi, Phil. 4.2.

Tertius, Slave and person who wrote the Epistle to the Romans, Rom. 16.22.

Timothy, A young man of Lystra with a Jewish mother and Greek father who labored on with Paul in his ministry, Acts 16.1;17.14, 15; 18.5; 19.22; 20.4; Rom. 16.21; 1 Cor. 4.17; 16.10; 2 Cor. 1.1, 19; Phil. 1.1; 2.19; Col. 1.1; 1 Thess. 1.1; 3.2, 6; 2 Thess. 1.1; 1 Tim. 1.2, 18; 6.20; 2 Tim. 1.2; Philem. 1; Heb. 13.23.

Titus, Greek disciple and co-laborer of Paul, 2 Cor. 2.13; 7.6, 13, 14; 8.6, 16, 23; 12.18; Gal. 2.1, 3; 2 Tim. 4.10; Titus 1.4.

Trophimus, Ephesian disciple who accompanied Paul to Jerusalem from Greece, Acts 20.4; 21.29; 2 Tim. 4.20.

Tryphena and Tryphosa, Female disciples of Rome, probably twins, who Paul calls laborers in the Lord, Rom. 16.12.

Tychicus, A disciple of Asia Minor who accompanied Paul in various trips, Acts 20.4; Eph. 6.21; Col. 4.7; 2 Tim. 4.12; Titus 3.12.

Urbanus, Roman disciple and aid to Paul, Rom. 16.9.

APPENDIX 18
Nurturing Authentic Christian Leadership
Rev. Dr. Don L. Davis

Cliff On-One-Side	Cliff On-the-Other-Side
Laying on hands too quickly	Always postponing delegation to the indigenous
Ignoring culture in leadership training	Elevating culture above truth
Demoting doctrine and theology	Supposing doctrine and theology as only criteria
Highlighting skills and gifts above availability and character	Substituting availability and character for genuine giftedness
Emphasizing administrative abilities above spiritual dynamism	Ignoring administration's role in spiritual vitality and power
Equating readiness with Christian perfection	Ignoring the importance of biblical standards
Limiting candidacy for leadership based on gender and ethnicity	Setting quotas of leadership based on gender and ethnicity
Seeing everyone as a leader	Seeing virtually no one as worthy to lead

APPENDIX 19
The Role of Women in Ministry
Dr. Don L. Davis

While it is plain that God has established a clearly designed order of responsibility within the home, it is equally clear that women are called and gifted by God, led by his own Spirit to bear fruit worthy of their calling in Christ. Throughout the NT, commands are directed specifically to women to submit, with the particular Greek verb *hupotasso*, occurring frequently which means "to place under" or "to submit" (cf. 1 Tim. 2.11). The word also translated into our English word "subjection" is from the same root. In such contexts these Greek renderings ought not to be understood in any way except as positive admonitions towards God's designed framework for the home, where women are charged to learn quietly and submissively, trusting and working within the Lord's own plan.

This ordering of the woman's submission in the home, however, must not be misinterpreted to mean that women are disallowed from ministering their gifts under the Spirit's direction. Indeed, it is the Holy Spirit through Christ's gracious endowment who assigns the gifts as he wills, for the edification of the Church (1 Cor. 12.1-27; Eph. 4.1-16). The gifts are not given to believers on the criteria of gender; in other words, there is no indication from the Scriptures that some gifts are for men only, and the others reserved for women. On the contrary, Paul affirms that Christ provided gifts as a direct result of his own personal victory over the devil and his minions (cf. Eph. 4.6ff.). This was his own personal choice, given by his Spirit to whomever he wills (cf. 1 Cor. 12.1-11). In affirming the ministry of women we affirm the right of the Spirit to be creative in all saints for the well-being of all and the expansion of his Kingdom, as he sees fit, and not necessarily as we determine (Rom. 12.4-8; 1 Pet. 4.10-11).

Furthermore, a careful study of the Scriptures as a whole indicates that God's ordering of the home in no way undermines his intention for men and women to serve Christ as disciples and laborers together, under Christ's leading. The clear NT teaching of Christ as head of the man, and the man of the woman (see 1 Cor. 11.4) shows God's esteem for godly spiritual representation within the home. The apparent forbidding of women to hold teaching/ruling positions appears to be an admonition to protect God's assigned lines of responsibility and authority within the home. For instance, the particular Greek term in the highly debated passage in 1 Timothy 2.12, *andros*, which has often times been translated "man," may also be

The Role of Women in Ministry (continued)

translated "husband." With such a translation, then, the teaching would be that a wife ought not to rule over her husband.

This doctrine of a woman who, in choosing to marry, makes herself voluntarily submissive to "line up under" her husband is entirely consistent with the gist of the NT teaching on the role of authority in the Christian home. The Greek word *hupotasso*, which means to "line up under" refers to a wife's voluntary submission to her own husband (cf. Eph. 5.22, 23; Col. 3.18; Titus 2.5; 1 Pet. 3.1). This has nothing to do with any supposed superior status or capacity of the husband; rather, this refers to God's design of godly headship, authority which is given for comfort, protection, and care, not for destruction or domination (cf. Gen. 2.15-17; 3.16; 1 Cor. 11.3). Indeed, that this headship is interpreted in light of Christ's headship over the Church signifies the kind of godly headship that must be given, that sense of tireless care, service, and protection required from godly leadership.

Of course, such an admonition for a wife to submit to a husband would not in any way rule out that women be involved in a teaching ministry (e.g., Titus 2.4), but, rather, that in the particular case of married women, that their own ministries would come under the protection and direction of their respective husbands (Acts 18.26). This would assert that a married woman's ministry in the Church would be given serving, protective oversight by her husband, not due to any notion of inferior capacity or defective spirituality, but for the sake of, as one commentator has put it, "avoiding confusion and maintaining orderliness" (cf. 1 Cor. 14.40).

In both Corinth and Ephesus (which represent the contested Corinthian and Timothy epistolary comments), it appears that Paul's restriction upon women's participation was prompted by occasional happenings, issues which grew particularly out of these contexts, and therefore are meant to be understood in those lights. For instance, the hotly-contested test of a women's "silence" in the church (see both 1 Cor. 14 and 1 Tim. 2) does not appear in any way to undermine the prominent role women played in the expansion of the Kingdom and development of the Church in the first century. Women were involved in the ministries of prophecy and prayer (1 Cor. 11.5), personal instruction (Acts 18.26), teaching (Titus 2.4,5), giving testimony (John 4.28, 29), offering hospitality (Acts 12.12), and serving as co-laborers with the Apostles in the cause of the Gospel (Phil. 4.2-3). Paul did not relegate women to an inferior role or hidden status but served side-by-side with women for the sake of Christ "I urge Euodia and I urge Syntyche to live in harmony in the Lord. Indeed, true companion, I ask you also to help these women

The Role of Women in Ministry (continued)

who have shared my struggle in *the cause of* the Gospel, together with Clement also and the rest of my fellow workers, whose names are in the book of life" (Phil. 4.2-3).

Furthermore, we must be careful in subordinating the personage of women *per se* (that is, their nature as women) versus their subordinated role in the marriage relationship. Notwithstanding the clear description of the role of women as heirs together of the grace of life in the marriage relationship (1 Pet. 3.7), it is equally plain that the Kingdom of God has created a dramatic shift in how women are to be viewed, understood, and embraced in the kingdom community. It is plain that in Christ there is now no difference between rich and poor, Jew and Gentile, barbarian, Scythian, bondman and freemen, as well as man and woman (cf. Gal. 3.28; Col. 3.11). Women were allowed to be disciples of a Rabbi (which was foreign and disallowed at the time of Jesus), and played prominent roles in the NT church, including being fellow laborers side by side with the Apostles in ministry (e.g., see Euodia and Syntyche in Phil. 4.1ff.), as well as hosting a church in their houses (cf. Phoebe in Rom. 16.1-2, and Apphia in Philem. 1).

In regards to the issue of pastoral authority, I am convinced that Paul's understanding of the role of equippers (of which the pastor-teacher is one such role, cf. Eph. 4.9-15) is not gender specific. In other words, the decisive and seminal text for me on the operation of gifts and the status and function of offices are those NT texts which deal with the gifts (1 Cor. 12.1-27; Rom. 12.4-8; 1 Pet. 4.10-11, and Eph. 4.9-15). There is no indication in any of these formative texts that gifts are gender-specific. In other words, for the argument to hold decisively that women were never to be in roles that were pastoral or equipping in nature, the simplest and most effective argument would be to show that the Spirit simply would never even consider giving a woman a gift which was not suited to the range of callings which she felt a calling towards. Women would be forbidden from leadership because the Holy Spirit would never grant to a woman a calling and its requisite gifts because she was a woman. Some gifts would be reserved for men, and women would never receive those gifts.

A careful reading of these and other related texts show no such prohibition. It appears that it is up to the Holy Spirit to give any person, man or woman, any gift that suits him for any ministry he wishes them to do, as he wills (1 Cor. 12.11 "But one and the same Spirit works all these things, distributing to each one individually as he wills"). Building upon this point, Terry Cornett has even written a fine theological essay showing how the NT Greek for the word "apostle" is

The Role of Women in Ministry (continued)

unequivocally applied to women, most clearly shown in the rendering of the female noun, "Junia" applied to "apostle" in Romans 16.7, as well as allusions to co-laboring, for instance, with the twins, Tryphena and Tryphosa, who "labored" with Paul in the Lord (16.12).

Believing that every God-called, Christ-endowed, and Spirit-gifted and led Christian ought to fulfill their role in the body, we affirm the role of women to lead and instruct under godly authority that submits to the Holy Spirit, the Word of God, and is informed by the tradition of the Church and spiritual reasoning. We ought to expect God to give women supernatural endowments of grace to carry out his bidding on behalf of his Church, and his reign in the Kingdom of God. Since men and women both reflect the *Imago Dei* (i.e., image of God), and both stand as heirs together of God's grace (cf. Gen. 1.27; 5.2; Matt. 19.4; Gal. 3.28; 1 Pet. 3.7), they are given the high privilege of representing Christ together as his ambassadors (2 Cor. 5.20), and through their partnership to bring to completion our obedience to Christ's Great Commission of making disciples of all nations (Matt. 28.18-20).

APPENDIX 20

Discerning the Call: The Profile of a Cross-Cultural Urban Church Planter

Rev. Dr. Don L. Davis

	Commission	Character	Community	Competence
Definition	Recognizes the call of God and replies with prompt obedience to his lordship and leading	Reflects the character of Christ in their personal convictions, conduct, and lifestyle	Regards multiplying disciples in the body of Christ as the primary role of ministry	Responds in the power of the Spirit with excellence in carrying out their appointed tasks and ministry
Key Scripture	2 Tim. 1.6-14; 1 Tim. 4.14; Acts 1.8; Matt. 28.18-20	John 15.4-5; 2 Tim. 2.2; 1 Cor. 4.2; Gal. 5.16-23	Eph. 4.9-15; 1 Cor. 12.1-27	2 Tim. 2.15; 3.16-17; Rom. 15.14; 1 Cor. 12
Critical Concept	The Authority of God: God's leader acts on God's recognized call and authority, acknowledged by the saints and God's leaders	The Humility of Christ: God's leader demonstrates the mind and lifestyle of Christ in his or her actions and relationships	The Growth of the Church: God's leader uses all of his or her resources to equip and empower the body of Christ for his/her goal and task	The Power of the Spirit: God's leader operates in the gifting and anointing of the Holy Spirit
Central Elements	A clear call from God Authentic testimony before God and others Deep sense of personal conviction based on Scripture Personal burden for a particular task or people Confirmation by leaders and the body	Passion for Christlikeness Radical lifestyle for the Kingdom Serious pursuit of holiness Discipline in the personal life Fulfills role-relationships as bondslave of Jesus Christ Provides an attractive model for others in their conduct, speech, and lifestyle (the fruit of the Spirit)	Genuine love for and desire to serve God's people Disciples faithful individuals Facilitates growth in small groups Pastors and equips believers in the congregation Nurtures associations and networks among Christians and churches Advances new movements among God's people locally	Endowments and gifts from the Spirit Sound discipling from an able mentor Skill in the spiritual disciplines Ability in the Word Able to evangelize, follow up, and disciple new converts Strategic in the use of resources and people to accomplish God's task
Satanic Strategy to Abort	Operates on the basis of personality or position rather than on God's appointed call and ongoing authority	Substitutes ministry activity and/or hard work and industry for godliness and Christlikeness	Exalts tasks and activities above equipping the saints and developing Christian community	Functions on natural gifting and personal ingenuity rather than on the Spirit's leading and gifting
Key Steps	Identify God's call Discover your burden Be confirmed by leaders	Abide in Christ Discipline for godliness Pursue holiness in all	Embrace God's Church Learn leadership's contexts Equip concentrically	Discover the Spirit's gifts Receive excellent training Hone your performance
Results	Deep confidence in God arising from God's call	Powerful Christlike example provided for others to follow	Multiplying disciples in the Church	Dynamic working of the Holy Spirit

APPENDIX 21
How to PLANT a Church
Don L. Davis

Evangelize

Mark 16.15-18 (ESV) - And he said to them, "Go into all the world and proclaim the gospel to the whole creation. [16] Whoever believes and is baptized will be saved, but whoever does not believe will be condemned. [17] And these signs will accompany those who believe: in my name they will cast out demons; they will speak in new tongues; [18] they will pick up serpents with their hands; and if they drink any deadly poison, it will not hurt them; they will lay their hands on the sick, and they will recover."

I. Prepare

Luke 24.46-49 (ESV) - and he said to them, "Thus it is written, that the Christ should suffer and on the third day rise from the dead, [47] and that repentance and forgiveness of sins should be proclaimed in his name to all nations, beginning from Jerusalem. [48] You are witnesses of these things. [49] And behold, I am sending the promise of my Father upon you. But stay in the city until you are clothed with power from on high."

A. Form a church-plant team.

B. Pray.

C. Select a target area and population.

D. Do demographic and ethnographic studies.

II. Launch

Gal. 2.7-10 (ESV) - On the contrary, when they saw that I had been entrusted with the gospel to the uncircumcised, just as Peter had been entrusted with the gospel to the circumcised [8] (for he who worked through Peter for his apostolic ministry to the circumcised worked also through me for mine to the Gentiles), [9] and when James and Cephas and John, who seemed to be pillars, perceived the grace that was given to me, they gave the right hand of fellowship to Barnabas and me, that we should go to the Gentiles and they to the circumcised. [10] Only, they asked us to remember the poor, the very thing I was eager to do.

How to PLANT a Church (continued)

    A. Recruit and train volunteers.

    B. Conduct evangelistic events and door-to-door evangelism.

Eph. 4.11-16 (ESV) - And he gave the apostles, the prophets, the evangelists, the pastors and teachers, [12] to equip the saints for the work of ministry, for building up the body of Christ, [13] until we all attain to the unity of the faith and of the knowledge of the Son of God, to mature manhood, to the measure of the stature of the fullness of Christ, [14] so that we may no longer be children, tossed to and fro by the waves and carried about by every wind of doctrine, by human cunning, by craftiness in deceitful schemes. [15] Rather, speaking the truth in love, we are to grow up in every way into him who is the head, into Christ, [16] from whom the whole body, joined and held together by every joint with which it is equipped, when each part is working properly, makes the body grow so that it builds itself up in love.

    Equip

III. Assemble

Acts 2.41-47 (ESV) - So those who received his word were baptized, and there were added that day about three thousand souls. [42] And they devoted themselves to the apostles' teaching and fellowship, to the breaking of bread and the prayers. [43] And awe came upon every soul, and many wonders and signs were being done through the apostles. [44] And all who believed were together and had all things in common. [45] And they were selling their possessions and belongings and distributing the proceeds to all, as any had need. [46] And day by day, attending the temple together and breaking bread in their homes, they received their food with glad and generous hearts, [47] praising God and having favor with all the people. And the Lord added to their number day by day those who were being saved.

    A. Form cell groups, Bible studies, etc. to follow up new believers, to continue evangelism, and to identify and train emerging leaders.

    B. Announce the birth of a new church to the neighborhood and meet regularly for public worship, instruction and fellowship.

How to PLANT a Church (continued)

IV. Nurture

1 Thess. 2.5-9 (ESV) - For we never came with words of flattery, as you know, nor with a pretext for greed— God is witness. [6] Nor did we seek glory from people, whether from you or from others, though we could have made demands as apostles of Christ. [7] But we were gentle among you, like a nursing mother taking care of her own children. [8] So, being affectionately desirous of you, we were ready to share with you not only the gospel of God but also our own selves, because you had become very dear to us. [9] For you remember, brothers, our labor and toil: we worked night and day, that we might not be a burden to any of you, while we proclaimed to you the gospel of God.

A. Develop individual and group discipleship.

B. Fill key roles in the church: identify and use spiritual gifts.

Empower

Acts 20.28 (ESV) - Pay careful attention to yourselves and to all the flock, in which the Holy Spirit has made you overseers, to care for the church of God, which he obtained with his own blood.

Acts 20.32 (ESV) - And now I commend you to God and to the word of his grace, which is able to build you up and to give you the inheritance among all those who are sanctified.

V. Transition

Titus 1.4-5 (ESV) - To Titus, my true child in a common faith: Grace and peace from God the Father and Christ Jesus our Savior. [5] This is why I left you in Crete, so that you might put what remained into order, and appoint elders in every town as I directed you—

A. Transfer leadership to indigenous leaders so they become self-governing, self-supporting and self-reproducing (appoint elders and pastors).

B. Finalize decisions about denominational or other affiliations.

C. Commission the church.

D. Foster association with World Impact and other urban churches for fellowship, support, and mission ministry.

How to PLANT a Church (continued)

How to PLANT a Church

PREPARE 　　　　　　　　　　　　　　　　　　　　　　　　　　　Evangelize

- Form a church-plant team.
- Pray.
- Select a target area and population.
- Do demographic and ethnographic studies.

LAUNCH

- Recruit and train volunteers
- Conduct evangelistic events and door-to-door evangelism

ASSEMBLE 　　　　　　　　　　　　　　　　　　　　　　　　　　　Equip

- Form cell groups, Bible studies, etc. to follow up new believers, to continue evangelism, and to identify and train emerging leaders.
- Announce the birth of a new church to the neighborhood and meet regularly for public worship, instruction and fellowship.

NURTURE

- Develop individual and group discipleship.
- Fill key roles in the church; identify and use spiritual gifts.

TRANSITION 　　　　　　　　　　　　　　　　　　　　　　　　　　Empower

- Transfer leadership to indigenous leaders so they become self-governing, self-supporting and self-reproducing (appoint elders and pastors).
- Finalize decisions about denominational or other affiliations.
- Commission the church.
- Foster association with World Impact and other urban churches for fellowship, support and mission ministry.

How to PLANT a Church (continued)

Pauline Precedents From Acts: The Pauline Cycle

1. Missionaries Commissioned: Acts 13.1-4; 15.39-40. Ga. 1.15-16.

2. Audience Contacted: Acts 13.14-16; 14.1; 16.13-15; 17.16-19.

3. Gospel Communicated: Acts 13.17-41; 16.31; Rom. 10.9-14; 2 Tim. 2.8.

4. Hearers Converted: Acts. 13.48; 16.14-15; 20.21; 26.20; 1 Thess. 1.9-10.

5. Believers Congregated: Acts 13.43; 19.9; Rom 16.4-5; 1 Cor. 14.26.

6. Faith Confirmed: Acts 14.21-22; 15.41; Rom 16.17; Col. 1.28; 2 Thess. 2.15; 1 Tim. 1.3.

7. Leadership Consecrated; Acts 14.23; 2 Tim. 2.2; Titus 1.5.

8. Believers Commended; Acts 14.23; 16.40; 21.32 (2 Tim. 4.9 and Titus 3.12 by implication).

9. Relationships Continued: Acts 15.36; 18.23; 1 Cor. 16.5; Eph. 6.21-22; Col. 4.7-8.

10. Sending Churches Convened: Acts 14.26-27; 15.1-4.

The "Pauline Cycle" terminology, stages, and diagram are taken from David J. Hesselgrave, Planting Churches Cross-Culturally, 2nd ed. Grand Rapids: Baker Book House, 2000.

"Evangelize, Equip, and Empower" and "P.L.A.N.T." schemas for church planting taken from Crowns of Beauty: Planting Urban Churches Conference Binder Los Angeles: World Impact Press, 1999.

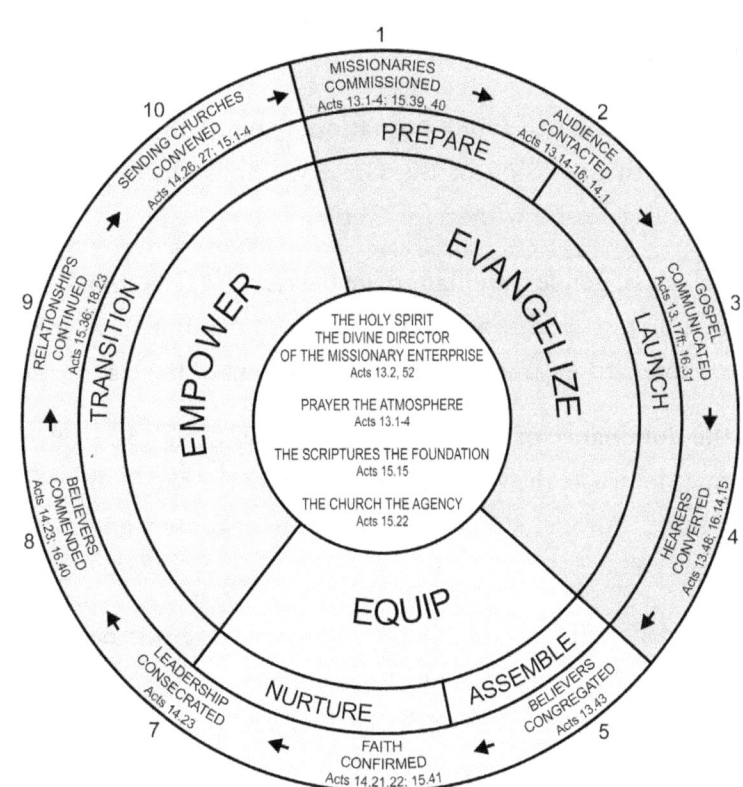

How to PLANT a Church (continued)

Ten Principles of Church Planting

1. **Jesus is Lord.** (Matt. 9.37-38) All church plant activity is made effective and fruitful under the watch care and power of the Lord Jesus, who himself is the Lord of the harvest.

2. **Evangelize, Equip, and Empower unreached people to reach people.** (1 Thess. 1.6-8) Our goal in reaching others for Christ is not only for solid conversion but also for dynamic multiplication; those who are reached must be trained to reach others as well.

3. **Be inclusive: whosoever will may come.** (Rom. 10.12) No strategy should forbid any person or group from entering into the Kingdom through Jesus Christ by faith.

4. **Be culturally neutral: Come just as you are.** (Col. 3.11) The Gospel places no demands on any seeker to change their culture as a prerequisite for coming to Jesus; they may come just as they are.

5. **Avoid a fortress mentality.** (Acts 1.8) The goal of missions is not to create an impregnable castle in the midst of an unsaved community, but a dynamic outpost of the Kingdom which launches a witness for Jesus within and unto the very borders of their world.

6. **Continue to evangelize to avoid stagnation.** (Rom. 1.16-17) Keep looking to the horizons with the vision of the Great Commission in mind; foster an environment of aggressive witness for Christ.

7. **Cross racial, class, gender, and language barriers.** (1 Cor. 9.19-22) Use your freedom in Christ to find new, credible ways to communicate the kingdom message to those farthest from the cultural spectrum of the traditional church.

8. **Respect the dominance of the receiving culture.** (Acts 15.23-29) Allow the Holy Spirit to incarnate the vision and the ethics of the Kingdom of God in the words, language, customs, styles, and experience of those who have embraced Jesus as their Lord.

9. **Avoid dependence.** (Eph. 4.11-16) Neither patronize nor be overly stingy towards the growing congregation; do not underestimate the power of the Spirit in the midst of even the smallest Christian community to accomplish God's work in their community.

How to PLANT a Church (continued)

10. **Think reproducibility.** (2 Tim. 2.2; Phil. 1.18) In every activity and project you initiate, think in terms of equipping others to do the same by maintaining an open mind regarding the means and ends of your missionary endeavors.

Resources for Further Study

Cornett, Terry G. and James D. Parker. *"Developing Urban Congregations: A Framework for World Impact Church Planters."* World Impact Ministry Resources. Los Angeles: World Impact Press, 1991.

Davis, Don L. and Terry G. Cornett. *"An Outline for a Theology of the Church."* Crowns of Beauty: Planting Urban Churches (Training Manual). Los Angeles: World Impact Press, 1999.

Hesselgrave, David J. *Planting Churches Cross Culturally: A Biblical Guide.* Grand Rapids: Baker Book House, 2000.

Hodges, Melvin L. *The Indigenous Church: A Handbook on How to Grow Young Churches.* Springfield, MO: Gospel Publishing House, 1976.

Shenk, David W. And Ervin R. Stutzman. *Creating Communities of the Kingdom: New Testament Models of Church Planting.* Scottsdale, PA: Herald Press, 1988.

APPENDIX 22
Defining the Leaders and Members of a Church Plant Team
Rev. Dr. Don L. Davis

CD - City Director   TL - Team Leader   MTL - Multiple Team Leader

	Team Member	Team Leader	Multiple Team Leader
Definition	Member of cross-cultural church planting team	Leader of cross-cultural church plant team	Facilitator and coordinator of multiple teams
Relationship to World Impact	May be a staff member or volunteer	May be a staff member or volunteer	May be a World Impact staff member or experienced planter
Responsibility	To employ gifts to enhance the ministry of the team as it plants a viable church	To facilitate the effective operation of the team	To provide counsel, resources, and support to all teams in a given area
Training	Initial training and ongoing team input	Specialized training curriculum, personal mentoring and TUMI	TUMI course work, mentoring and regional training, and specialized input
Accountable to Whom?	Team Leader	City Director (support from MTL)	Regional VP and City Director
Time Commitments	Associated with team to plant for specified period of time as core or support member	Throughout the duration of the church plant	Regular review and substantive ministry assessment at end of CPT time
Resources	Team members and leaders, CPT "kit" (initial resource allotment)	Team members, ministry budget, access to MTL and CD	Access to sites of CPTs, access to team leaders for training and support ministries
Authority	To pursue those steps necessary to evangelize, disciple, and plant - reports to the team leader	To lead the team in its operations as it seeks to plant a church - reports to the CD and MTL	To support the team during its charter period, and decide at the end if the plant warrants further time and effort
Assignment	By CD and TL for particular time and role	By CD for duration of the church plant	By Regional VP and CD as they determine necessary
Composition	Primary members, support members, and/or volunteers	Individual or co-leaders (interns)	Individual selected by Regional VP and CD

APPENDIX 23
Equipping the Church Plant Team Member
Developing Workable Training Strategies
Rev. Dr. Don L. Davis

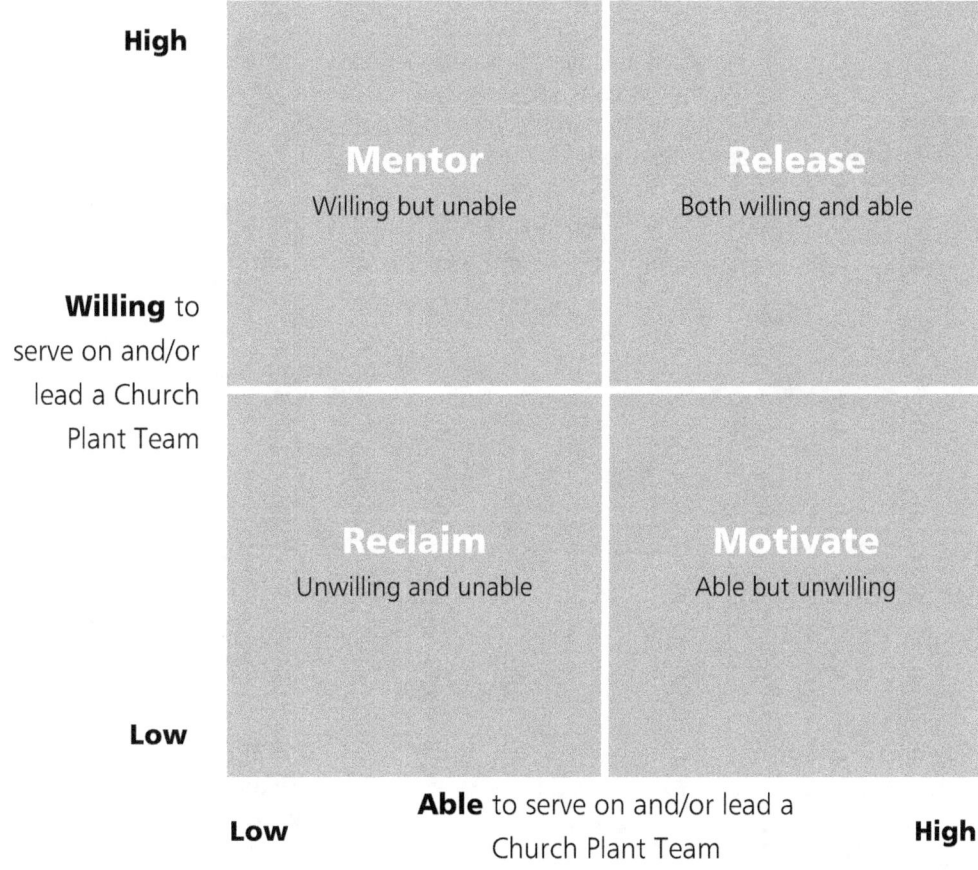

APPENDIX 24
The Communal Context of Authentic Christian Leadership
Rev. Dr. Don L. Davis

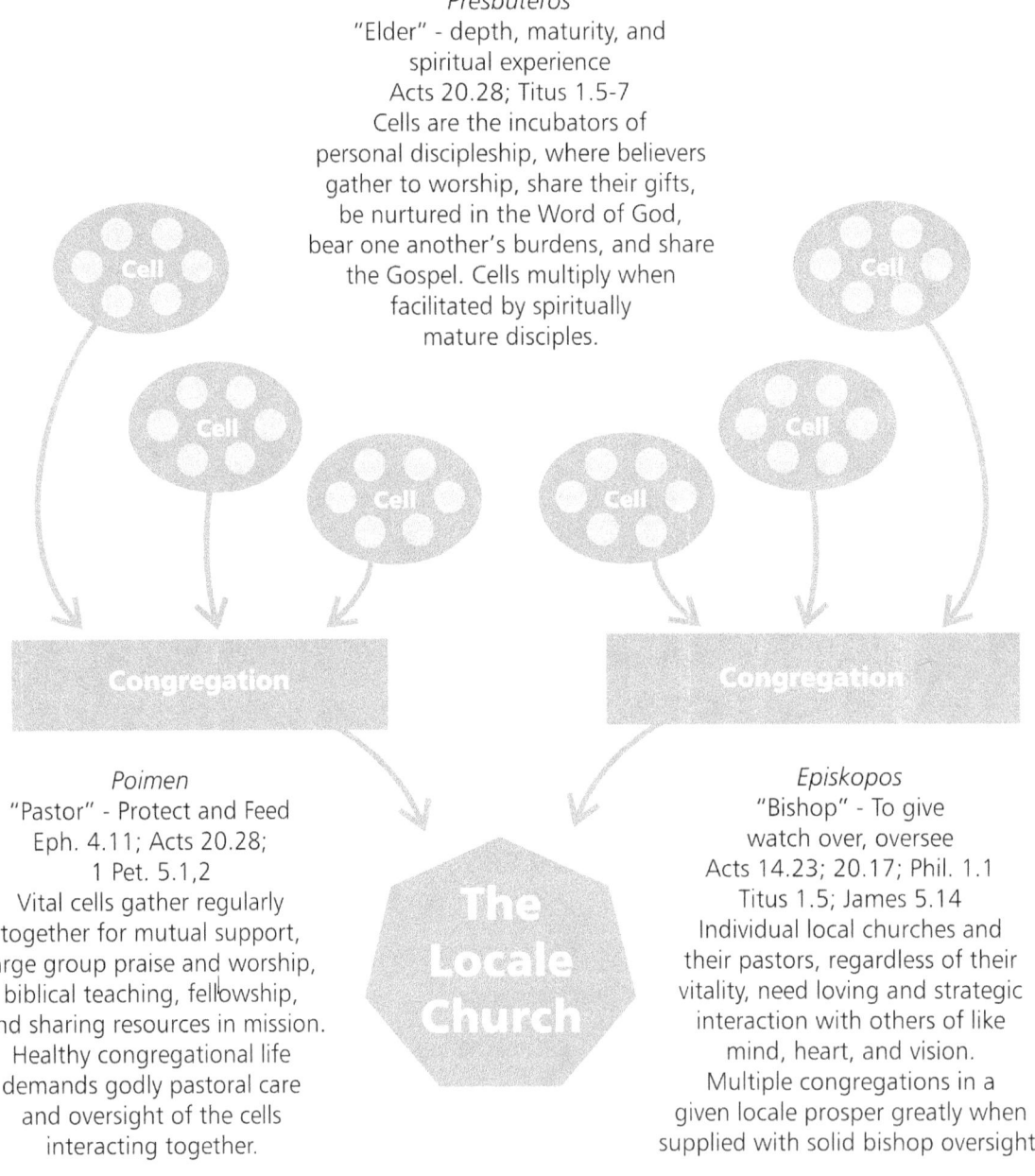

Presbuteros
"Elder" - depth, maturity, and spiritual experience
Acts 20.28; Titus 1.5-7
Cells are the incubators of personal discipleship, where believers gather to worship, share their gifts, be nurtured in the Word of God, bear one another's burdens, and share the Gospel. Cells multiply when facilitated by spiritually mature disciples.

Poimen
"Pastor" - Protect and Feed
Eph. 4.11; Acts 20.28; 1 Pet. 5.1,2
Vital cells gather regularly together for mutual support, large group praise and worship, biblical teaching, fellowship, and sharing resources in mission. Healthy congregational life demands godly pastoral care and oversight of the cells interacting together.

Episkopos
"Bishop" - To give watch over, oversee
Acts 14.23; 20.17; Phil. 1.1 Titus 1.5; James 5.14
Individual local churches and their pastors, regardless of their vitality, need loving and strategic interaction with others of like mind, heart, and vision. Multiple congregations in a given locale prosper greatly when supplied with solid bishop oversight.

Presbuteros, "an elder" is another term for the same person as bishop or overseer . . . . The term "elder" indicates the mature spiritual experience and understanding of those so described; the term "bishop" or "overseer," indicates the character of the work undertaken. According to the divine will and appointment, as in the NT, there were to be bishops in every local church, Acts 14.23; 20.17; Phil. 1.1; Titus 1.5; James 5.14." - *Vines Complete Expository Dictionary*. Nashville: Thomas Nelson Publishers, 1996. p. 195

APPENDIX 25
Church Planting Models
Rev. Dr. Don L. Davis

The following questions are designed to help us explore the various options available to the cross-cultural urban church planter in establishing congregations among the poor. Our dialogue today hopefully will isolate some of the critical issues necessary for a church plant team to think through in order to make its selection as to what particular kind of church they ought to plant, given the culture, population, and other factors encountered in its particular mission field.

1. What is the definition of the phrase "church planting models"? Why might it be important to consider various options in planting a church among the poor in the city?

2. How would you characterize the various models (or other) which are available to an urban church plant team? What would you consider to be its strengths and/or weaknesses in regard to planting churches among the poor in the city?

   a. Founding pastor model - a leader moves into a community with a commitment to lead and shepherd the church that is planted.

   b. Church split model?! - a new church is formed due to fundamental disagreement over some issue of morality, Bible interpretation, or schism.

   c. Colonization model - a central assembly commissions an entire group (usually with leadership and members already organized) into an unreached community as a kind of ready-made nucleus of the church which is to be formed.

   d. Beachhead or Mother Church model - a strong, central congregation determines to become a kind of sending center and nurturing headquarters for new churches planted through its oversight and auspices, in the immediate area and/or beyond.

   e. Cell Church model - once centralized assembly which considers the heart of its life and ministry to occur in the cells which are connected structurally and pastorally to the central congregation; their participation together constitutes the church.

Church Planting Models (continued)

    f. Home Church model - a church, which although similar to a cell church model, is intentionally planted with greater attention given to the authority and autonomy of the gathering of Christians who meet regularly in their respective homes.

    g. Missionary model - a church where a cross-cultural church planter seeks to plant a church among an unreached people with an intent from the beginning to help the church to be self-propagating, self-governing, and self-supporting.

3. What are the critical issues (e.g., culture, the tradition of the church planters, and contextualization) which ought to be factored most into selecting the appropriate model for in planting a church cross-culturally in the city?

4. Of all the things which a church planter may be aware of, what do you believe is the central element he or she must understand in order to choose the "right" option for them?

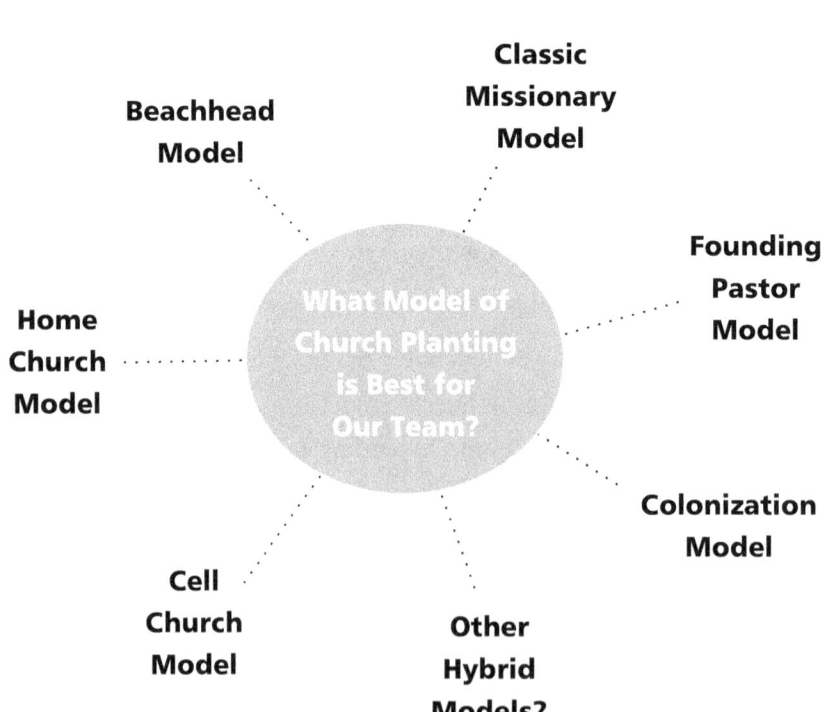

APPENDIX 26
From Deep Ignorance to Credible Witness
Rev. Dr. Don L. Davis

Witness - Ability to give witness and teach 2 Tim. 2.2 Matt. 28.18-20 1 John 1.1-4 Prov. 20.6 2 Cor. 5.18-21 *And the things you have heard me say in the presence of many witnesses entrust to reliable men who will also be qualified to teach others. - 2 Tim. 2.2*	8
Lifestyle - Consistent appropriation and habitual practice based on beliefs Heb. 5.11-6.2 Eph. 4.11-16 2 Pet. 3.18 *And Jesus increased in wisdom and in stature, and in favor* 1 Tim. 4.7-10 *with God and man. - Luke 2.52*	7
Demonstration - Expressing conviction in corresponding conduct, speech, and behavior James 2.14-26 2 Cor. 4.13 *Nevertheless, at your word I will let down the net.* 2 Pet. 1.5-9 *- Luke 5.5* 1 Thess. 1.3-10	6
Conviction - Committing oneself to think, speak, and act in light of information Heb. 2.3-4 Heb. 11.1, 6 *Do you believe this?* Heb. 3.15-19 *- John 11.26* Heb. 4.2-6	5
Discernment - Understanding the meaning and implications of information John 16.13 Eph. 1.15-18 *Do you understand what you are reading?* Col. 1.9-10 *- Acts 8.30* Isa. 6.10; 29.10	4
Knowledge - Ability to recall and recite information 2 Tim. 3.16-17 1 Cor. 2.9-16 *For what does the Scripture say?* 1 John 2.20-27 *- Rom. 4.3* John 14.26	3
Interest - Responding to ideas or information with both curiosity and openness Ps. 42.1-2 Acts 9.4-5 *We will hear you again on this matter.* John 12.21 *- Acts 17.32* 1 Sam. 3.4-10	2
Awareness - General exposure to ideas and information Mark 7.6-8 Acts 19.1-7 *At that time, Herod the tetrarch heard about the fame of Jesus.* John 5.39-40 *- Matt. 14.1* Matt. 7.21-23	1
Ignorance - Unfamiliarity with information due to naivete, indifference, or hardness Eph. 4.17-19 Ps. 2.1-3 *Who is the Lord that I should heed his voice?* Rom. 1.21; 2.19 *- Exod. 5.2* 1 John 2.11	0

APPENDIX 27
Different Traditions of African-American Response
Interpreting a Legacy, Shaping an Identity, and Pursuing a Destiny as a Minority Culture Person
Adapted from and informed by Cornell West's Prophecy Deliverance

I. **Exceptionalism — Afro-centrism and Superiority - "Above"**

   A. Definition: tendency to respond in terms of exalted, superior, and even romanticized view of one's own cultural and racial roots

   B. Example: Louis Farrakhan, W.E.B. DuBois

   C. Issues

   1. Pendulum swing: same bigotry as oppressive group, only inverted ("Same shoe, different foot")

   2. Isolationist and separatistic; have no desire to be in relationship with people of majority culture and/or race

   3. See separation and segregation as an essential step on the road to a full personhood as a minority group

   4. To gain one's own identity is the prime goal, not relating to people of another culture

II. **Assimilationism: Adopting the Predominant Culture as One's Primary (and in some cases) Only Culture - "Behind"**

   A. Definition: the tendency to ignore or bypass one's particular cultural roots in order to identify with a more general, broad, and accepted majority culture identity

   B. Example: Shelby Steele, Alan Keyes

   C. Issues

   1. Advocate a full blown adoption of the predominant cultural identity (e.g., "I am not Black, but American")

   2. Tends to ignore the specialness of difference

Different Traditions of African American Response (continued)

    3. Need not be committed to obliterating culture, only ignoring difference in order that we may all meld into one common pot

    4. Perpetually defers to the cultural mores and habits of the dominant culture

III. Marginalism: Inferiority, Shame and Hatred, Denial - "Outside"

  A. Definition: tendency to deny, overlook, or even reject one's own cultural legacy as pathological, insignificant, and even detrimental to one's own growth and prosperity

  B. Example: Joseph Washington, E. Franklin Frazier

  C. Issues

    1. Breeds contempt for oneself; self-deprecation is not viewed as a negative in reference to the overall badness of the culture

    2. Ignores God's role in shaping culture

    3. Oversimplifies one's own cultural legacy as either insignificant or immoral

IV. Integrationism: Modern-day Multi-culturalism - "Among"

  A. Definition: tendency to strive for a multi-cultural integration of peoples within society that guarantees the rights and privileges of citizenry, equality, and justice

  B. Example: Jesse Jackson, Thurgood Marshall, traditional civil rights vision

  C. Issues

    1. Focus on attaining distributive justice in society among all the people groups within it ("equal treatment under the law", and "cut the societal pie correctly")

    2. Seeks limited goods within the society of equality and fairness under the law, and does not focus (usually) on friendship but equal treatment

Different Traditions of African American Response (continued)

    3. Appeals mainly to issues related to economic issues, distribution of wealth, and the overall benefits of society

    4. May focus on establishing coalitions of people of different culture in order to sway the hand of government and society for equal and just treatment

    5. Legislates its agenda, does not emphasize relationship

V. Celebrationism: Acknowledgment, Delight, Critique and Relationship "Alongside"

  A. Definition: tendency to see all cultures as significant and unique, and intentionally celebrates the differences between cultures while 1) critiquing its immoral elements according to a biblical vision and, 2) arguing against exclusion and bigotry on the basis of the differences.

  B. Example: Martin Luther King, Jr.

  C. Issues

    1. Grounded in a Christian vision of God's creation

    2. Ethic of a Christian community, and its prophetic message

    3. Affirms culture as a distinctly human phenomenon

    4. Attaches no pejorative connotation to cultural identity or preference

APPENDIX 28
Targeting Unreached Groups in Churched Neighborhoods
Mission Frontiers

Many Different Peoples!

Many Homogenous Congregations

**The Extent of Normal "Outreach":
Incorporating and Gathering
According to Culture**

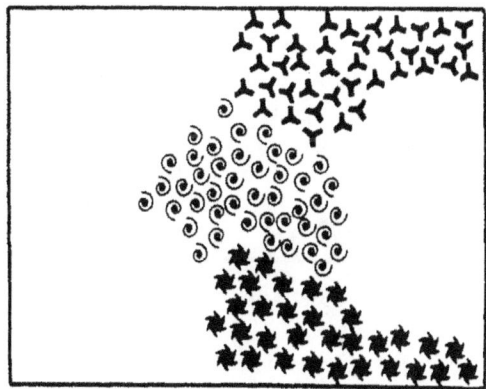

**"So Close and Yet so Far Away":
The Unreached, Unaffected
Neighbors**

APPENDIX 29
Dealing With Old Ways
Adapted from Paul Hiebert

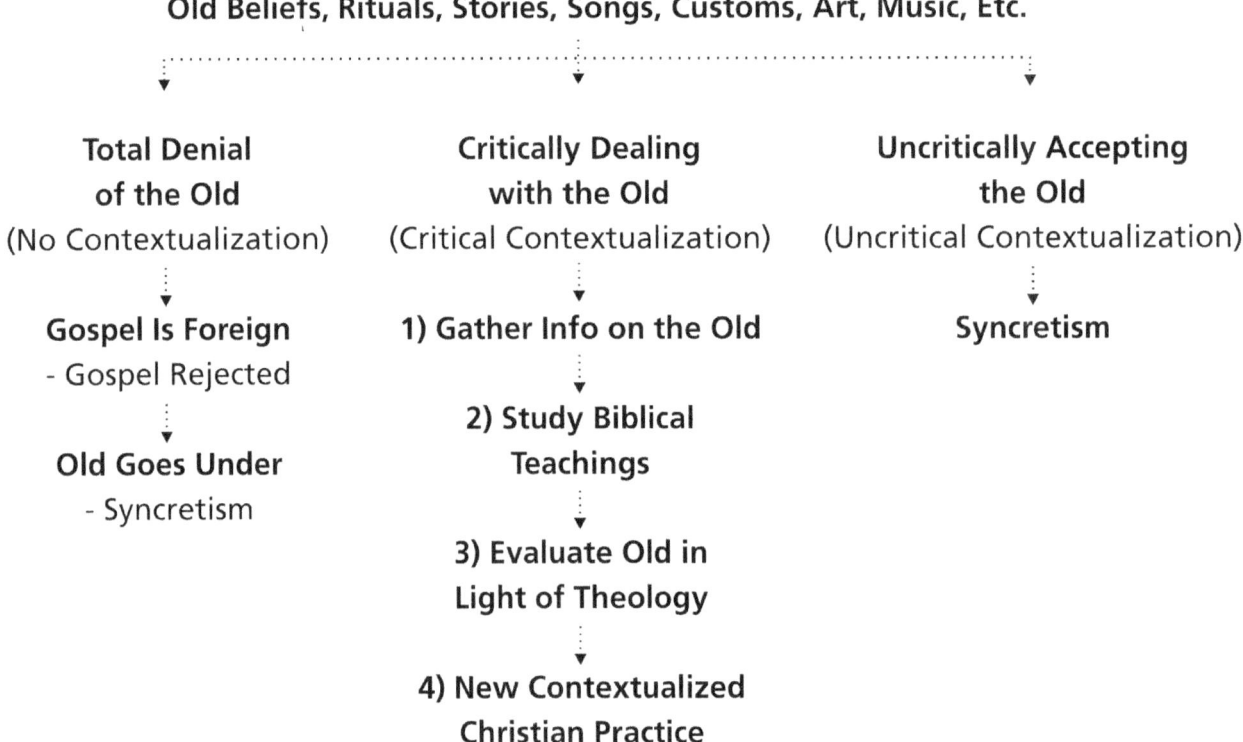

APPENDIX 30
Overview Plant to Birth Models
Rev. Dr. Don L. Davis

World Impact Model	Phases of Church Planting Compared to Childbirth	Emphasis During Particular Phase of Childbearing
Prepare	Commitment to Parent	Commitment to give birth and to parent secured from qualified parents
Prepare	Conception	Core team, volunteers gathered/prepared, parenting church engaged, target population and community selected, studied, canvassed
Launch	Prenatal Care	Ongoing outreach, small group community, structured in-reach of nucleus
Assemble	Birth	Announcement of public gathering and worship, celebration of gathered groups
Nurture	Growth Toward Maturity	Building foundations, developing vital ministries, forming systems, achieving leadership autonomy
Transition	Reproduction	Congregational "adulthood," new church as kingdom outpost: spiritual DNA planting new congregations

APPENDIX 31

Overview of Church Plant Planning Phases

Rev. Dr. Don L. Davis

	Prepare	Launch	Assemble	Nurture	Transition
Definition	Forming a team of called members who ready themselves to plant a church under the Holy Spirit's direction	Penetrating the selected community by conducting evangelistic events among the target population	Gathering the cells of converts together to form a local assembly of believers, announcing the new church to the neighbors in the community	Nurturing member and leadership discipleship, enabling members to function in their spiritual gifts, and establishing solid infrastructure within the Christian assembly	Empowering the church for independence by equipping leaders for autonomy, transferring authority, and creating structures for financial independence
Purpose	Seek God regarding the target population and community, the formation of your church plant team, organizing strategic intercession for the community, and doing research on its needs and opportunities	Mobilize team and recruit volunteers to conduct ongoing evangelistic events and holistic outreach to win associates and neighbors to Christ	Form cell groups, Bible studies, or home fellowships for follow-up, continued evangelism, and ongoing growth toward public birth of the church	Develop individual and group discipleship by filling key roles in the body based on burden and gifting of members	Commission members and elders, install pastor, and foster church associations
Parent-Child Metaphor	Decision and Conception	Pre-natal Care	Childbirth	Growth and Parenting	Maturity to Adulthood
Question Focus During Dialogue	**Questions about:** • Preparing your team • The target community • Strategic prayer initiatives • Demographic studies	**Questions about:** • Character and number of evangelistic events • Communication and advertisement of events • Recruiting and coordinating volunteers • Identity and name of the outreach	**Questions about:** • Follow-up and incorporation of new believers • Make-up of small group life • The character of public worship • Initial church structures and procedures • Initial body life and growth • Cultural friendliness of church	**Questions about:** • Discipling individuals and leaders • Helping members identify gifts and burdens (teams) • Credentials for leadership • Church order, government and discipline	**Questions about:** • Incorporation • Affiliations and associations • Transferring leadership • Missionary transition • Ongoing reproduction
Cardinal Virtue	Openness to the Lord	Courage to engage the community	Wisdom to discern God's timing	Focus upon the faithful core	Dependence on the Spirit's ability
Cardinal Vices	Presumption and "paralysis of analysis"	Intimidation and haughtiness	Impatience and cowardice	Neglect and micromanagement	Paternalism and quick release
Bottom Line	Cultivate a period of listening and reflecting	Initiate your engagement with boldness and confidence	Celebrate the announcement of your body with joy	Concentrate on investing in the faithful	Pass the baton with confidence in the Spirit's continued working

APPENDIX 32

Investment, Empowerment, and Assessment

How Leadership as Representation Provides Freedom to Innovate

Rev. Dr. Don L. Davis

ASSESS: Evaluate and Review

Accountability for Results Within an Agreed Upon Time Frame

Ministry oversight measure results here

- Evaluation by sending authority
- Review of results in light of task
- Faithfulness and loyalty assessed
- Overall evaluation of plan and strategy
- Critical evaluation of leadership performance
- Formal determination of operation's "success"
- Reassignment in light of evaluation

EMPOWER

Freedom to innovate under the oversight of godly local leadership and the guidance of the Holy Spirit

Ministry oversight provides resources, prayer, and counsel

INVEST: Preparation and Resources

Selection and Investment of Leaders and Team Members

Ministry oversight provides support, resources and authority here

- Formal leadership selection
- Acknowledgment of personal call
- Determination of task and assignment
- Training in spiritual warfare
- Authorization to act defined and given
- Necessary resources given and logistics planned
- Commissioning: deputization formally recognized

FOCUS ON REPRODUCTION

APPENDIX 33
Five Views of the Relationship between Christ and Culture

*Based on **Christ and Culture** by H. Richard Niebuhr. New York: Harper and Row, 1951.*

Christ Against Culture	Christ and Culture in Paradox	Christ the Transformer of Culture	Christ Above Culture	The Christ of Culture
Opposition	Tension	Conversion	Cooperation	Acceptance
Therefore come out from them and be separate, says the Lord. Touch no unclean thing, and I will receive you. - 2 Cor. 6.17 (cf. 1 John 2.15)	Give to Caesar what is Caesar's, and to God what is God's. - Matt. 22.21 (cf. 1 Pet. 2.13-17)	In putting everything under him, God left nothing that is not subject to him. Yet at present we do not see everything subject to him. - Heb. 2.8 (cf. Col. 1.16-18)	Indeed, when Gentiles, who do not have the law, do by nature things required by the law, they are a law for themselves. - Rom. 2.14 (cf. Rom. 13.1, 5-6)	Every good and perfect gift is from above, coming down from the Father of the heavenly lights, who does not change like shifting shadows. - James 1.17 (cf. Phil. 4.8)
Culture is radically affected by sin and constantly opposes the will of God. Separation and opposition are the natural responses of the Christian community which is itself an alternative culture.	Culture is radically affected by sin but does have a role to play. It is necessary to delineate between spheres: Culture as law (restrains wickedness), Christianity as grace (gives righteousness). Both are an important part of life but the two cannot be confused or merged.	Culture is radically affected by sin but can be redeemed to play a positive role in restoring righteousness. Christians should work to have their culture acknowledge Christ's lordship and be changed by it.	Culture is a product of human reason and is part of a God-given way to discover truth. Although culture can discern real truth, sin limits its capacities which must be aided by revelation. Seeks to use culture as a first step toward the understanding of God and his revelation.	Culture is God's gift to help man overcome his bondage to nature and fear and advance in knowledge and goodness. Human culture is what allows us to conserve the truth humanity has learned. Jesus' moral teaching moves human culture upward to a new level.
Tertullian, Menno Simons Anabaptists	Martin Luther Lutherans	St. Augustine, John Calvin Reformed	Thomas Aquinas Roman Catholic	Peter Abelard, Immanual Kant Liberal Protestant

APPENDIX 34
That We May Be One
Elements of an Integrated Church Planting Movement Among the Urban Poor
Rev. Dr. Don L. Davis

> *It is a most invaluable part of that blessed "liberty wherewith Christ hath made us free," that in his worship different forms and usages may without offence be allowed, provided the substance of the Faith be kept entire; and that, in every Church, what cannot be clearly determined to belong to Doctrine must be referred to Discipline; and therefore, by common consent and authority, may be altered, abridged, enlarged, amended, or otherwise disposed of, as may seem most convenient for the edification of the people, "according to the various exigency of times and occasions."*
> ~ 1789 Preface to the Book of Common Prayer. 1928 Episcopal edition.

Church Planting Movements among the Urban Poor = an integrated and aggressive advance of the Kingdom of God among the urban poor resulting in a significant increase of indigenous churches which fundamentally share in common a constellation of elements which provides them with a distinct and unique identity, purpose, and practice.

Ministry among the urban poor must be grounded in a vision and understanding of the liberty we have in Christ to conceive of coherent, integrated movements of followers of Jesus who because of shared experience, proximity, culture, and history *determine to reflect their unique faith and practice in a way consistent with the historic faith but distinct to their life and times.* This is not an arbitrary act; movements cannot ignore the nature of the one (unity), holy (sanctity), catholic (universality), and apostolic (apostolicity) Church, the one true people of God.

Nevertheless, as was affirmed by the emerging leaders of the then American Episcopal Church, the freedom that we have in Christ allows for different forms and usages of worship in the body of Christ without any offense whatsoever, as long as we are faithful to the historic orthodox beliefs of the Church as taught to us by the prophets and apostles of our Lord. Doctrine must remain anchored and complete; discipline, however, can be based on the contingencies and exigencies of the people who embrace them, as long as all that is shaped and conceived builds up the body of Christ, and glorifies God our Father through our Lord Jesus Christ.

"The congregations in an Integrated Church Planting Movement Among the Urban Poor *will exhibit together:*"

1. *A shared history and identity* (i.e., *a common name and heritage*). CPMs among the urban poor will seek to link themselves to and identify themselves by a well defined and joyfully shared history and persona that all members and congregations share.

That We May Be One (continued)

2. *A shared liturgy and celebration* (i.e., *a common worship*). CPMs among the urban poor should reflect a shared hymnody, practice of the sacraments, theological focus and imagery, aesthetic vision, vestments, liturgical order, symbology, and spiritual formation that enables us to worship and glorify God in a way that lifts up the Lord and attracts urbanites to vital worship.

3. *A shared membership, well-being, welfare, and support* (i.e., *a common order and discipline*). CPMs among the urban poor must be anchored in evangelical and historically orthodox presentations of the Gospel that result in conversions to Jesus Christ and incorporation into local churches.

4. *A shared catechism and doctrine* (i.e., *a common faith*). CPMs among the urban poor must embrace a common biblical theology and express it practically in a Christian education that reflects their commonly-held faith.

5. *A shared church government and authority* (i.e., *a common polity*). CPMs among the urban poor must be organized around a common polity, ecclesial management, and submit to flexible governing policies that allow for effective and efficient management of their resources and congregations.

6. *A shared leadership development structure* (i.e., *a common pastoral strategy*). CPMs among the urban poor are committed with supplying each congregation with godly undershepherds, and seek to identify, equip, and support its pastors and missionaries in order that their members may grow to maturity in Christ.

7. *A shared financial philosophy and procedure* (i.e., *a common stewardship*). CPMs among the urban poor strive to handle all of their financial affairs and resources with wise, streamlined, and reproducible policies that allow for the good management of their monies and goods, locally, regionally, and nationally.

8. *A shared care and support ministry* (i.e., *a common service*). CPMs among the urban poor seek to practically demonstrate the love and justice of the Kingdom among its members and towards others in the city in ways that allow individuals and congregations to love their neighbors as they love themselves.

9. *A shared evangelism and outreach* (i.e., *a common mission*): CPMs among the urban poor network and collaborate among their members in order to clearly present Jesus and his Kingdom to the lost in the city in order to multiply new congregations in unreached urban areas as quickly as possible.

That We May Be One (continued)

10. *A shared vision for connection and association* (i.e., *a common partnership*). CPMs among the urban poor must seek to make fresh connections, links, and relationships with other movements for the sake of regular communication, fellowship, and mission.

These principles of belonging, camaraderie, and identity lay the foundation for a new paradigm of authentic ecumenical unity, the kind that can lead to partnerships and collaboration of grand scope and deep substance. Below is a short overview of the TUMI biblical basis for the kind of partnerships which can fuel and sustain credible church planting movements among the urban poor.

God's Partners and Fellow Workers

1 Cor. 3.1-9 (ESV) - But I, brothers, could not address you as spiritual people, but as people of the flesh, as infants in Christ. [2] I fed you with milk, not solid food, for you were not ready for it. And even now you are not yet ready, [3] for you are still of the flesh. For while there is jealousy and strife among you, are you not of the flesh and behaving only in a human way? [4] For when one says, "I follow Paul," and another, "I follow Apollos," are you not being merely human? [5] What then is Apollos? What is Paul? Servants through whom you believed, as the Lord assigned to each. [6] I planted, Apollos watered, but God gave the growth. [7] So neither he who plants nor he who waters is anything, but only God who gives the growth. [8] He who plants and he who waters are one, and each will receive his wages according to his labor. [9] For we are God's fellow workers. You are God's field, God's building.

To Facilitate Pioneer Church Planting Movements Among America's Unreached C_1 Communities

As a ministry of World Impact, TUMI is dedicated to generating and strategically facilitating dynamic, indigenous C_1 church planting movements targeted to reach the 80% Window of America's inner cities. In order to attain this purpose, we will help form strategic alliances between and among urban missionaries and pastors, theologians and missiologists, churches and denominations, and other kingdom-minded individuals and organizations in order to trigger robust pioneer

That We May Be One (continued)

church planting movements that multiply thousands of culturally-conducive evangelical C₁ churches among America's urban poor. We will offer our expertise to assure that these churches in every way glorify God the Father in their Christ-centered identity, Spirit-formed worship and community life, historically orthodox doctrine, and kingdom-oriented practice and mission.

I. Partnership₁ Involves Recognizing our Fundamental Unity in Christ: We Share the Same Spiritual DNA.

    A. *Our faith in Jesus has made us one together.*

        1. 1 John 1.3 (ESV) - that which we have seen and heard we proclaim also to you, so that you too may have fellowship with us; and indeed our fellowship is with the Father and with his Son Jesus Christ.

        2. John 17.11 (ESV) - And I am no longer in the world, but they are in the world, and I am coming to you. Holy Father, keep them in your name, which you have given me, that they may be one, even as we are one.

    B. *The organic unity between the Father and Son, and the people of God,* John 17.21-22 (ESV) - that they may all be one, just as you, Father, are in me, and I in you, that they also may be in us, so that the world may believe that you have sent me. [22] The glory that you have given me I have given to them, that they may be one even as we are one.

    C. *Our unity leads to a common effort in glorifying God the Father of our Lord,* Rom. 15.5-6 (ESV) - May the God of endurance and encouragement grant you to live in such harmony with one another, in accord with Christ Jesus, [6] that together you may with one voice glorify the God and Father of our Lord Jesus Christ.

    D. *God's will for the body is unity in mind and judgment,* 1 Cor. 1.10 (ESV) - I appeal to you, brothers, by the name of our Lord Jesus Christ, that all of you agree and that there be no divisions among you, but that you be united in the same mind and the same judgment.

    E. *The Holy Spirit's baptism has made us of one spiritual body and spirit,* 1 Cor. 12.12-13 (ESV) - For just as the body is one and has many members, and all the members of the body, though many, are one body, so it is with Christ.

That We May Be One (continued)

[13] For in one Spirit we were all baptized into one body— Jews or Greeks, slaves or free—and all were made to drink of one Spirit.

F. *The very essence of biblical faith is unity*, Eph. 4.4-6 (ESV) - There is one body and one Spirit—just as you were called to the one hope that belongs to your call [5] one Lord, one faith, one baptism, [6] one God and Father of all, who is over all and through all and in all.

G. *Our bond of partnership precludes unity with those not united to Christ*, 2 Cor. 6.14-16 (ESV) - Do not be unequally yoked with unbelievers. For what partnership has righteousness with lawlessness? Or what fellowship has light with darkness? [15] What accord has Christ with Belial? Or what portion does a believer share with an unbeliever? [16] What agreement has the temple of God with idols? For we are the temple of the living God; as God said, "I will make my dwelling among them and walk among them, and I will be their God, and they shall be my people.

II. **Partnership$_2$ Involves the Sharing of Monies, Persons, and Resources to Fund a Common Cause: We Share a Common Source, Table, and Pot.**

A. *The partnership between those who share the Word and receive it involves concrete blessing and giving.*

1. *The taught share with the teacher*, Gal. 6.6 (ESV) - One who is taught the word must share all good things with the one who teaches.

2. *Illustrated in the relationship of the Jew to the Gentile in the body*, Rom. 15.27 (ESV) - They were pleased to do it, and indeed they owe it to them. For if the Gentiles have come to share in their spiritual blessings, they ought also to be of service to them in material blessings.

B. *The power of unity extends to those who are appointed by God to serve his people*, Deut. 12.19 (ESV) - Take care that you do not neglect the Levite as long as you live in your land.

C. *Those who labor deserve the generous supply of those who benefit from that labor.*

1. *Christ's exhortation to the disciples*, Matt. 10.10 (ESV) - No bag for your journey, nor two tunics nor sandals nor a staff, for the laborer deserves his food.

That We May Be One (continued)

    2. *Illustrated from OT Scripture and analogy*, 1 Cor. 9.9-14 (ESV) - For it is written in the Law of Moses, "You shall not muzzle an ox when it treads out the grain." Is it for oxen that God is concerned? [10] Does he not speak entirely for our sake? It was written for our sake, because the plowman should plow in hope and the thresher thresh in hope of sharing in the crop. [11] If we have sown spiritual things among you, is it too much if we reap material things from you? [12] If others share this rightful claim on you, do not we even more? Nevertheless, we have not made use of this right, but we endure anything rather than put an obstacle in the way of the gospel of Christ. [13] Do you not know that those who are employed in the temple service get their food from the temple, and those who serve at the altar share in the sacrificial offerings? [14] In the same way, the Lord commanded that those who proclaim the gospel should get their living by the gospel.

    3. *Double honor: respect and sharing of resources*, 1 Tim. 5.17-18 (ESV) - Let the elders who rule well be considered worthy of double honor, especially those who labor in preaching and teaching. [18] For the Scripture says, "You shall not muzzle an ox when it treads out the grain," and, "The laborer deserves his wages."

D. *The Philippian relationship with Paul is a prototype of this kind of essential partnership.*

    1. *From the beginning they shared tangibly with Paul*, Phil. 1.3-5 (ESV) - I thank my God in all my remembrance of you, [4] always in every prayer of mine for you all making my prayer with joy, [5] because of your partnership in the gospel from the first day until now.

    2. *Epaphroditus was their messenger to transport their aid to Paul*, Phil. 2.25 (ESV) - I have thought it necessary to send to you Epaphroditus my brother and fellow worker and fellow soldier, and your messenger and minister to my need

    3. *The Philippians were completely engaged in the support of Paul's ministry from the first*, Phil. 4.15-18 (ESV) - And you Philippians yourselves know that in the beginning of the gospel, when I left Macedonia, no church entered into partnership with me in giving and receiving, except you only. [16] Even in Thessalonica you sent me help for my needs once

That We May Be One (continued)

and again. [17] Not that I seek the gift, but I seek the fruit that increases to your credit. [18] I have received full payment, and more. I am well supplied, having received from Epaphroditus the gifts you sent, a fragrant offering, a sacrifice acceptable and pleasing to God.

III. Partnership$_3$ Involves Collaborating Together as Co-workers and Co-laborers in the Work of Advancing the Kingdom: We Share a Common Cause and Task.

A. *Partnership assumes that each person and congregation brings their unique experience, perspective, and gifting to the table for use*, Gal. 2.6-8 (ESV) - And from those who seemed to be influential (what they were makes no difference to me; God shows no partiality)—those, I say, who seemed influential added nothing to me. [7] On the contrary, when they saw that I had been entrusted with the gospel to the uncircumcised, just as Peter had been entrusted with the gospel to the circumcised [8] (for he who worked through Peter for his apostolic ministry to the circumcised worked also through me for mine to the Gentiles).

B. *Authentic partnerships involve discerning the Lord's leading, opportunity, and blessing on those who are called to represent his interests in the places where he has led them*, Gal. 2.9-10 (ESV) - and when James and Cephas and John, who seemed to be pillars, perceived the grace that was given to me, they gave the right hand of fellowship to Barnabas and me, that we should go to the Gentiles and they to the circumcised. [10] Only, they asked us to remember the poor, the very thing I was eager to do.

C. *Partnership in terms of co-working and co-laboring involves a shared vision and commitment to a common cause*, e.g., Timothy, Phil. 2.19-24 (ESV) - I hope in the Lord Jesus to send Timothy to you soon, so that I too may be cheered by news of you. [20] For I have no one like him, who will be genuinely concerned for your welfare. [21] They all seek their own interests, not those of Jesus Christ. [22] But you know Timothy's proven worth, how as a son with a father he has served with me in the gospel. [23] I hope therefore to send him just as soon as I see how it will go with me, [24] and I trust in the Lord that shortly I myself will come also.

That We May Be One (continued)

    D. *Paul's unique words for his partners in the Gospel*

        1. Co-worker (*synergos*), Rom. 16.3, 7, 9, 21; 2 Cor. 8.23; Phil. 2.25; 4.3; Col. 4.7, 10, 11, 14; Philem. 1, 24.

        2. Co-prisoner (*synaichmalotos*), Col. 4.10; Philem. 23

        3. Co-slave (*syndoulos*), Col. 1.7, 4.7

        4. Co-soldier (*systratiotes*) Phil. 2.25; Philem. 2

        5. Co-laborer (*synatheleo*), Phil. 4.2-3

    E. A brief listing of Paul's partners in ministry (these accompanied him at every phase and effort of the work, with diverse backgrounds, giftings, tasks, and responsibilities along the way of his ministry)

        1. John Mark (Col. 4.10; Philem. 24)

        2. Artistarchus (Col. 4.10; Philem. 24)

        3. Andronicus and Junia (Rom. 16.7)

        4. Philemon (Philem. 1)

        5. Epaphroditus (same as Epaphras) (Col. 1.7; Philem. 23; Phil. 2.25)

        6. Clement (Phil. 4.3)

        7. Urbanus (Rom. 16.9)

        8. Jesus (Justus) (Col. 4.11)

        9. Demas (who later apostocized in the world), (Col. 4.14; Philem. 24; 2 Tim. 4.20)

        10. Tychicus (Col. 4.7; Phil. 4.3)

        11. Archippus (Philem. 2)

        12. Euodia (Phil. 4.2-3)

        13. Syntyche (Phil. 4.2-3)

        14. Tertius (Rom. 16.22)

That We May Be One (continued)

15. Phoebe (Rom. 16.1)

16. Erastus (Rom. 16.23)

17. Quartus (Rom. 16.23)

18. Tryphaena (Rom. 16.12)

19. Tryphosa (Rom. 16.12)

20. Persis (Rom. 16.12)

21. Mary (Rom. 16.6)

22. Onesiphorus (2 Tim. 1.16-18)

IV. Implications of Partnership Principles in Light of TUMI's Visions

To Facilitate Pioneer Church Planting Movements Among America's Unreached C_1 Communities

As a ministry of World Impact, TUMI is dedicated to generating and strategically facilitating dynamic, indigenous C_1 church planting movements targeted to reach the 80% Window of America's inner cities. In order to attain this purpose, we will help form strategic alliances between and among urban missionaries and pastors, theologians and missiologists, churches and denominations, and other kingdom-minded individuals and organizations in order to trigger robust pioneer church planting movements that multiply thousands of culturally-conducive evangelical C_1 churches among America's urban poor. We will offer our expertise to assure that these churches in every way glorify God the Father in their Christ-centered identity, Spirit-formed worship and community life, historically orthodox doctrine, and kingdom-oriented practice and mission.

A. *TUMI will help form strategic alliances to trigger urban church plant movements.*

B. *TUMI seeks to support dynamic movements which produce and sustain healthy C_1 churches.*

That We May Be One (continued)

    C. Clear implications of this for us

        1. We don't recruit people to ourselves, but to participate in Christ's kingdom advance.

        2. We don't own the vision, it is God's desire to impact the world, and we contribute alongside others.

        3. Our contribution is no better or worse than others: we are co-laborers with others.

        4. The work that others do will probably be more critical and fruitful than our own.

Bottom Line

There is virtually no limit to what we can accomplish if we as a team are willing to give our all for the sake of our common cause, if we do not care what role we have to play in order to win, nor care who gets the credit after the victory.

APPENDIX 35

Advancing the Kingdom in the City
Multiplying Congregations with a Common Identity
Rev. Dr. Don L. Davis

Acts 2:41-47 (ESV) - So those who received his word were baptized, and there were added that day about three thousand souls. [42] And they devoted themselves to the apostles' teaching and fellowship, to the breaking of bread and the prayers. [43] And awe came upon every soul, and many wonders and signs were being done through the apostles. [44] **And all who believed were together and had all things in common.** *[45] And they were selling their possessions and belongings and distributing the proceeds to all, as any had need. [46] And day by day, attending the temple together and breaking bread in their homes, they received their food with glad and generous hearts, [47] praising God and having favor with all the people.* **And the Lord added to their number day by day those who were being saved.**

koinonia (pronunciation: [koy-nohn-ee'-ah])

Trinitarian Principle: Unity • Diversity • Equality

World Impact seeks to plant churches that are kingdom-oriented communities where Christ is exalted as Lord and the Kingdom of God is advanced in every facet of community life, and, we seek to do this in a way that respects and acknowledges the validity and significance of incarnating this community life in the receiving culture. In order to ensure the viability, protection, and flourishing of these congregations, we ought to explore forming close-knit associations between congregations where a common identity, confession, and faith are practiced, under a common oversight and governance, that connects in a fundamental way the resources and visions of each church without lording over them.

Following is a chart that sketches what might be the elements of such a common coalition of churches which would link their lives in a strategic way for the well-being and enrichment of the entire fellowship of churches. (Cf. *Imagining a Unified, Connected C1 Church Planting Movement* [see *www.tumi.org/Capstone* under the header *Appendices*] which in a comprehensive way suggests what may be included along ecclesial and missional, liturgical, and catechetical lines in such a fellowship).

Advancing the Kingdom in the City (continued)

Sharing a Common Identity, Purpose, and Mission	
A Common Name and Association	Understanding the churches as fundamentally linked in history, identity, legacy, and destiny
A Common Confession of Faith	Developing a common theological and doctrinal vision
A Common Celebration and Worship	Practicing a common liturgy with shared worship approaches
A Common Discipleship and Catechism	Sharing a common curriculum and process for welcoming, incorporating, and discipling new believers into our fellowship
A Common Governance and Oversight	Answering to a common accountability for leadership and care
A Common Service and Missionary Outreach	Developing integrated processes and programs of justice, good works, outreach, evangelism, and missions, both at home and throughout the world
A Common Stewardship and Partnership	Combining resources through consistent mutual contribution to maximize impact for the entire association

Benefits of a Common Movement
1. Sense of belonging through a shared faith and identity
2. Efficiency and economy of effort
3. Ability to plant multiple plants in many different venues and populations
4. Cultivating genuine unity and diversity, with a spirit of mutuality and equality among the congregations
5. Increased productivity and viability within our missions efforts and churches
6. Interchangability and cross pollination
7. Ongoing support and encouragement of our leaders
8. Provide leverage for new projects and new initiatives
9. Standardized processes and procedures for incorporation and training
10. Greater opportunities for convocation and exposure to other like-minded believers

APPENDIX 36
Creating Coherent Urban Church Planting Movements
Discerning the Elements of Authentic Urban Christian Community
Rev. Dr. Don L. Davis

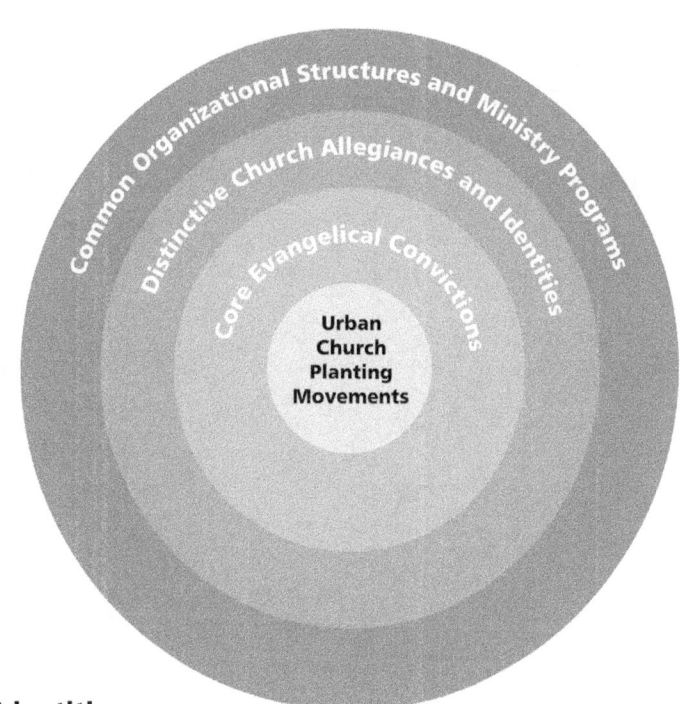

Core Evangelical Convictions

This circle represents *its most fundamental convictions and commitments*, its Affirmation of Faith, its commitment to the Gospel and those truths contained in the early Christian creeds (i.e., The Nicene Creed). These convictions are anchored in its confidence in the Word of God, and represent our unequivocal commitment to historic orthodoxy.

As members of the one, holy, apostolic, and catholic (universal) body of Christ, movements must be **ready and willing to die for their core evangelical convictions**. These convictions serve as the connection of the movements to the historic Christian faith, and as such, can never be compromised or altered.

Distinctive Church Allegiances and Identities

This circle represents their distinctive *church allegiances and identities.* Urban church plant movements will coalesce around their own distinctive traditions, overseen by leaders who provide those movements with vision, instruction, and direction as they move forward together to represent Christ and his Kingdom in the inner city.

Specific traditions seek to express and live out this faithfulness to the Authoritative and Great Traditions through their worship, teaching, and service. They seek to make the Gospel clear within new cultures or sub-cultures, speaking and modeling the hope of Christ into new situations shaped by their own set of questions posed in light of their own unique circumstances. These movements, therefore, seek to contextualize the Authoritative Tradition in a way that faithfully and effectively leads new groups of people to faith in Jesus Christ, and incorporates those who believe into the community of faith that obeys his teachings and gives witness of him to others.

Urban church plant movements must be **ready and willing to articulate and defend their unique distinctives** as God's kingdom community in the city.

Common Organizational Structure and Ministry Programs

This circle represents the ways in which coherent urban church plant movements express their convictions and identity *through their own distinct organizational structures and ministry programs*. These structures and programs are designed and executed through their own specific strategies, policies, decisions, and procedures. The structures and programs represent their self-chosen methods of fleshing out their understanding of the faith as it pertains to their community purpose and mission. These are subject to change under their own legitimate processes as they apply accumulated wisdom in *how best* to accomplish their purposes in the city.

As a communities of faith in Christ, urban church movements must be encouraged to **dialogue about their structures and ministry programs** in order to discover the best possible means to contextualize the Gospel and advance the Kingdom of God among their neighbors.

APPENDIX 37

The *Oikos* Factor
Spheres of Relationship and Influence
Rev. Dr. Don L. Davis

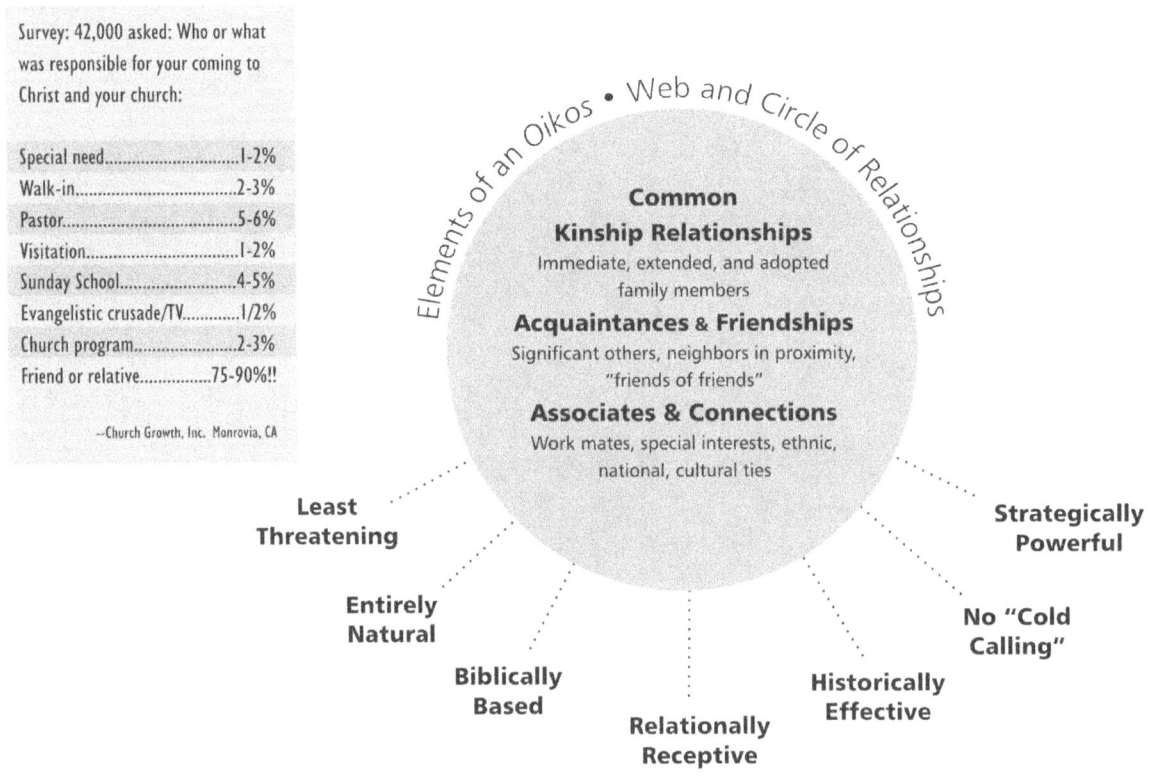

Survey: 42,000 asked: Who or what was responsible for your coming to Christ and your church:

Special need	1-2%
Walk-in	2-3%
Pastor	5-6%
Visitation	1-2%
Sunday School	4-5%
Evangelistic crusade/TV	1/2%
Church program	2-3%
Friend or relative	75-90%!!

--Church Growth, Inc. Monrovia, CA

Elements of an Oikos • Web and Circle of Relationships

Common Kinship Relationships
Immediate, extended, and adopted family members

Acquaintances & Friendships
Significant others, neighbors in proximity, "friends of friends"

Associates & Connections
Work mates, special interests, ethnic, national, cultural ties

- Least Threatening
- Entirely Natural
- Biblically Based
- Relationally Receptive
- Historically Effective
- No "Cold Calling"
- Strategically Powerful

Oikos (household) in the OT
"A household usually contained four generations, including men, married women, unmarried daughters, slaves of both sexes, persons without citizenship, and "sojourners," or resident foreign workers." – *Hans Walter Wolff, Anthology of the Old Testament.*

Oikos (household) in the NT
Evangelism and disciple making in our NT narratives are often described as following the flow of the relational networks of various people within their *oikoi* (households), that is, those natural lines of connection in which they resided and lived (c.f., Mark 5.19; Luke 19.9; John 4.53; 1.41-45, etc.). Andrew to Simon (John 1.41-45), and both Cornelius (Acts 10-11) and the Philippian jailer (Acts 16) are notable cases of evangelism and discipling through *oikoi*.

Oikos (household) among the urban poor
While great differences exist between cultures, kinship relationships, special interest groups, and family structures among urban populations, it is clear that urbanites connect with others far more on the basis of connections through relationships, friendships, and family than through proximity and neighborhood alone. Often times the closest friends of urban poor dwellers are not immediately close-by in terms of neighborhood; family and friends may dwell blocks, even miles away. Taking the time to study the precise linkages of relationships among the dwellers in a certain area can prove extremely helpful in determining the most effective strategies for evangelism and disciple making in inner city contexts.

APPENDIX 38
The Complexity of Difference: Race, Culture, Class
Don L. Davis and Terry Cornett

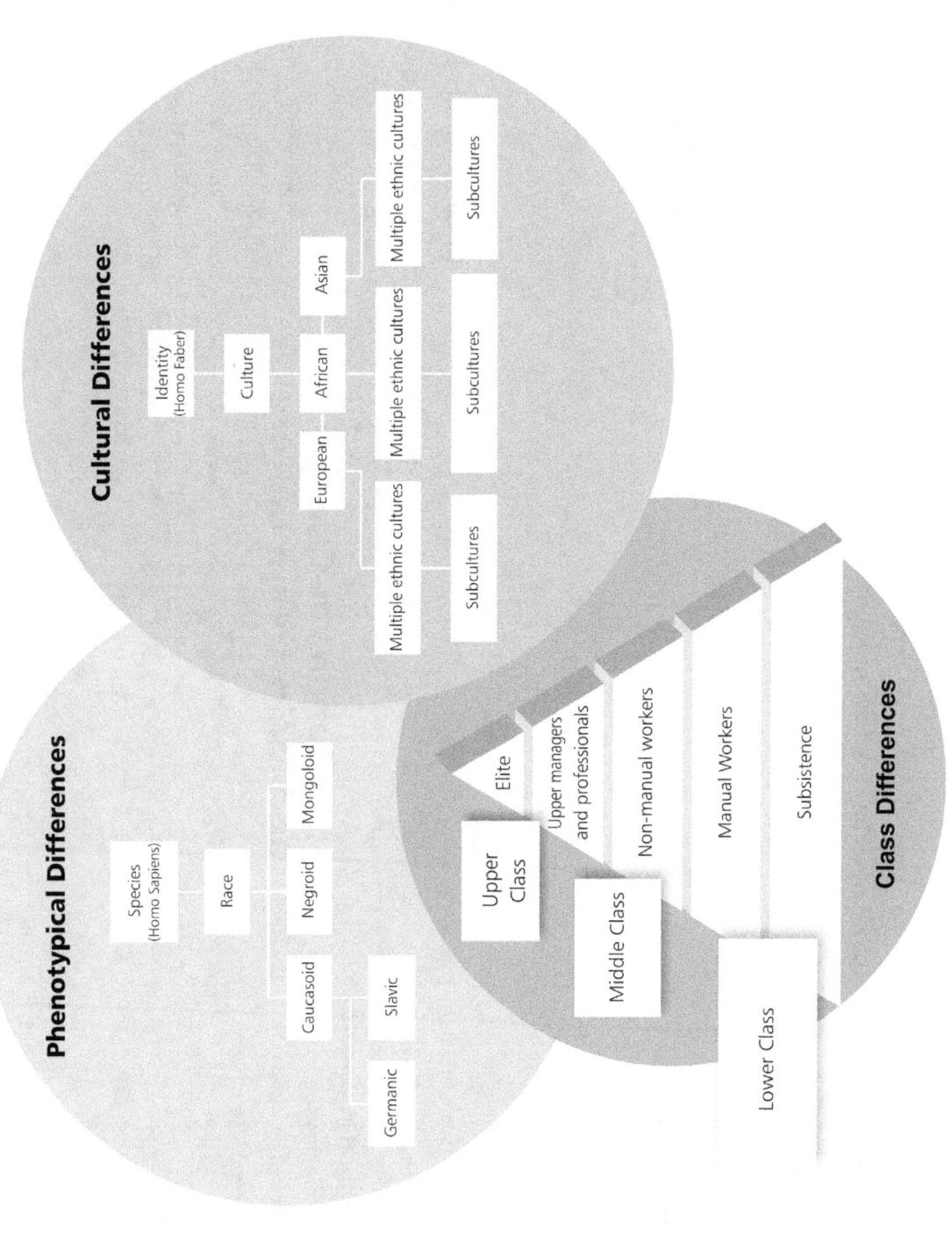

APPENDIX 39
Culture, Not Color: Interaction of Class, Culture, and Race
World Impact Inc.

Asian

Hispanic

White

African-American

C_1, C_2, C_3

Dominant Class and Mainstream Culture

Major Cultural Indicators:
- Where they live
- Where they work
- Where educated

Other Indicators of Culture:
1. Kinship and friendships
2. Upbringing
3. Values and norms
4. Language habits
5. Socio-economic background
6. Education
7. Customs

APPENDIX 40
Authentic Freedom in Jesus Christ
Rev. Dr. Don L. Davis

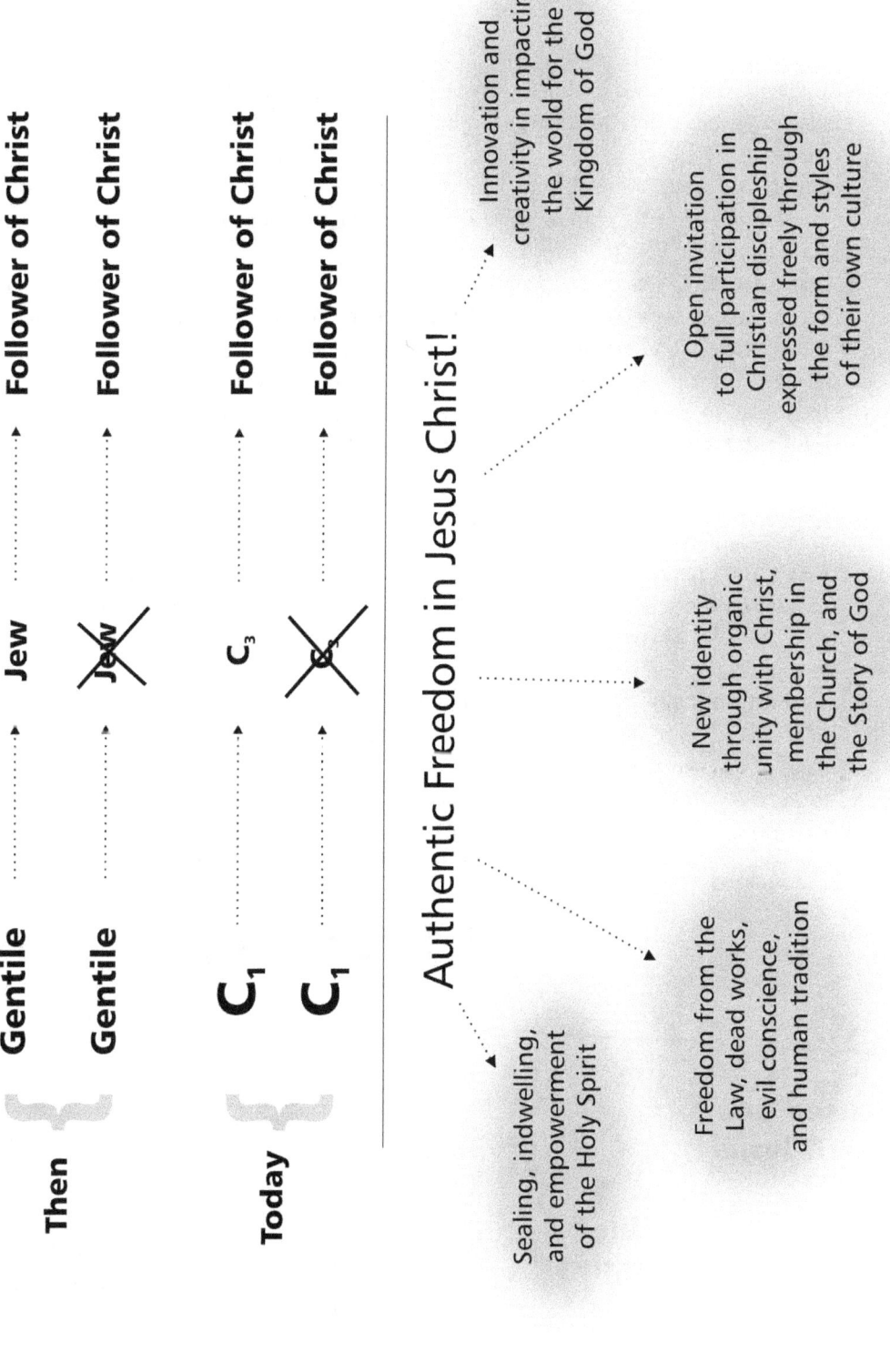

APPENDIX 41

Apostolicity

The Unique Place of the Apostles in Christian Faith and Practice

Rev. Dr. Don L. Davis

Gal. 1.8-9 (ESV) - But even if we or an angel from heaven should preach to you a gospel contrary to the one we preached to you, let him be accursed. **[9]** As we have said before, so now I say again: If anyone is preaching to you a gospel contrary to the one you received, let him be accursed.

2 Thess. 3.6 (ESV) - Now we command you, brothers, in the name of our Lord Jesus Christ, that you keep away from any brother who is walking in idleness and not in accord with the tradition that you received from us.

Luke 1.1-4 (ESV) - Inasmuch as many have undertaken to compile a narrative of the things that have been accomplished among us, **[2]** just as those who from the beginning were eyewitnesses and ministers of the word have delivered them to us, **[3]** it seemed good to me also, having followed all things closely for some time past, to write an orderly account for you, most excellent Theophilus, [4] that you may have certainty concerning the things you have been taught.

John 15.27 (ESV) - And you also will bear witness, because you have been with me from the beginning.

Acts 1.3 (ESV) - To them he presented himself alive after his suffering by many proofs, appearing to them during forty days and speaking about the kingdom of God.

Acts 1.21-22 (ESV) - So one of the men who have accompanied us during all the time that the Lord Jesus went in and out among us, **[22]** beginning from the baptism of John until the day when he was taken up from us—one of these men must become with us a witness to his resurrection.

1 John 1.1-3 (ESV) - That which was from the beginning, which we have heard, which we have seen with our eyes, which we looked upon and have touched with our hands, concerning the word of life— **[2]** the life was made manifest, and we have seen it, and testify to it and proclaim to you the eternal life, which was with the Father and was made manifest to us— **[3]** that which we have seen and heard we proclaim also to you, so that you too may have fellowship with us; and indeed our fellowship is with the Father and with his Son Jesus Christ.

"Apostolicity"

- **Focused on Messiah Jesus**
- **Infallible (Authoritative)**
- **Universally acknowledged among the churches**
- **Clear standard for credentialing ordained leaders**
- **Standard for NT canon**

APPENDIX 42
Apostolic Band
Cultivating Outreach for Dynamic Harvest
Rev. Dr. Don L. Davis

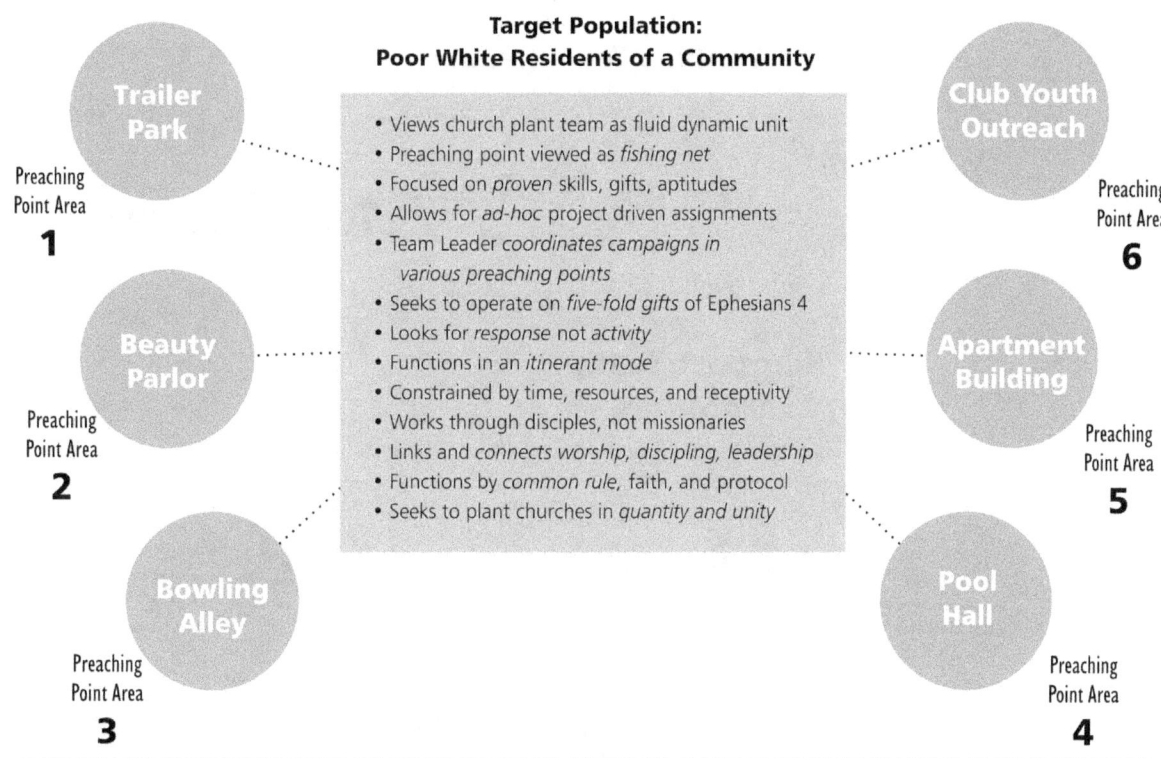

Target Population: Poor White Residents of a Community

- Views church plant team as fluid dynamic unit
- Preaching point viewed as *fishing net*
- Focused on *proven* skills, gifts, aptitudes
- Allows for *ad-hoc* project driven assignments
- Team Leader *coordinates campaigns in various preaching points*
- Seeks to operate on *five-fold gifts* of Ephesians 4
- Looks for *response* not *activity*
- Functions in an *itinerant mode*
- Constrained by time, resources, and receptivity
- Works through disciples, not missionaries
- Links and *connects worship, discipling, leadership*
- Functions by *common rule,* faith, and protocol
- Seeks to plant churches in *quantity and unity*

Preaching Point Area 1 — Trailer Park
Preaching Point Area 2 — Beauty Parlor
Preaching Point Area 3 — Bowling Alley
Preaching Point Area 4 — Pool Hall
Preaching Point Area 5 — Apartment Building
Preaching Point Area 6 — Club Youth Outreach

Principle Concepts

1. Itinerancy- an apostolic band functions in multiple-contexts simultaneously organized around a common target population
2. Commonality- an apostolic band uses similar forms, methods, and protocols to win and build converts
3. Authority- an apostolic band functions under a common authority structure and leadership core
4. Identity- an apostolic band plants churches of a kind with shared doctrine, practice, structures and traditions
5. Gifting- an apostolic band is organized around the proven gifts of the band, not availability and assignment alone
6. Fluidity- an apostolic band invests in contacts who respond in preaching points, giving the receptive their critical attention
7. Coordination- an apostolic band will draft and employ select individuals for contribution at critical times for particular projects
8. Consolidation- an apostolic band consolidates the fruit in an area with an eye toward movement and growth, not permanence
9. Discipline- an apostolic band functions according to an order and structure, equipping disciples in the disciplines of the faith
10. Germinal- an apostolic band seeks to inaugurate and initiate spiritual birth and formation, entrusting the lion's share of the congregation's growth and maturity to pastoral oversight

DEFINITION OF TERMS:

Apostolic Band—a fluid team of gifted, available, and committed workers assigned to play particular roles or accomplish specific tasks contributing to the outreach to a population

Preaching Point—a distinct area, venue, or place where people of the target population live or gather

Team Charter—a fluid agreement based on the prospective time and resources necessary to present the Gospel credibly to a target population in a given venue

Project Management—putting together a temporary group of people, strategies, and resources to complete a particular task, outreach, or event

APPENDIX 43
The Church Plant Team
Forming an Apostolic Band
World Impact, Inc.

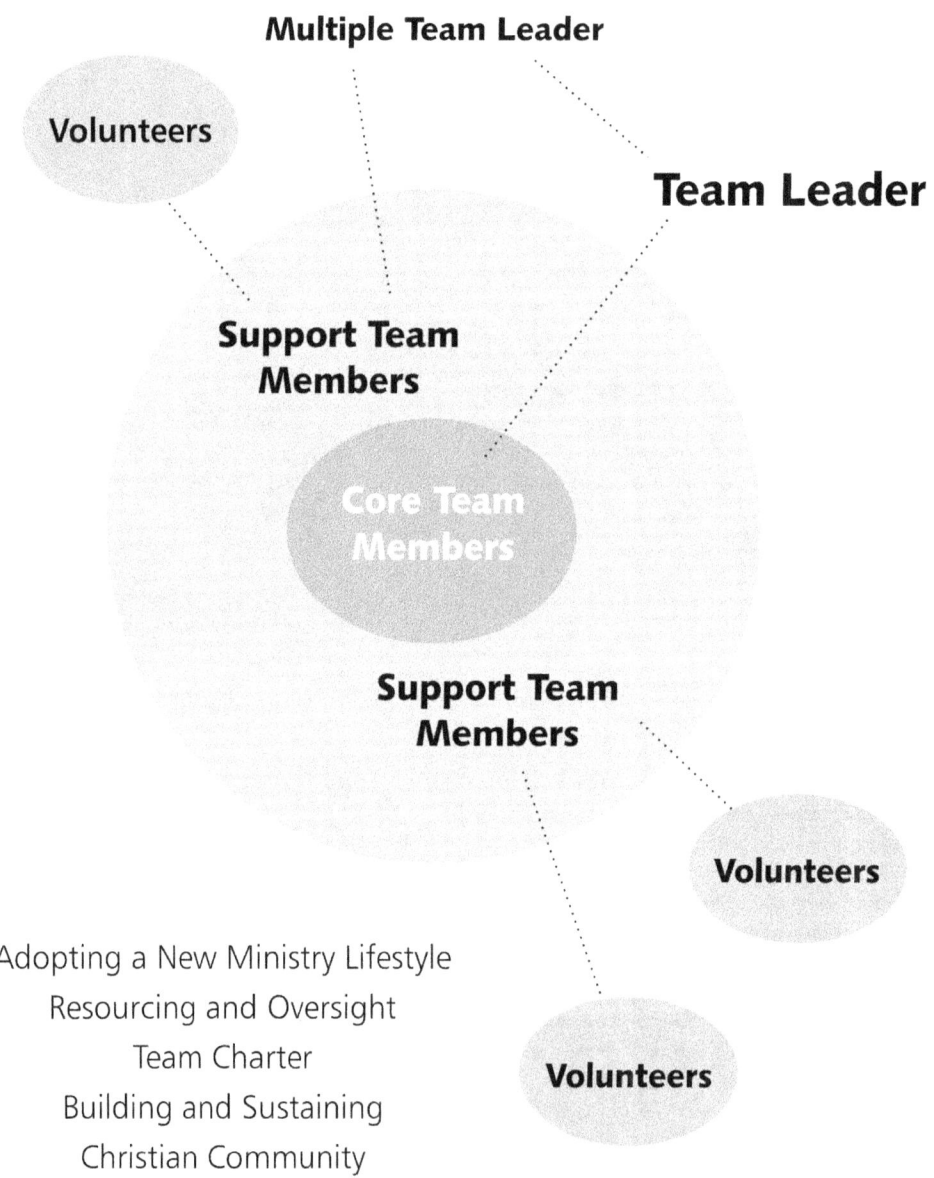

Adopting a New Ministry Lifestyle
Resourcing and Oversight
Team Charter
Building and Sustaining
Christian Community

APPENDIX 44
Translating the Story of God
Rev. Dr. Don L. Davis

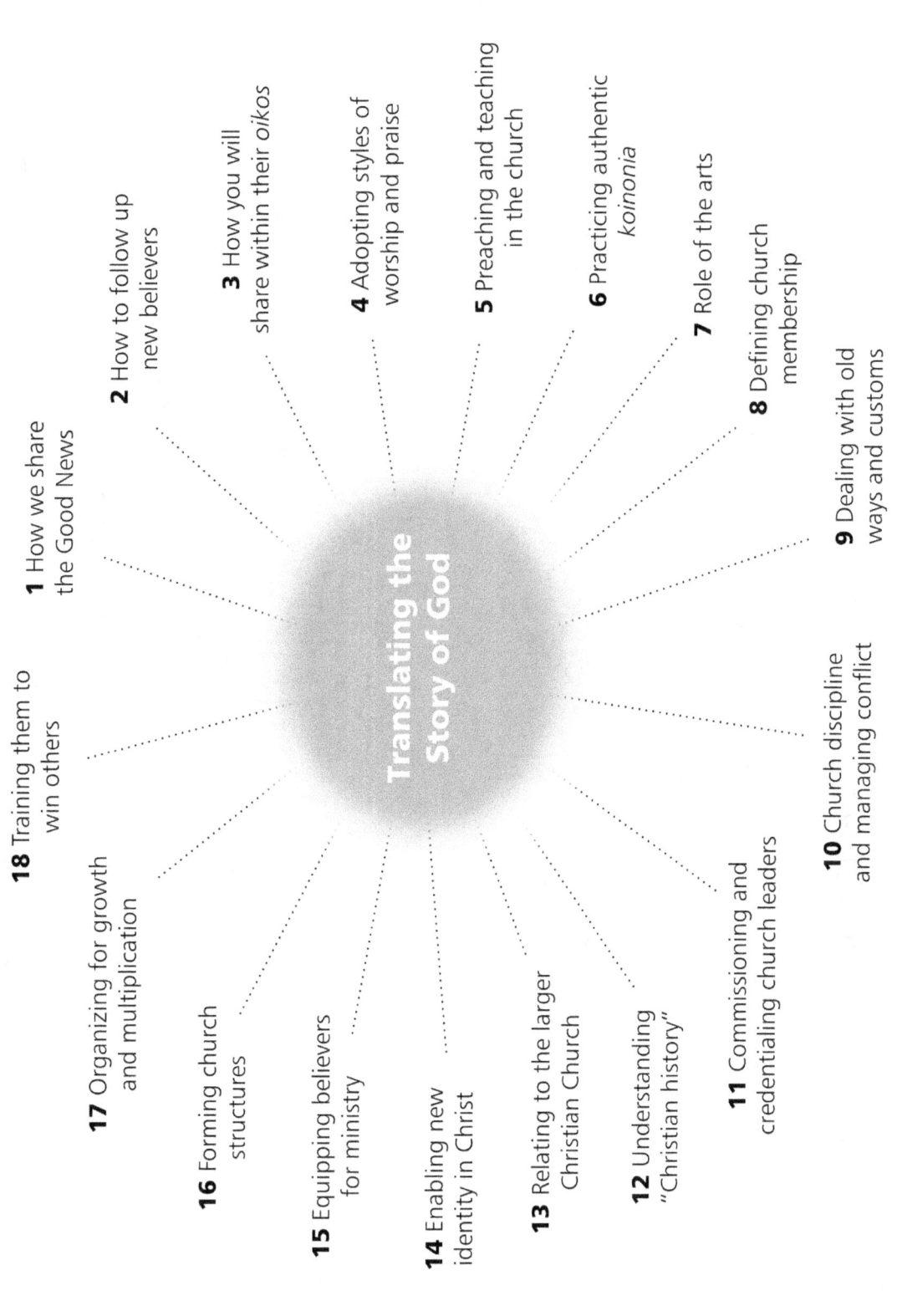

Translating the Story of God

1. How we share the Good News
2. How to follow up new believers
3. How you will share within their *oikos*
4. Adopting styles of worship and praise
5. Preaching and teaching in the church
6. Practicing authentic *koinonia*
7. Role of the arts
8. Defining church membership
9. Dealing with old ways and customs
10. Church discipline and managing conflict
11. Commissioning and credentialing church leaders
12. Understanding "Christian history"
13. Relating to the larger Christian Church
14. Enabling new identity in Christ
15. Equipping believers for ministry
16. Forming church structures
17. Organizing for growth and multiplication
18. Training them to win others

266 / Capstone Curriculum FOCUS ON REPRODUCTION

APPENDIX 45
Three Levels of Ministry Investment
Rev. Dr. Don L. Davis

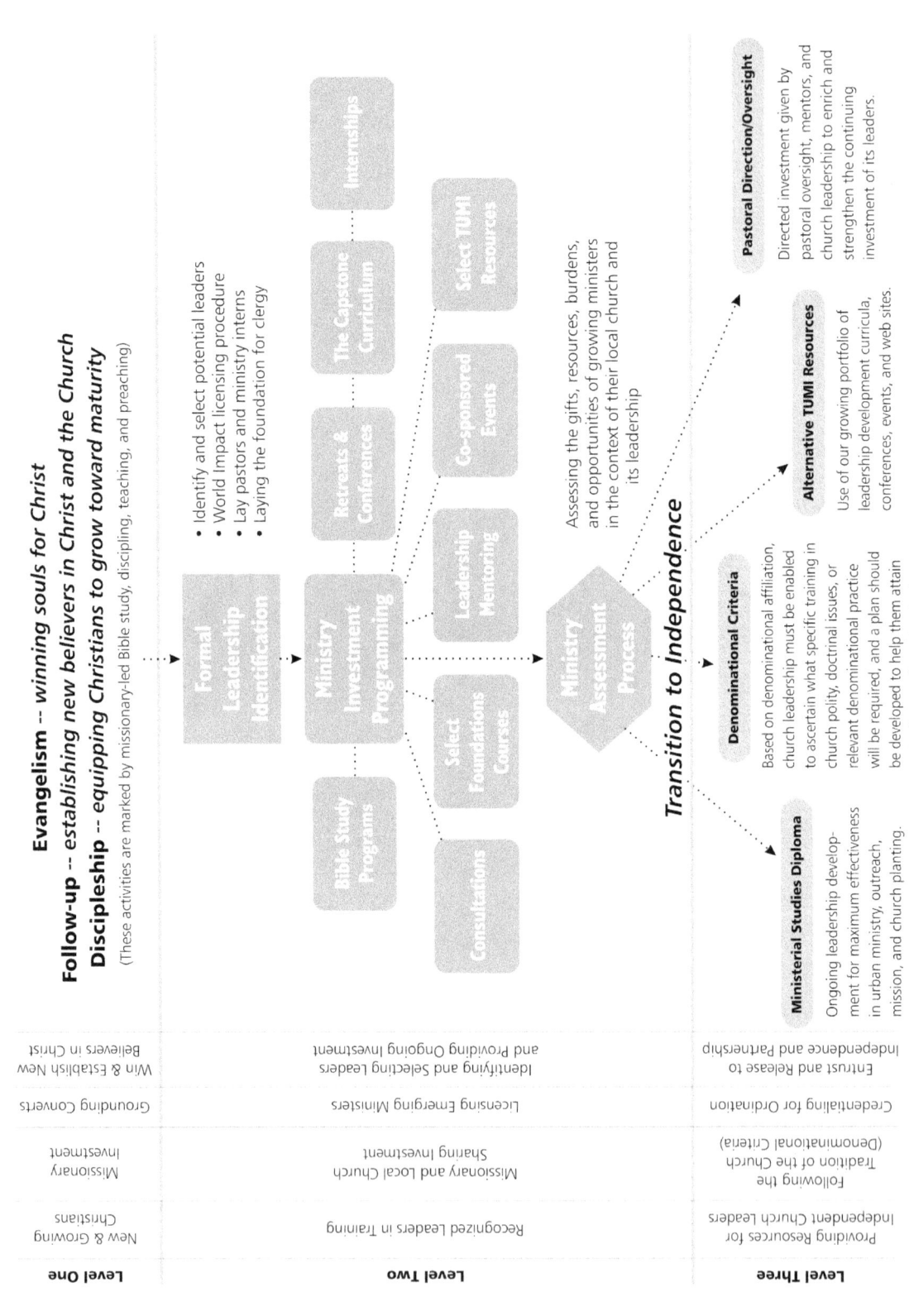

APPENDIX 46
World Impact's Vision: Toward a Biblical Strategy to Impact the Inner City

World Impact, Inc.

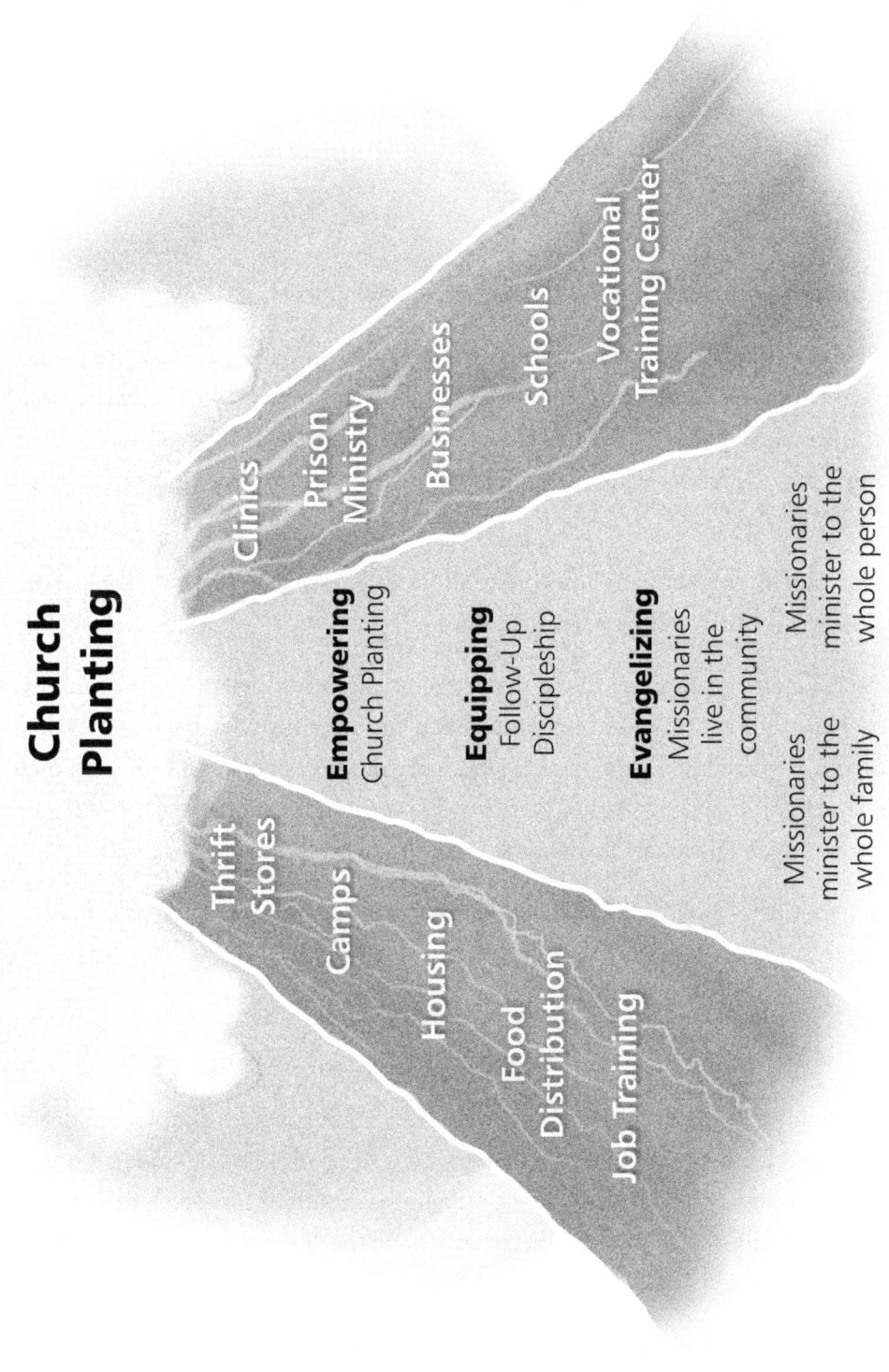

APPENDIX 47
Editorial
Ralph D. Winter

This article was taken from Mission Frontiers: The Bulletin of the US Center for World Mission, Vol. 27, No. 5; September-October 2005; ISSN 0889-9436.
Copyright 2005 by the U.S. Center for World Mission. Used by permission. All Rights Reserved.

Ralph D. Winter is the Editor of Mission Frontiers and the General Director of the Frontier Mission Fellowship.

Dear Reader,

This time you must learn a new phrase: Insider Movements.

This idea as a mission strategy was so shockingly new in Paul's day that almost no one (either then or now) gets the point. That's why we are devoting this entire issue to "Insider Movements." That's why the 2005 annual meeting of the International Society for Frontier Missiology is devoted to the same subject. (See *www.ijfm.org/isfm*.)

First of all, be warned: many mission donors and prayer warriors, and even some missionaries, heartily disagree with the idea.

One outstanding missionary found that even his mission board director could not agree. He was finally asked to find another mission agency to work under. Why? His director was a fine former pastor who had never lived among a totally strange people. After a couple of years of increasingly serious correspondence between the director and the missionary family, the relationship had to come to an end.

Okay, so this is serious business. Why is *Insider Movements* such a troubling concept?

Well, everywhere Paul went "Judaizers" followed him and tried to destroy the Insider Movement he had established.

Some of those Judaizers were earnest followers of Christ who simply could not imagine how a Greek – still a Greek in dress, language and culture – could become a believer in Jesus Christ without casting off a huge amount of his Greek culture, get circumcised, follow the "kosher" dietary rules and the "new moons and Sabbaths", etc.

The flagrant language of Paul's letter to the Galatians is one result. The very serious text of his letter to the Romans is another. Years ago the scales fell off my eyes when I read that "Israel, who pursued a law of righteousness, has not attained it ... Why

Ralph D. Winter Editorial (continued)

not? Because they pursued it not by faith but as if it were by works" (Rom. 9:32 NIV).

Paul was not saying the Jewish religious culture was defective or that the Greek culture was superior. He was emphasizing that heart faith is the key element in any culture—that *forms* were not the key thing but the *faith*. Greeks who yielded in heart faith to the Gospel did not need to become Jews culturally and follow Jewish forms.

Paul said, in effect, "I am very, very proud of a Gospel that is the power of God to save people who obey God in faith, no matter whether they follow Jewish or Greek customs" (Rom. 1:16).

But the real trick is not simply for people of faith in every culture to stay and stagnate in their own cultural cul-de-sac, but both to retain their own culture and at the same time recognize the validity of versions of the faith within other cultures and the universality of the Body of Christ.

Different sources of European Christianity flowed over into the United States, producing some 200 different "flavors" of Christianity—some born here (Mormons, Jehovah's Witnesses), some quite biblical, some not so biblical, some very strange.

The same thing happens on the mission field: a lot of different movements emerge. The ideal is for the Gospel to become effectively expressed within the language and culture of a people and not just be a transplant from the missionary's culture.

H. Richard Niebhur's famous book, *Social Sources of Denominationalism*, is known for pointing out that different denominations did not just have doctrinal differences (often very minor) but usually reflected, at least for a time, social differences that were the real difference. Note, however, the Christian faith was in many cases an "Insider Movement" and was expressed within different social streams, taking on characteristics of those different streams.

But, back to missions. The Jewish/Greek thing is far more and far "worse" than the differences between Methodists who pray that their trespasses be forgiven and Presbyterians who pray that their debts be forgiven!

No, in Paul's day circumcision was undoubtedly a major barrier to adult Greek men becoming culturally Jewish followers of Christ. Another sensitive point was the question of eating meat that had been offered to idols, and so on.

Ralph D. Winter Editorial (continued)

Later in history, the Jewish/Greek tension was paralleled by a Latin/German tension. This time, we see a profound difference in attitudes toward clerical marriage vs. celibacy and the use of Latin in church services.

For centuries Latin was *the language* of Europe, enabling ministers, attorneys, medical doctors, and public officials to read the books of their trade in a single language. That lasted a long time! For centuries a unifying reading language did a lot of good. But the Bible did not come into its own until it was translated into the heart languages of Europe.

The deep rumbling that modernized Europe was the unleashed Bible.

It is an exciting and maybe disturbing thing—the idea that biblical faith can be clothed in any language and culture. Witness the awesome reality in the so-called mission lands today. Whether Africa, India or China, it may well be that the largest number of genuine believers in Jesus Christ do not show up in what we usually call Christian churches!

Can you believe it? They may still consider themselves Muslims or Hindus (in a cultural sense).

Alas, today Christianity itself is identified with the cultural vehicle of the civilization of the West. People in mission lands who do not wish to be "westernized" feel they need to stay clear of the Christian Church, which in their own country is often a church highly Western in its culture, theology, interpretation of the Bible, etc.

For example, in Japan there are "churches" that are so Western that in the last forty years they have not grown by a single member. Many astute observers have concluded that there is not yet "a Japanese form of Christianity." When one emerges, it may not want to associate with the Western Christian tradition except in a fraternal way.

In India we now know that there are actually millions of Hindus who have chosen to follow Christ, reading the Bible daily and worshipping at the household level, but not often frequenting the West-related Christian churches of that land.

In some places thousands of people who consider themselves Muslims are nevertheless heart-and-soul followers of Jesus Christ who carry the New Testament with them into the mosques.

Ralph D. Winter Editorial (continued)

In Africa there are more than 50 million believers (of a sort) within a vast sphere called "the African Initiated Churches." The people in the more formally "Christian church" may not regard these others as Christians at all. Indeed, some of them are a whole lot further from pure biblical faith than Mormons. But, if they revere and study the Bible, we need to let the Bible do its work. These groups range from the wildly heretical to the seriously biblical within over ten thousand "denominations" which are not related to any overt Christian body.

Thus, not all "insider" movements are ideal. Our own Christianity is not very successfully [*sic*] "inside" our culture, since many "Christians" are Christian in name only. Even mission "church planting" activities may or may not be "insider" at all, and even if they are they may not be ideal.

Around the world some of these movements do not baptize. In other cases they do. I have been asked, "Are you promoting the idea of non-baptized believers?" No, in reporting the existence of these millions of people, we are reporting on the incredible power of the Bible. We are not promoting all the ideas they reflect or the practices they follow. The Bible is like an underground fire burning out of control! In one sense we can be very happy.

APPENDIX 48

When "Christian" Does Not Translate
Frank Decker

This article was taken from Mission Frontiers: The Bulletin of the US Center for World Mission, Vol. 27, No. 5; September-October 2005; ISSN 0889-9436.
Copyright 2005 by the U.S. Center for World Mission. Used by permission. All Rights Reserved.

"I grew up as a Muslim, and when I gave my life to Jesus I became a Christian. Then I felt the Lord saying, 'Go back to your family and tell them what the Lord has done for you.'" Such was the beginning of the testimony of a sweet sister in Christ named Salima. As she stood before the microphone at a conference held recently in Asia, I thought about how her story would have been applauded by my Christian friends back home.

But then she said something that would have probably shocked most American Christians. She told us that in order to share Christ with her family, she now identifies herself as a Muslim rather than a Christian. "But," she added, "I could never go back to Islam without Jesus whom I love as my Lord."

Like this woman, countless people, primarily in Asia, who live in Muslim, Buddhist, and Hindu contexts are saying *yes* to Jesus, but *no* to Christianity. As Westerners, we assume that the word "Christian" *ipso facto* refers to someone who has given his or her life to Jesus, and a "non-Christian" is an unbeliever. However, in the words of one Asian attendee, "The word 'Christian' means something different here in the East."

Consider the story of Chai, a Buddhist from Thailand. "Thailand has not become a Christian country, because in the eyes of the Thai, to become a Christian means you can no longer be Thai. That's because in Thailand 'Christian' equals 'foreigner.'" So when Chai gave his life to Jesus, he began referring to himself as a "Child of God" and a "new Buddhist." He then related a subsequent incident in which he had a conversation with a Buddhist monk on a train. "After I listened to his story, I told him that he was missing one thing in life. He asked me what that was and I told him it was Jesus."

Chai continued to tell us the story in which the monk not only gave his life to Christ, but also invited Chai to come to his Buddhist temple to share about Jesus. Then Chai said, "At the beginning of our conversation the monk asked me, 'Are you a Christian?' and I said *no*. I explained that Christianity and Jesus are two

A former missionary in Ghana, Frank Decker currently serves as Vice President for Field Operations for the Mission Society for United Methodists.

When "Christian" Does Not Translate (continued)

different things. Salvation is in Jesus, not in Christianity. If I had said I was a 'Christian,' the conversation would have ended at that point." But it didn't end. And the monk now walks with Jesus.

Indeed, an American missionary that has been working in Asia for about two decades said, "For the first five or seven years of our ministry in [a Muslim country] we were frustrated because we were trying to get people to change their religion." He went on to say how in evangelical circles we talk a lot about how it is not our religion that saves us; it is *Jesus*. "If we really believe that, why do we insist that people change their religion?"

Asif is a brother in Christ with whom I have spent time in his village in a country that is 90 percent Muslim. Traditional Christian organizations in that country have only had a significant impact on the other ten percent that has never been Muslim. Make no mistake – Asif is sold out to Jesus, as are the other members of this Muslim Background Believers (MBB) movement. I will never forget seeing the tears stream down Asif's face as he told me how he and his brother, also a believer in Jesus, were beaten in an attack that his brother did not survive. These are Muslims who walk with Jesus and openly share with their Muslim friends about the Lord, who in Arabic is referred to as "Isa al-Masih" (Jesus the Messiah).

These "insider movements" are not intended to *hide* a believer's spiritual identity, but rather to enable those within the movement to *go deeper* into the cultural community – be it Islamic, Hindu, or Buddhist – and be witnesses for Jesus within the context of that culture. In some countries, such movements are just getting started. In other places, estimates of adherents are in the hundreds of thousands.

As the Body of Christ, we should be very careful that the things we uphold as sacred are not post-biblical accoutrements, but are indeed transcendent. If we are not open to "new wineskins," we may unwittingly find ourselves attached to traditions, as were the Pharisees in the day of Jesus.

The names in this story have been changed. This article is excerpted by permission from the May/June 2005 issue of Good News Magazine, a renewal ministry within the United Methodist Church (www.goodnewsmag.org).

APPENDIX 49
Pursuing Faith, Not Religion
The Liberating Quest for Contextualization
Charles Kraft

This article was taken from Mission Frontiers: The Bulletin of the US Center for World Mission, Vol. 27, No. 5; September-October 2005; ISSN 0889-9436.
Copyright 2005 by the U.S. Center for World Mission. Used by permission. All Rights Reserved.

The following is excerpted from chapters 5 and 6 of **Appropriate Christianity** *(William Carey Library Publishers, 2005).*

It is not widely understood either outside of or even inside of Christianity that our faith is intended to be different from the religions in its relationship to the culture of the people who practice it. Whereas religions such as Islam, Buddhism and Hinduism require a sizeable chunk of the culture in which they were developed, Christianity rightly understood does not. Jesus came to bring life (Jn. 10:10), not a religion. It is people who have reduced our faith to a religion and exported it as if it is simply a competitor with the religions. And so, those receiving our message tend to interpret Christianity as if it was simply another religion—a culturally-encapsulated religion—rather than a faith that can be expressed in terms of any culture.

But Christianity correctly understood is commitment- and meaning-based, not form-based. A commitment to Jesus Christ and the meanings associated with that commitment can, therefore, be practiced in a wide variety of cultural forms. This is what contextualization is all about. And this is an important feature of Christianity that is often misunderstood by advocates as well as potential receptors.

Still another part of the reputation of Christianity worldwide is that it is more a matter of thinking than of practicality. For many, our faith has little to do with the issues of real life such as how to gain protection from evil spirits, how to gain and keep physical health and how to maintain good family relationships. Instead, Christianity is often seen as a breaker-up of families. And when the issue is a need for spiritual power and protection, even Christians need to keep on good terms with a shaman, priest or medicine man/woman since, in spite of biblical promises, Christian pastors can only recommend secular approaches to healing and protection.

A Christianity that is appropriate both to the Bible and to the receiving culture will confront these misperceptions and, hopefully, get them changed.

Dr. Charles H. Kraft has served as a missionary in Nigeria, taught African languages and linguistics at Michigan State University and UCLA for ten years, and taught Anthropology and Intercultural Communication in the School of Intercultural Studies, Fuller Seminary for the past 35 years. He travels widely, has pioneered in the field of Contextualization, and is widely used in a ministry of inner healing. He is the author or editor of many books, including Appropriate Christianity (William Carey Library Publishers, 2005).

Pursuing Faith, Not Religion (continued)

Traditions Die Hard

Any discussion of this topic needs to take into account the fact that the situations most cross-cultural workers are working in nowadays are seldom pioneer situations. Thus, we who teach contextualization are dealing primarily with those whose major concern will have to be on how to bring about change in already existing situations rather than on how to plant culturally appropriate churches.

Typically, then, those who learn what contextualization is all about find themselves working with churches that are quite committed to their Western approach to Christianity. This has become their tradition and they are not open to changing it.

The leaders of many such churches may never have seen culturally appropriate Christianity and probably lack the ability to imagine it. And if they can imagine such an approach, they are unlikely to want to risk what they are familiar with in hopes of gaining greater cultural appropriateness. For many, the risk of losing their position may be very real since their colleagues, committed to preserving the "sacred" tradition, may turn against them and oust them from their parishes.

We need to learn, then, not only the principles of cultural appropriateness, but the principles of effective communication. And this needs to be coupled with patience and prayer plus a readiness to make the right kind of suggestions if asked to.

Fear of Syncretism

A major hindrance to many, especially those who have received theological instruction, is the fear that they might open the door to an aberrant form of Christianity. They see Latin American "christo-paganism" and shy away from what is called Christian but is not really. Fearing that if they deviate from the Western Christianity that they have received they are in danger of people carrying things too far, they fall back on the familiar and do nothing to change it, no matter how much misunderstanding there might be in the community of unbelievers concerning the real meanings of Christianity.

There are, however, at least two roads to syncretism: an approach that is too nativistic and an approach that is too dominated by foreignness. With respect to the latter, it is easy to miss the fact that Western Christianity is quite syncretistic when it is very intellectualized, organized according to foreign patterns, weak on the Holy Spirit and spiritual power, strong on Western forms of communication (e.g.,

Pursuing Faith, Not Religion (continued)

preaching) and Western worship patterns and imposed on non-Western peoples as if it were scriptural. It is often easier to conclude that a form of Christian expression is syncretistic when it looks too much like the receiving culture than when it looks "normal," that is, Western.

But Western patterns are often farther from the Bible than non-Western patterns. And the amount of miscommunication of what the gospel really is can be great when people get the impression that ours is a religion rather than a faith and that, therefore, foreign forms are a requirement. To give that impression is surely syncretistic and heretical. I call this "communicational heresy."

But, what about the concept of syncretism? Is this something that can be avoided or is it a factor of human limitations and sinfulness? I vote for the latter and suggest that there is no way to avoid it. Wherever there are imperfect understandings made by imperfect people, there will be syncretism. That syncretism exists in all churches is not the problem. Helping people to move from where they are to more ideal expressions of Christian faith is what we need to address.

As long as we fear something that is inevitable, however, we are in bondage. I remember the words of one field missionary who was studying with us, "Until I stopped worrying about syncretism, I could not properly think about contextualization." Our advice to national leaders (and to missionaries), then, is to stop fearing syncretism. Deal with it in its various forms as a starting point, whether it has come from the receiving society or from the source society and help people to move toward more ideal expressions of their faith ....

Domestication and "Cultural Christianity"

[Down] through the centuries, those who have come to Christ have tended to "domesticate" their Christianity. Just as the early Jewish Christians who disagreed with Paul required Gentiles to accept Christ in a Jewish cultural package, so Romans and Germans and Americans have pressured those who convert to Christ to also convert to the culture of those who bring the message.

Thus, our faith has come to be known as primarily a cultural thing, a religion wrapped in the cultural forms of the group in power. And from about the fourth century on it has been seen largely as a European cultural thing—captured by our European ancestors and domesticated in cultures very different from that in which

Pursuing Faith, Not Religion (continued)

the faith was originally planted. Converts to Christianity, then, are seen as those who have abandoned their own cultural religion and chosen to adopt the religion and, usually, many of the forms of European culture. Often such converts are regarded as traitors to their own people and their ways.

If ours is simply a "form religion," ... it can be *adapted but not contextualized*, it can be in *competition with other forms of religion* but not flow through those forms because by definition it seeks to replace those forms. But biblical Christianity is not simply a set of cultural forms. Cultural Christianity, however, is. And we get tangled up in our discussions because it is often not clear whether we are speaking of essential, biblical Christianity or of the traditional religion of Western societies that is also called Christianity. In one of my books (1979a) I have attempted to make this distinction by spelling biblical Christianity with a capital C and cultural christianity with a small c....

I would ... call religion a form thing, the expression through cultural forms of deep-level (worldview) assumptions and meanings. Religious forms are culture-specific and, if the religion has been borrowed from another cultural context, it requires certain of the forms of that other culture to be borrowed. Islam, for example, requires certain forms of prayer, a specific pilgrimage, an untranslatable Arabic book, even clothing styles. Likewise Judaism, Hinduism, Buddhism and cultural christianity. These are religions.

Essential biblical Christianity, however, requires none of the original cultural forms. That's how it can be "captured" by the West and be considered Western even though its origin is not Western. *Essential Christianity is an allegiance, a relationship, from which flow a series of meanings that are intended to be expressed through the cultural forms of any culture*. These forms are intended, then, to be chosen for their appropriateness to convey proper biblical meanings in the receptors' contexts.

I believe Christianity is intended to be "a faith," not a set of cultural forms and therefore different in essence from the religions. Religions, because they are cultural things, can be *adapted* to new cultures. Adaptation is an external thing resulting in smaller or larger changes in the forms of the religion. Christianity, however, can be *contextualized*, a process in which appropriate meanings may be carried by quite different forms in various cultures. Unfortunately, due to the interference of cultural christianity, we have not seen all the variety that is possible ....

APPENDIX 50

Contextualization Among Muslims, Hindus, and Buddhists: A Focus on "Insider Movements"

John and Anna Travis

This article was taken from Mission Frontiers: The Bulletin of the US Center for World Mission, Vol. 27, No. 5; September-October 2005; ISSN 0889-9436. Copyright 2005 by the U.S. Center for World Mission. Used by permission. All Rights Reserved.

The following is excerpted by permission of the authors. A larger version of this article is found in chapter 23 of **Appropriate Christianity** *(William Carey Library Publishers, 2005).*

Much has been written over the past 25 years on the application of contextualization in ministry among Muslims. In 1998 I (John) wrote an article for the *Evangelical Missions Quarterly* in which I presented a model for comparing six different types of *ekklesia* or congregations (which I refer to as "Christ-centered communities") found in the Muslim world today (Travis 1998). These six types of Christ-centered communities are differentiated in terms of three factors: language, cultural forms, and religious identity. This model, referred to as the C1-C6 spectrum (or continuum), has generated much discussion, especially around the issue of fellowships of "Muslim followers of Jesus" (the C5 position on the scale).

Parshall (1998), an advocate of contextualization, feels that C5 crosses the line and falls into dangerous syncretism. In subsequent writings many of Parshall's concerns have been addressed (see Massey 2000, Gilliland 1998, Winter 1999, Travis 1998 and 2000). *Yet in spite of concerns that some may have on this issue, the fact remains that in a number of countries today, there are groups of Muslims who have genuinely come to faith in Jesus Christ, yet have remained legally and socio-religiously within the local Muslim community....*

We will not be contending that C5 is the best or only thing God is doing in the Muslim world today; indeed God is bringing Muslims to Himself in a great diversity of ways, some of which we may only understand in eternity. What we will argue, however, is that one way God is moving at this point in salvation history, is by sovereignly drawing Muslims to Himself, revolutionizing them spiritually, yet calling them to remain as salt and light in the religious community of their birth....

In recent years we have had the privilege of meeting a number of C5 Muslims, and although our religious backgrounds and forms of worship are quite different, we have experienced sweet fellowship in Isa the Messiah. There is no question in our

---

John and Anna Travis, along with their two children, have lived in a tight-knit Asian Muslim neighborhood for nearly 20 years. They are involved in contextualized sharing of the good news, Bible translation and the ministry of prayer for inner healing. They have also helped train field workers in a number of Asian, Middle Eastern and North African countries. Both are pursuing graduate degrees, with John a Ph.D. candidate.

Contextualization Among Muslims, Hindus, and Buddhists (continued)

minds that these C5 Muslims are born-again members of the Kingdom of God, called to live out the Gospel inside the religious borders of their birth. As we have continued to see the limits of C4 in our context, and as our burden for lost Muslims only grows heavier, we have become convinced that a C5 expression of faith could actually be viable for our precious Muslim neighbors and probably large blocs of the Muslim world. We ourselves, being "Christian-background-believers," maintain a C4 lifestyle, but we believe God has called us to help "birth a C5 movement" in our context . . . .

We have attended many Muslim funerals. We grieve every time we see another Muslim friend buried, having passed into eternity without salvation in Christ. As we have seen the resistance toward changing religions and the huge gap between the Muslim and Christian communities, we feel that fighting the religion-changing battle is the wrong battle. We have little hope in our lifetime to believe for a major enough cultural, political and religious change to occur in our context such that Muslims would become open to entering Christianity on a wide scale.

But we do have great hope, as great as the promises of God, to believe that an "insider movement" could get off the ground – that vast numbers could discover that salvation in Isa the Messiah is waiting for every Muslim who will believe. We sense the desire of Jesus Himself to take the "yeast" of His Gospel to the inner chambers of Muslim communities, calling men, women and children to walk with Him as Lord and Savior, remaining vital members of their families and Muslim communities.

Theoretical and Theological Issues Regarding C5 Movements

. . . Our intent is not to prove if C5 *can* happen, as case studies already indicate that it *is* happening. Rather, we hope to help build a framework from which to understand this phenomenon and to answer some of the questions which have arisen such as: From a biblical perspective, can a person be truly saved and continue to be a Muslim? Doesn't a follower of Christ need to identify himself as a Christian and officially join the Christian faith? Can a Muslim follower of Christ retain all Muslim practices, in particular praying in the mosque toward Mecca and continuing to repeat the Muslim creed? This section will be framed around ten premises [elaborated in the full version of this article].

Contextualization Among Muslims, Hindus, and Buddhists (continued)

- *Premise 1*: For Muslims, culture, politics and religion are nearly inseparable, making changing religions a total break with society.

- *Premise 2*: Salvation is by grace alone through relationship / allegiance to Jesus Christ. Changing religions is not a prerequisite for nor a guarantee of salvation.

- *Premise 3*: Jesus' primary concern was the establishment of the Kingdom of God, not the founding of a new religion.

- *Premise 4*: The very term "Christian" is often misleading – not all called Christian are in Christ and not all in Christ are called Christian.

- *Premise 5*: Often gaps exist between what people actually believe and what their religion or group officially teaches.

- *Premise 6*: Some Islamic beliefs and practices are in keeping with the Word of God; some are not.

- *Premise 7*: Salvation involves a process. Often the exact point of transfer from the kingdom of darkness to the Kingdom of light is not known.

- *Premise 8*: A follower of Christ needs to be set free by Jesus from spiritual bondages in order to thrive in his/her life with Him.

- *Premise 9*: Due to the lack of Church structure and organization, C5 movements must have an exceptionally high reliance on the Spirit and the Word as their primary source of instruction.

- *Premise 10*: A contextual theology can only properly be developed through a dynamic interaction of actual ministry experience, the specific leading of the Spirit and the study of the Word of God.

A Look Beyond the Islamic Milieu

. . . An amazing book has just been republished by William Carey Library – *Churchless Christianity* (Hoefer 2001). The author, while formerly teaching at a seminary in India, began hearing stories of Hindus who in fact were worshipping and following Jesus in the privacy of their own homes. Knowing that there are many Hindus who have high regard for Jesus as a teacher, he set out to determine if

---

"The Church Emerges from the Inside"
A missionary couple working in Asia report, "In 1990 we were sent out into the field as church planters. But over the last year we have observed that when the gospel is sown on fertile soil within already established social groupings – like a circle of close neighbor friends, or the multi-generations an extended household – the church emerges from the inside. It is not so much that we are planting a church but that we are planting the gospel, and as the gospel seed grows, the church or churches form to the shape of existing networks."

Contextualization Among Muslims, Hindus, and Buddhists (continued)

indeed they had accepted Him as Lord and Savior or only as an enlightened guru. His quest became the basis of a doctoral dissertation in which he interviewed 80 such Hindu and Muslim families in the area of Madras, India.

Hoefer found that that a large number of these families, which have never been baptized or joined churches, indeed have a true relationship with Christ and pray and study His Word fervently. Hoefer says that most want baptism, but have never seen a baptism which is not one in the same with becoming an official member of a particular church. His conclusion after a very extensive process of interviews and statistical analysis is that in Madras there are 200,000 Hindus and Muslims who worship Jesus – an amount equal to the total number of Christians in that city!

It is instructive to note that 200 years ago, William Carey referred to Hindu followers of Jesus as "Christian Hindoos." Apparently this was due to the strong linkage in the minds of the Indians (and presumably William Carey) between being Hindu and being Indian (etymologically the word India comes from Hindia, the land of the Hindus). Rather than Hinduism being close to monotheistic faiths, it is just the opposite: adherents can worship any number of gods and goddesses. It appears that this openness allows room to exclusively worship the God of the Bible as the one true God (note the words of Joshua in Joshua 24:14-15).

In the early 1900s, Indian evangelist Sadhu Sundar Singh ran into hidden groups of Jesus followers among Hindus. As he preached the Gospel in Benares, his listeners told him of a Hindu holy man who had been preaching the same message. Singh spent the night at the man's home and heard his claim that his Hindu order had been founded long ago by the apostle Thomas, and now had up to 40,000 members. Singh later observed their services (including worship, prayer, baptism and communion) which were held in places which looked exactly like Hindu shrines and temples, minus the idols. "When Sundar tried to persuade them that they should openly declare themselves as Christians, they assured him that they were doing a more effective work as secret disciples, accepted as ordinary sadhus, but drawing men's minds toward the true faith in readiness for the day when open discipleship became possible" (Davey 1950:80) [*sic*].

Recently, we met a man doing outreach among Buddhists, among whom there is an extremely high fusion of culture and religion. To my surprise he had taken the C1-C6 continuum and adapted it to a Buddhist context. Though it appears impossible for the Gospel to thrive inside Buddhism, might there not be millions of Buddhists who are nominal believers and who are only Buddhist due to birth and

Contextualization Among Muslims, Hindus, and Buddhists (continued)

nationality? As Kraft has stated (1996:212-213), once this principle of true spiritual allegiance versus formal religion is grasped, "we begin to discover exciting possibilities for working within, say, Jewish or Islamic or Hindu or Buddhist or animistic cultures to reach people who will be culturally Jewish or Muslim or Hindu or animist to the end of their days but Christian in their faith allegiance". (Note: in his book Kraft defines Christian with a capital "C" as follower of Christ verses *christian* with a small "c" referring to the religious institution).

What is all of this leading to? Is there not blatant idolatry in traditional Hinduism? Yes, but not among those Hindu followers of Christ described by Hoefer and Davey. Is there not a denial by most Muslims that Jesus died on the cross? Yes, but not by those Muslims we have known who have put their faith in Christ. Is it not true that Jews teach the Messiah is yet to come? Yes, but thousands of Jews go to Messianic synagogues and believe, as did thousands of Jews in the first century, that Yeshua is indeed the long awaited Son of David.

We are tentatively coming to the conviction that God is doing a new thing to reach these remaining nations (*ta ethne*) dominated by mega-faiths. If Bosch had it right that faith in Christ wasn't meant to be a religion, could it be that we are witnessing some of the first fruits of vast movements where Jesus is causing the Gospel to break out of "Christianity"? Where those who know Jesus remain as a sweet fragrance inside the religion of their birth, and eventually the number of born-again adherents grows so large that a reform movement from inside that religion is birthed?

The process may be theologically messy, but we see no alternative. If we view both culture and religion as a person's own skin, we can look beyond it to the millions of human hearts longing for God yet longing to remain in community with their own people. This is in no way universalism (the belief that in the end all will be saved). Rather, this is a call to take much more seriously Christ's final words to go into all the world – Hindu, Buddhist, Muslim, Christian – and make disciples of all nations.

References

Bosch, David J. 1991 *Transforming Mission*. Maryknoll, NY: Orbis Books.

Davey, Cyril J. 1980 *Sadhu Sundar Singh*. Kent, UK: STL Books.

Contextualization Among Muslims, Hindus, and Buddhists (continued)

Gilliland, Dean S. 1998 "Context is Critical in Islampur Case." *Evangelical Missions Quarterly* 34(4): 415-417.

Hoefer, Herbert E. 2001 *Churchless Christianity*. Pasadena, CA: William Carey Library.

Kraft, Charles H. 1996 *Anthropology for Christian Witness*. Maryknoll, NY: Orbis Books.

Massey, Joshua. 2000 "God's Amazing Diversity in Drawing Muslims to Christ." *International Journal of Frontier Missions* 17 (1): 5-14.

Parshall, Phil. 1998 "Danger! New Directions in Contextualization." *Evangelical Missions Quarterly*. 43(4): 404-406, 409-410.

Travis, John. 1998 "Must all Muslims Leave Islam to Follow Jesus?" *Evangelical Missions Quarterly* 34(4): 411-415.

------. 2000 "Messianic Muslim Followers of Isa: A Closer Look at C5 Believers and Congregations." *International Journal of Frontier Missions* 17 (1): 53-59.

Winter, Ralph. 1999 "Going Far Enough? Taking Some Tips from the Historical Record." In *Perspectives on the World Christian Movement*. Ralph Winter and Steven Hawthorne, eds. Pp. 666-617. Pasadena, CA: William Carey Library.

APPENDIX 51
A People Reborn
Foundational Insights on People Movements
Donald McGavran

This article was taken from Mission Frontiers: The Bulletin of the US Center for World Mission, Vol. 27, No. 5; September-October 2005; ISSN 0889-9436.
Copyright 2005 by the U.S. Center for World Mission. Used by permission. All Rights Reserved.

Editor's note: What follows are excerpts from the late Donald McGavran's foreword to the English edition of Christian Keysser's classic book, A People Reborn (William Carey Library, 1980). McGavran's pen portraits and autobiographical notes reveal the extent to which, consciously or not, today's proponents of either insider movements or church-planting movements are building on foundations laid by pioneers such as Keysser, McGavran, and others in the first half of the 20th century. Note, in the final paragraph, McGavran's prescient observations about mission in the 21st century.

[Christian Keysser] was born in Bavaria in 1877, went to Kaiser Wilhelm Land (East New Guinea) in 1899, and remained in or near Sattelberg as a missionary till 1921, when he returned to Germany.... A literal translation of [Keysser's book] is *A New Guinean Congregation*. A truer, better title is: *A People Reborn: Caring Communities, Their Birth and Development*. . . .

People Movements to Christ

. . . Around 1900 Keysser found himself evangelizing the Kate (pronounced Kawtai or kotte) tribe in the mountains near the sea.... Keysser's genius recognized that Christianization ought to preserve this people consciousness, and transform it into Tribal Christianity or Folk Christianity. . . .

In 1935, largely through [Waskom] Pickett's writings and lectures, I woke to a discipling of ethnic units. I accompanied him while he studied missions in Mid-India and contributed several chapters to his *Christian Missions in Mid-India*, 1938. I, too, saw that the goal was not one-by-one conversion out of the castes and tribes, but rather the conversion of social units which remained part of the caste or tribe, and continued living in their ancestral homes. For the next two decades I worked at encouraging a Satnami people movement to develop – and failed. In 1955, my *Bridges of God* called castewise or tribal movements to Christian Faith "people

A People Reborn (continued)

movements".... What Keysser, Pickett and [Bruno] Gutmann had described in New Guinea, India and Tanganyika – *Bridges of God* – indebted only to Pickett, described in universal terms.

The discovery of all of us was that group decisions, which preserved the corporate life of the society and enabled men and women to become Christians without social dislocation, was the route by which most humans have moved to Christian Faith from non-Christian Faith, and was a good route. For all four of us, the discovery was difficult because missionaries came out of the most dedicated parts of the Western Church. They had learned that real Christians are those who individually and at great cost believe in Jesus Christ, love Him, obey His word, and venture out alone across the seven seas to do His bidding. They believed that "one-by-one-against-the-tide" was the right, the best, and often the only way for men and women to become Christians. . . .

Keysser's discovery in 1903 should be seen against his common erroneous conviction. He broke through that mindset to see that for a people to come to Christ "with social structure intact" was the best possible way. He, of course, went on immediately to describe the way in which such a people movement should be nurtured, guarded against formalism, fed on the Word, and made strong through constant exercise of its Christian options. This is his great contribution. His book is essential reading for any who wish to understand a) that discipling ethnic units is a splendid way for multitudes to become Christian, and b) how discipling and perfecting can be done so they result in genuine Christians in a truly Christian Congregation – a true Homogeneous Unit Church.

The Objective Thinker

. . . The people movement really began to roll. The outlying clans and villages clamored to become Christian, precisely because they saw that the Christians had become *greatly changed for the better*. This is the fundamental reason why people movements occur. Human beings are highly intelligent. After all, man is homo sapiens. When he sees that the new order, the Church, is actually different from and *superior* to the old order, then homo sapiens in corporate decisions moves to Christian Faith. A chain reaction runs through the tribal fabric. Congregations multiply. In general, it may be said that the higher the standard of Christianity

A People Reborn (continued)

achieved by the first groups to become Christian, the more influential is their example. Keysser, the objective thinker, saw this. . . .

Forming a True Congregation

[Another reason] why missiologists will profit from this book is Keysser's determined emphasis on the privilege and duty of the missionary *to form a Christian congregation out of various villages and clans.* By this he does not mean taking individuals, as separate pebbles, and forming them into a new organization called the church. Rather, he means taking the social organism, which the clan or village had been from time immemorial, and by exposing it to God's will and God's Word, and by leading it to act in a Christian fashion *transforming it into a Christian tribe.* This is not done simply by baptizing it. Hearing the Gospel, seeing the Gospel, receiving ample instruction, some of it in dramatic form, being baptized with clanal approval, and then for years led by the missionary and the Word, thinking through what in specific circumstances Christ requires the village, clan or tribe (the Christian Congregation) to do – all these steps are required to transform non-Christian social units into a Christian congregation. . . .

Dr. Keysser's adverse judgments concerning the churches in Germany must be seen as part of his convictions concerning the True Church. Throughout this volume he criticizes congregations in Germany for not being true communities, i.e. true *congregations.* . . . When in 1922 Keysser went back to Germany, he experienced culture shock in reverse. He found "churches" which as churches exercised little if any pastoral care of their members. . . . The congregations were not real communities. . . .

Today, when the establishment of caring communities in western churches has become one of the main purposes of contemporary Christianity, Keysser's comments about the German Church are particularly pertinent. They can be affirmed about the Church in most developed nations. When society becomes fragmented, individualism rages out of control and loneliness afflicts millions. The Church must provide loving, caring, powerful *communities*. Life is richest when lived in such. In the ancient world New Testament churches were such communities. Churches can again become such in New Guinea and New York, in Tokyo and Berlin, and in short, in every land. *True Churches are functioning communities.*

A People Reborn (continued)

. . . Professor Keysser has given the world of mission many insights which will be of great use in the coming century. In his day, animistic tribes were turning to Christ by people movements and forming genuine communities (congregations) in the Christian fold. In the twenty-first century, we shall see great segments of developing *and developed* nations turn to Christian Faith without social dislocation. They will remain real communities in becoming real congregations. Modern missiology is indebted to Christian Keysser.

APPENDIX 52

Missions in the 21st Century
Working with Social Entrepreneurs?
Rebecca Lewis

This article was taken from Mission Frontiers: The Bulletin of the US Center for World Mission, Vol. 27, No. 5; September-October 2005; ISSN 0889-9436.
Copyright 2005 by the U.S. Center for World Mission. Used by permission. All Rights Reserved.

The challenge is this: how to catalyze an "insider movement" to Christ in a society closed to traditional mission work? For this to happen, the gospel needs to spread through pre-existing social networks, which become the "church." People should not be drawn out of their families or communities into new social structures in order to become believers. God seems to be opening a new avenue of opportunity into closed societies through working with community agents of change – entrepreneurs working for social reform.

Historically, the most successful model for achieving lasting social change has been neither government nor business but the voluntary society (also known as the "citizen sector" or "civil society"). The idea of citizens banding together to reform society took a great step forward during the Evangelical Awakening, initiated by John Wesley in the 18th century. Out of this revival, and the Second Great Awakening in the early 19th century, came hundreds of voluntary, cross-denominational associations or "societies." Founded by visionary social entrepreneurs, each society attacked a certain issue, everything from abolishing slavery to creating special "Sunday schools" to teach reading to children who worked all week. Why not harness this successful model as a vehicle for advancing God's purposes among today's least-reached people groups?

Today the door is wide open in most countries to people who would catalyze grass-roots initiatives to address social problems. During the 1990s the number of international non-profit organizations jumped from 6000 to 26,000, a growth rate of over 400%. Likewise, hundreds of thousands of national NGOs (non-government organizations) have been formed in non-Western countries. Why the sudden growth? First, since the fall of the Soviet Union, many governments have been releasing control of the economy and nurturing the private sector. Second, social entrepreneurs and the civil society sector are now widely recognized for their success in solving formerly intractable problems.

Rebecca Lewis spent eight years in Morocco on a church planting team and currently creates curricula to help young people see how they can live their lives for God's purposes.

Missions in the 21st Century: Working with Social Entrepreneurs? (continued)

Third, governments are increasingly embarrassed if they try to block non-profit initiatives, because a global value for "empathy" has been established by the rapidly-spreading evangelical movement and the incorporation of Christian values in secular education worldwide. Fourth, there is a new openness to change in general. As people in remote places have become exposed to the rest of the world through mass media, they are reconsidering their behavior patterns and traditional beliefs. People everywhere are putting their hope in education and valuing progress as never before. As a result, local communities, as well as national governments, are getting behind citizen organizations seeking to implement solutions to systemic problems.

If the goal is to produce insider movements to Christ, why work with social entrepreneurs? Christian workers can build extensive relationships with leaders and families within a community by assisting social entrepreneurs (whether they are believers or not) with their vision to attack a problem. These types of broad relational networks – proactively bringing change to the community – form an excellent basis for the spread of the gospel in a way that leads to insider movements. Through helping the civil sector, workers have a role that is understandable and beneficial both in the eyes of the local people and the government. Also, like Jesus, they can announce the Kingdom in the context of bringing healing to the community.

To those who would like to learn more about finding and assisting social entrepreneurs, I recommend David Bornstein's fascinating book, *How to Change the World: Social Entrepreneurs and the Power of New Ideas* (Oxford University Press, 2003).

APPENDIX 53

Documenting Your Work
A Guide to Help You Give Credit Where Credit Is Due
The Urban Ministry Institute

Plagiarism is using another person's ideas as if they belonged to you without giving them proper credit. In academic work it is just as wrong to steal a person's ideas as it is to steal a person's property. These ideas may come from the author of a book, an article you have read, or from a fellow student. The way to avoid plagiarism is to carefully use "notes" (textnotes, footnotes, endnotes, etc.) and a "Works Cited" section to help people who read your work know when an idea is one you thought of, and when you are borrowing an idea from another person.

Avoiding Plagiarism

A citation reference is required in a paper whenever you use ideas or information that came from another person's work.

All citation references involve two parts:

- Notes in the body of your paper placed next to each quotation which came from an outside source.

- A "Works Cited" page at the end of your paper or project which gives information about the sources you have used

Using Citation References

There are three basic kinds of notes: parenthetical notes, footnotes, and endnotes. At The Urban Ministry Institute, we recommend that students use parenthetical notes. These notes give the author's last name(s), the date the book was published, and the page number(s) on which you found the information. Example:

> In trying to understand the meaning of Genesis 14.1-24, it is important to recognize that in biblical stories "the place where dialogue is first introduced will be an important moment in revealing the character of the speaker . . ." (Kaiser and Silva 1994, 73). This is certainly true of the character of Melchizedek who speaks words of blessing. This identification of Melchizedek as a positive spiritual influence is reinforced by the fact that he is the King of Salem, since Salem means "safe, at peace" (Wiseman 1996, 1045).

Using Notes in Your Paper

Documenting Your Work (continued)

Creating a Works Cited Page

A "Works Cited" page should be placed at the end of your paper. This page:

- lists every source you quoted in your paper
- is in alphabetical order by author's last name
- includes the date of publication and information about the publisher

The following formatting rules should be followed:

1. Title

The title "Works Cited" should be used and centered on the first line of the page following the top margin.

2. Content

Each reference should list:

- the author's full name (last name first)
- the date of publication
- the title and any special information (Revised edition, 2nd edition, reprint) taken from the cover or title page should be noted
- the city where the publisher is headquartered followed by a colon and the name of the publisher

3. Basic form

- Each piece of information should be separated by a period.
- The second line of a reference (and all following lines) should be indented.
- Book titles should be underlined (or italicized).
- Article titles should be placed in quotes.

Example:

Fee, Gordon D. 1991. *Gospel and Spirit: Issues in New Testament Hermeneutics.* Peabody, MA: Hendrickson Publishers.

Documenting Your Work (continued)

4. Special Forms

A book with multiple authors:

Kaiser, Walter C., and Moisés Silva. 1994. *An Introduction to Biblical Hermeneutics: The Search for Meaning.* Grand Rapids: Zondervan Publishing House.

An edited book:

Greenway, Roger S., ed. 1992. *Discipling the City: A Comprehensive Approach to Urban Mission.* 2nd ed. Grand Rapids: Baker Book House.

A book that is part of a series:

Morris, Leon. 1971. *The Gospel According to John.* Grand Rapids: Wm. B. Eerdmans Publishing Co. The New International Commentary on the New Testament. Gen. ed. F. F. Bruce.

An article in a reference book:

Wiseman, D. J. "Salem." 1982. In *New Bible Dictionary.* Leicester, England - Downers Grove, IL: InterVarsity Press. Eds. I. H. Marshall and others.

(An example of a "Works Cited" page is located on the next page.)

Standard guides to documenting academic work in the areas of philosophy, religion, theology, and ethics include:

Atchert, Walter S., and Joseph Gibaldi. 1985. *The MLA Style Manual.* New York: Modern Language Association.

The Chicago Manual of Style. 1993. 14th ed. Chicago: The University of Chicago Press.

Turabian, Kate L. 1987. *A Manual for Writers of Term Papers, Theses, and Dissertations.* 5th edition. Bonnie Bertwistle Honigsblum, ed. Chicago: The University of Chicago Press.

For Further Research

Documenting Your Work (continued)

Works Cited

Fee, Gordon D. 1991. *Gospel and Spirit: Issues in New Testament Hermeneutics*. Peabody, MA: Hendrickson Publishers.

Greenway, Roger S., ed. 1992. *Discipling the City: A Comprehensive Approach to Urban Mission*. 2nd ed. Grand Rapids: Baker Book House.

Kaiser, Walter C., and Moisés Silva. 1994. *An Introduction to Biblical Hermeneutics: The Search for Meaning*. Grand Rapids: Zondervan Publishing House.

Morris, Leon. 1971. *The Gospel According to John*. Grand Rapids: Wm. B. Eerdmans Publishing Co. *The New International Commentary on the New Testament*. Gen. ed. F. F. Bruce.

Wiseman, D. J. "Salem." 1982. In *New Bible Dictionary*. Leicester, England-Downers Grove, IL: InterVarsity Press. Eds. I. H. Marshall and others.

Mentoring
The Capstone Curriculum

Before the Course Begins

- First, read carefully the Introduction of the Module found on page 5, and browse through the Mentor's Guide in order to gain an understanding of the content that will be covered in the course. The Student's Workbook is identical to your Mentor's Guide. Your guide, however, also contains a section of additional material and resources for each lesson, called *Mentor's Notes*. References to these instructions are indicated by a symbol in the margin: 📖. The Quizzes, Final Exam, and Answer Keys can all be found on the TUMI Satellite Gateway. (This is available to all approved satellites.)

- Second, you are strongly encouraged to view the teaching on both DVDs prior to the beginning of the course.

- Third, you should read any assigned readings associated with the curriculum, whether textbooks, articles or appendices.

- Fourth, it may be helpful to review the key theological themes associated with the course by using Bible dictionaries, theological dictionaries, and commentaries to refresh your familiarity with major topics covered in the curriculum.

- Fifth, please know that the students *are not tested on the reading assignments*. These are given to help the students get a fuller understanding of what the module is teaching, but it is not required that your students be excellent readers to understand what is being taught. For those of you who are receiving this module in any translation other than English, the required reading might not be available in your language. Please select a book or two that is available in your language - one that you think best represents what is being taught in this module - and assign that to your students instead.

- Finally, begin to think about key questions and areas of ministry training that you would like to explore with students in light of the content that is being covered.

Before Each Lesson

Prior to each lesson, you should once again watch the teaching content that is found on the DVD for that class session, and then create a *Contact* and *Connection* section for this lesson.

Review the Mentor's Guide to understand the lesson objectives and gather ideas for possible Contact activities. (Two to three Contacts are provided which you may use, or feel free to create your own, if that is more appropriate.)

Then, create a Contact section that introduces the students to the lesson content and captures their interest. As a rule, Contact methods fall into three general categories.

Attention Focusers capture student attention and introduce them to the lesson topic. Attention focusers can be used by themselves with motivated learners or combined with one of the other methods described below. Examples:

- Singing an opening song related to the lesson theme.

- Showing a cartoon or telling a joke that relates to an issue addressed by the lesson.

- Asking students to stand on the left side of the room if they believe that it is easier to teach people how to be saved from the Gospels and to stand on the right side if they believe it is easier to teach people from the Epistles.

Story-telling methods either have the instructor tell a story that illustrates the importance of the lesson content or ask students to share their experiences (stories) about the topic that will be discussed. Examples:

- In a lesson on the role of the pastor, a Mentor may tell the story of conducting a funeral and share the questions and challenges that were part of the experience.

- In a lesson about evangelism, the Mentor may ask students to describe an experience they have had of sharing the Gospel.

Problem-posing activities raise challenging questions for students to answer and lead them toward the lesson content as a source for answering those questions, or they may ask students to list the unanswered questions that they have about the topic that will be discussed. Examples:

- Presenting case studies from ministry situations that call for a leadership decision and having students discuss what the best response would be.

Preparing the Contact Section

- Problems framed as questions such as "When preaching at a funeral, is it more important for a minister to be truthful or compassionate? Why?"

Regardless of what method is chosen, the key to a successful Contact section is making a transition from the Contact to the Content of the lesson. When planning the Contact section, Mentors should write out a transition statement that builds a bridge from the Contact to the lesson content. For example, if the lesson content was on the truth that the Holy Spirit is a divine Person who is a full member of the Godhead, the Contact activity might be to have students quickly draw a symbol that best represents the Holy Spirit to them. After having them share their drawings and discuss why they chose what they did, the Mentor might make a transition statement along the following lines:

> *Because the Holy Spirit is often represented by symbols like fire or oil in Scripture rather than with a human image like the Father or the Son, it is sometimes difficult to help people understand that the Spirit is a full person within the Godhead who thinks, acts, and speaks as personally as God the Father or Jesus Christ. In this lesson, we want to establish the scriptural basis for understanding that the Spirit is more than just a symbol for "God's power" and think about ways that we can make this plain to people in our congregations.*

This is a helpful transition statement because it directs the students to what they can expect from the lesson content and also prepares them for some of the things that might be discussed in the Connection section that comes later. Although you may adapt your transition statement based on student responses during the Contact section, it is important, during the planning time, to think about what will be said.

Three useful questions for evaluating the Contact section you have created are:

- Is it creative and interesting?
- Does it take into account the needs and interests of this particular group?
- Does it focus people toward the lesson content and arouse their interest in it?

Again, review the Mentor's Guide to understand the lesson objectives and gather ideas for possible Connection activities.

Then, create a Connection section that helps students form new associations between truth and their lives (implications) and discuss specific changes in their beliefs, attitudes, or actions that should occur as a result (applications). As you plan, be a little wary of making the Connection section overly specific. Generally this lesson section should come to students as an invitation to discover, rather than as a finished product with all the specific outcomes predetermined.

At the heart of every good Connection section is a question (or series of questions) that asks students how knowing the truth will change their thinking, attitudes, and behaviors. (We have included some Connection questions in order to "prime the pump" of your students, to spur their thinking, and help them generate their own questions arising from their life experience.) Because this is theological and ministry training, the changes we are most concerned with are those associated with the way in which the students train and lead others in their ministry context. Try and focus in on helping students think about this area of application in the questions you develop.

The Connection section can utilize a number of different formats. Students can discuss the implications and applications together in a large Mentor-led group or in small groups with other students (either open discussion or following a pre-written set of questions). Case studies, also, are often good discussion starters. Regardless of the method, in this section both the Mentor and the learning group itself should be seen as a source of wisdom. Since your students are themselves already Christian leaders, there is often a wealth of experience and knowledge that can be drawn on from the students themselves. Students should be encouraged to learn from each other as well as from the Mentor.

Several principles should guide the Connection discussions that you lead:

- First, the primary goal in this section is to bring to the surface the questions that students have. In other words, the questions that occur to students during the lesson take priority over any questions that the Mentor prepares in advance–although the questions raised by an experienced Mentor will

Preparing the Connection Section

still be a useful learning tool. A corollary to this is to assume that the question raised by one student is very often the unspoken question present among the entire group.

- Second, try and focus the discussion on the concrete and the specific rather than the purely theoretical or hypothetical. This part of the lesson is meant to focus on the actual situations that are being faced by the specific students in your classroom.

- Third, do not be afraid to share the wisdom that you have gained through your own ministry experience. You are a key resource to students and they should expect that you will make lessons you have learned available to them. However, always keep in mind that variables of culture, context, and personality may mean that what has worked for you may not always work for everyone. Make suggestions, but dialogue with students about whether your experience seems workable in their context, and if not, what adaptations might be made to make it so.

Three useful questions for evaluating the Connection section you have created are:

- Have I anticipated in advance what the general areas of implication and application are likely to be for the teaching that is given in the lesson?

- Have I created a way to bring student questions to the surface and give them priority?

- Will this help a student leave the classroom knowing what to do with the truth they have learned?

Finally, because the Ministry Project is the structured application project for the entire course, it will be helpful to set aside part of the Connection section to have students discuss what they might choose for their project and to evaluate progress and/or report to the class following completion of the assignment.

Steps in Leading a Lesson

- Take attendance.

- Lead the devotion.

- Say or sing the Nicene Creed and pray.

- Administer the quiz.

- Check Scripture memorization assignment.

- Collect any assignments that are due.

Opening Activities

- Use a Contact provided in the Mentor's Guide, or create your own.

Teach the Contact Section

- Present the Content of the lesson using the video teaching.

  Using the Video Segments
  Each lesson has two video teaching segments, each approximately 25 minutes in length. After teaching the Contact section (including the transition statement), play the first video segment for the students. Students can follow this presentation using their Student Workbook which contains a general outline of the material presented and Scripture references and other supplementary materials referenced by the speaker. Once the first segment is viewed, work with the students to confirm that the content was understood.

  Ensuring that the Content is Understood
  Segue
  Using the Mentor's Guide, check for comprehension by asking the questions listed in the "Student Questions and Response" section. Clarify any incomplete understandings that students may demonstrate in their answers.

  Ask students if there are any questions that they have about the content and discuss them together as a class. NOTE - The questions here should focus on

Oversee the Content Section

understanding the content itself rather than on how to apply the learning. Application questions will be the focus of the upcoming Connection section.

Take a short class break and then repeat this process with the second video segment.

Teach the Connection Section

- Summary of Key Concepts
- Student Application and Implications
- Case Studies
- Restatement of Lesson's Thesis
- Resources and Bibliographies
- Ministry Connections
- Counseling and Prayer

Remind Students of Upcoming Assignments

- Scripture Memorization
- Assigned Readings
- Other Assignments

Close Lesson

- Close with prayer
- Be available for any individual student's questions or needs following the class

Please see the next page for an actual "Module Lesson Outline."

The quizzes, the final exam, and their answer keys are located at the back of this book.

Module Lesson Outline

Lesson Title — Introduction
Lesson Objectives
Devotion
Nicene Creed and Prayer
Quiz
Scripture Memorization Review
Assignments Due

Contact (1-3) — Contact

Video Segment 1 Outline — Content
Segue 1 (Student Questions and Response)
Video Segment 2 Outline
Segue 2 (Student Questions and Response)

Summary of Key Concepts — Connection
Student Application and Implications
Case Studies
Restatement of Lesson's Thesis
Resources and Bibliographies
Ministry Connections
Counseling and Prayer

Scripture Memorization — Assignments
Reading Assignment
Other Assignments
Looking Forward to the Next Lesson

FOCUS ON REPRODUCTION Capstone Curriculum / 303

MENTOR'S NOTES
1

Church Growth
Reproducing in Number and Quality

📖 **1**
Page 13
Lesson Introduction

Welcome to the Mentor's Guide for Lesson 1, *Church Growth: Reproducing in Number and Quality*. The overall focus of the *Focus on Reproduction* module is to equip your students with an understanding of evangelism, discipleship, and church planting as it relates to the urban community. If urban anthropologists are correct, within the next 20-25 years, every person in three will be an urban-slum dweller! For the first time in human history, more people live in cities than in rural or agrarian areas; missions in the 21st century will, of necessity, be urban mission. The argument of this module is that the fastest, most effective, and most fruitful form of spiritual reproduction is urban cross-cultural church planting. Your role in this module is to challenge your students to prepare themselves for a new wave of ministry and missions, to become a part of that cadre of urban workers who, if they yield themselves to God with new abandon and focus, can impact, even transform thousands of communities as they go forward in mission, in the power of the Holy Spirit, with the message of Christ, for the glory of God the Father.

The lessons are structured carefully to walk your students through the process of planting churches in the urban community. In lesson one, we begin our study with the subject, *Church Growth, Reproducing in Number and Quality*. Here we affirm the single most critical concept in understanding mission in the city: the lordship of Jesus Christ. As risen Lord and God's Anointed Messiah, Jesus has been exalted to the position of head over all things to the Church and Lord of the harvest. In lesson two, *Planting Urban Churches, Sowing* we introduce the important concept of *oikos* in urban evangelism. Here we show how an *oikos* is that web of common kinship relationships, friendships, and associations that make up a person's larger social circle. Beginning with an outline of *oikos* in the NT, we then explore the meaning of this critical idea for urban cross-cultural evangelism. In lesson three we further outline the second main phase of church planting, *Equipping*, through the idea of *follow-up*, or incorporating new disciples into the Church. Arguing that the Church is God's means of bringing new Christians to maturity, we provide key elements and tips in the practice of following up new believers in Christ. In this lesson we will also look closely at the practice of discipling growing believers. Finally, in lesson four we consider our role in helping new churches progress toward independence through *Empowerment*, and the final phase of urban church planting: transition. We will define the purpose, plan, and perspectives related to empowering through four

biblical aspects of godly urban church leadership. Without a doubt, godly, servant leadership is critical to ensure a dynamic growing church in the city.

Throughout these lessons it will be important for you to emphasize and draw the student's attention to the objectives. Determine right away to emphasize them throughout the lesson, in every part and dimension, and especially during the discussions and interaction with the students. The more you can highlight the objectives throughout the class period, the better the chances are that they will understand and grasp the magnitude of these objectives.

Do not hesitate to discuss these objectives briefly before you enter into the class period. Draw the students' attention to the objectives, for, in a real sense, this is the heart of your educational aim for the class period in this lesson. Everything discussed and done ought to point back to these objectives. Find ways to highlight these at every turn, to reinforce them and reiterate them as you go.

📖 2
Page 13
Lesson Objectives

This devotion focuses on the significance of the Great Commission to the Apostles, and the way in which they took this calling seriously, even willing to risk persecution, rejection, and death in order to fulfill it. In a real sense this devotion is on the Great Commission itself, and a nice summary from J. B. Green may be helpful as you orient the students to the heart of Christian mission, which is Jesus' command to go and make disciples of all nations.

📖 3
Page 14
Devotion

> *Through the Great Commission of Matthew 28.16–20 Jesus focuses his followers on the ongoing importance of discipleship through the ages. . . Jesus committed his earthly ministry to "making disciples" within Israel (cf. John 4.1), and he commissioned his disciples to "make disciples" among the nations (Matt. 28.16–20; see Gentiles). The obvious meaning of "making disciples" is to proclaim the gospel message among those who have not yet received forgiveness of sins (Luke 24.46–47; John 20.21; see Forgiveness of Sins). The command finds remarkable verbal fulfillment in the activities of the early Church (e.g., Acts 14.21), where disciples went from Jerusalem to Judea, to Samaria (see Samaritans), to the ends of the earth*

proclaiming the message of Jesus and making disciples. In the early Church to believe in the gospel message was to become a disciple (cf. Acts 4.32 with 6.2). The injunction of the Great Commission is given at least to the eleven remaining disciples (cf. Matt. 28.16), but in their own role as disciples they are paradigms for all disciples. As Jesus addresses the disciples and commands them to "make disciples of all the nations," Jesus is telling them to continue the work he began with them.

~ J. B. Green. **Dictionary of Jesus and the Gospels.** (electronic ed.) Downers Grove, IL: InterVarsity, 1997. p. 188.

This challenge to the original Apostles is likewise a clarion call of the Lord to the entire generation of Christians in this age to go to the ends of the earth and testify to every people the good news of the Gospel. The Apostles reveal in this passage their uncompromising commitment to be faithful to the Commission, regardless of the opposition, whatever price that must be paid. This is where urban mission and ministry begins: an unconditional availability to do the will of Christ, whatever it takes.

📖 **4**
Page 16
Contact

Pay careful attention to the contact sections in these lessons. These portions are specifically designed to "prime the intellectual and spiritual pumps" of your students, to get them ready to consider the biblical content of the lesson, and the corollary implications connected to that content. Be careful that you guide your time well in your use of the contact information; although the incidents and ideas covered are intriguing, they can take a large amount of your lesson time, depending on how you have allocated your time for the lesson.

📖 **5**
Page 29
Student Questions and Response

These questions in the Segue section (pronounced *seg - way*) are designed to help you review the materials in the section just covered. More than that, it provides you with an opportunity to ensure that the students understand the principal objectives, facts, and ideas presented in the previous video segment. As always, you will want to gauge your time as you proceed through these various questions, especially if your students are intrigued with the concepts, and want to discuss their implications at length. Allow for the proper time to focus in on the main points, and still have enough time for a break before the next video segment is started.

Again, it cannot be overemphasized how important it is in teaching others to stay close by the objectives you have for a particular teaching moment. Your teaching will be more interesting, remembered with greater ease, and be more useful to your students if you insist on relating the matter under consideration to the objectives of the segment and the lesson.

Also notice at the end of these questions is an instrument, a tool that was developed by Charles Ridley to help denominations (many across North America) determine whether or not someone might succeed at church planting. These categories are included in interview materials where candidates are assessed as to their readiness to plant churches. Briefly discuss these standards with your students, and keep them in mind throughout the module. One of your tasks as mentor is to help students come to understand more clearly whether or not God has called them to actually plant churches in the city among the poor in a formal way as church planters themselves. These kinds of dialogues can keep such questions "front and center" in the minds of the students throughout your study of this module.

📖 6
*Page 46
Summary of
Key Concepts*

This section highlights the fundamental truths written in sentence form which the students should have received from this lesson, that is, from the videos and your guided discussion with them. Your aim should be to help your students come to understand the critical principles in proverb form, in a simple, declarative statement that allows them to summarize the material and pass it along to others.

The purpose of the study is to get to the "nuggets," those key principles of truth that they can evaluate, apply, and share in their lives and ministries. It is never a waste of time to make certain that the students are understanding the underlying truths which run through the material. Often, our ability to help our students grapple with these concepts will determine whether or not they are able to *use these truths* later, in their personal edification, their teaching and preaching, and their discipling of others. So, make sure that these concepts are clearly defined and carefully considered, for their quiz work and exams will be taken from these items directly.

📖 **7**
*Page 47
Student Application
and Implications*

While the first part of the lesson concentrates on the need for the students to *master the concepts in the material*, from this moment on the focus is on helping your students *master their own applications in their personal lives*. In other words, students need at least two modes of reflection as they go through the lesson. The first mode is intellectual and dialogical, and focuses on their ability to wrestle with difficult concepts to gain a sense of what the Scriptures actually teach on a particular subject. This mode is *critical*.

However, there is another mode, equally important, which has an entirely different focus. This second mode is personal and spiritual, and focuses on their ability to evaluate the meaning of the truths they have learned relative to their own life applications and ministries. This mode is primarily *creative*.

In light of these ideas, it will always be important at some time in the lesson to shift gears, so to speak, and enable the students to begin to think through their own situations with a greater focus and deliberation. The questions in this section are always designed to be "kindling" to ignite their own fires of inquiry, so to speak. What is significant here is not that they answer *the particular questions written below*, but that they engage the concepts in such a way that they turn their attention to their *evaluation* and *application* of the issues and themes to their own lives and ministries.

In your conversation with your students, seek to help them settle on a cadre of issues, concerns, questions, and ideas that flow directly from their experience, and relate to their lives and ministries. Do not hesitate to spend the majority of time on some question that arose from the video, or some special concern that is especially relevant in their ministry context right now. The goal of this section is for you to enable them to think critically and theologically in regards to their own lives and ministry contexts. Again, the questions below are provided as guides and primers, and ought not to be seen as absolute necessities. Pick and choose among them, or come up with your own. The key is relevance now, to their context and to their questions.

The case studies function somewhat like the "contact" sections above, with one major difference. Whereas the *Contact* section was given to help *introduce* your students to the ideas and issues covered in the lesson, the *Case Studies* are actual or probable events designed to help your students show that they can apply the truths in the context of real or probable life situations. Often they are based on true stories, and all the time they reflect the complexity and difficulty of ministering in urban communities.

A large part of the case study section is your ability to help the students become *wise in their application of the truth to particular situations*. Hopefully, your students will be able to apply biblical wisdom to these studies. In general, a three fold approach is helpful:

1. Make sure that the students understand the facts of the situation.

2. After the facts are clear, help your students determine what insights and principles apply to the situation, and how many *right answers* are possible in the situation.

3. Have them actually select solutions to the situations, or approaches they would take, given the insight into the situation and the biblical principles that apply.

This kind of reflection can help your students move from simply consideration of the truth, to its more fundamental application to their own lives and to the life situations of others.

📖 **8**
Page 49
Case Studies

This section again gives you the right to "pile-drive" the truths one final time into the hearts and minds of the students before you end the lesson.

Lest you think that this kind of approach is overkill, consider the following Scriptures:

> Phil. 3.1 - Finally, my brothers, rejoice in the Lord. To write the same things to you is no trouble to me and is safe for you.

📖 **9**
Page 50
Restatement of the Lesson's Thesis

2 Pet. 1.12-15 - Therefore I intend always to remind you of these qualities, though you know them and are established in the truth that you have. [13] I think it right, as long as I am in this body, to stir you up by way of reminder, [14] since I know that the putting off of my body will be soon, as our Lord Jesus Christ made clear to me. [15] And I will make every effort so that after my departure you may be able at any time to recall these things.

2 Pet. 3.1 - This is now the second letter that I am writing to you, beloved. In both of them I am stirring up your sincere mind by way of reminder.

2 Tim. 1.6 - For this reason I remind you to fan into flame the gift of God, which is in you through the laying on of my hands.

The ministry of "reminding" is one of the key ministries that the godly teacher can do. Do not hesitate to reiterate the fundamental truths at every turn. You will ensure that the students make these truths their very own.

📖 10
Page 52
Counseling and Prayer

Seek to make your times of study a time of *spiritual refreshment and awakening* as much as it is a time of *reflection and dialogue on the truth*. If at all possible, structure your time in such a way that you can allow for prayer for the students, and encourage the same in their lives. Prayer has profound power to intermingle with your teaching and produce fruit in their lives with powerful effect. The Lord is willing to help them grow to become more like his Son, and be as effective as they need to be as they learn and apply these truths.

📖 11
Page 52
Assignments

Above all, it is imperative on the assignments you provide that you be clear. Make certain that the students understand the assignment for next week, especially the written piece. This is not difficult; the goal is that they would read the material as best as they can and write a few sentences on what they take them to mean. This is a critical intellectual skill for your students to learn, so make sure that you encourage them in this process. Of course, for those students who might find this difficult, assure them of the intent behind this assignment, and emphasize their understanding of the material being the key, not their writing skills. We want to

improve their skills, but not at the expense of their encouragement and edification. Nor, however, do we want to sell them short. Strike to find the midpoint between challenge and encouragement here.

Excellence is to be expected from your students, and of course, we know that students will have different abilities to do intellectual work–reading, writing, and so on. While we want to emphasize credible academic performance, we do not wish to exalt these indicators over softness of heart, readiness to obey the Word of God, and availability to serve Christ as he leads by the Spirit. *Constantly monitor your own emphasis on grades, assignments and academic performance. These are important, but not all-important.* Focus on the main thing: unconditional availability to Christ to obey him in our lives as he directs us.

Planting Urban Churches
Sowing

MENTOR'S NOTES 2

📖 **1**
Page 57
Lesson Introduction

Welcome to the Mentor's Guide for Lesson 2, *Planting Urban Churches: Sowing*. The overall focus of this lesson is the introduction of the concept of *oikos* in urban evangelism. It is hard emphasize how important the idea of the *oikos* is for ministry, not just urban ministry, but all forms of outreach that are interested in multiplied impact on families, groups and communities. In this lesson we will cover in what ways an *oikos* is that web of common kinship relationships, friendships, and associations that make up a person's larger social circle. We will start with a general outline of the idea of *oikos* in the NT, and then, begin to explore the practical application of this meaning for urban cross-cultural evangelism.

D. N. Freedman's account of the *oikos* in Peter's epistle can give you some further background of the concept in the New Testament:

> *Among these various images of community, it is the identification and exhortation of Christians as members of the household or family of God which dominates the letter from beginning to end. In two key passages of the letter, 2.4–10 and 4.12–19, the community is explicitly called the "household (oikos) of the Spirit" (2.5) or the "household (oikos) of God" (4.17). In the former passage, this phrase interprets the covenantal epithet basileion (Exod. 19.6) cited in 2.9, and describes the eschatological community as the "house(hold) in which God's Spirit dwells" (Elliott 1981: 167-69). In the latter passage, "house(hold) of God" likewise identifies the community united with Christ and upon which God's Spirit rests. Consistent with this household metaphor are further instances of oikos-related terminology. The readers also are assured that they are being "built up" (oikodomeisthe, 2.5) by God and at the letter's conclusion this metaphor of construction and confirmation is repeated (5.10). In the household instruction of 2.18–3.7, the servant-slaves are addressed not with the conventional term for slaves (douloi, Eph. 6.5; Col. 3.22; Titus 2.9) but with the word for "household servants" (oiketai, 2.18). In its only NT occurrence, synoikein is used to exhort Christian husbands to "live together" with their wives in the knowledge that both spouses are co-heirs of the grace of life (3.7). Similarly, all the addressees are encouraged to practice hospitality, love, and mutual service as "household stewards (oikonomoi) of God's varied grace" (4.7-11).*
>
> ~ D. N. Freedman. **The Anchor Bible Dictionary**. Vol. 5. New York: Doubleday. pp. 275-276.

This focus on the household is crucial for you to comprehend as you seek to help your students get a grasp on the concept. You may want to obtain a copy of Arn and Arn's book, *The Master's Plan for Making Disciples,* which speaks of evangelism, discipleship, and church growth all with the concept of the *oikos in mind.*

As you go through this lesson, please notice again in the objectives that this focus on *oikos* highlighted clearly. Since this idea is central to every part of the lesson, you will have to ensure that this concept above all is understood throughout the lesson, and that you help them at every turn when it is clear that they do not fully grasp it. The clearer you can be on this concept, the better the students' understanding will be of the other sections of the material as well.

This devotion focuses on the power of the *oikos* for understanding the function of ministry. The example of the Philippian jailer provides a nice context for understanding how normal, natural, and personal sharing the Good News along the lines of the *oikos* can be.

📖 **2**
Page 57
Devotion

Perhaps the greatest challenge here will be the tendency to confuse the biblical term for household with our sense of the nuclear family–mother, father, and children. As you will see the concept of the *oikos* was a sophisticated network of friendships, kinfolk relationships, patrons, associates, and other parties which were considered a part of the head of the household's sphere of influence. Be careful to distinguish throughout the lesson between the two.

In these questions you will find the focus is upon mastering the data and the facts associated with the claims made in the first video segment. Concentrate on ensuring that the students understand the answers in light of the lesson aims of the first segment. Make certain that you watch the clock here, covering the questions below and those posed by your students, and watch for any tangents which may lead you from rehearsing the critical facts and main points.

📖 **3**
Page 71
Student Questions and Response

Notice, too, at the end of these Segue questions is included the record of the various churches which were planted in Acts. One thing that is clear is that many of these churches were planted in the *oikos* of the city in question. The dynamism of this concept is clearly seen in such a record, and deserves some discussion with the students.

4
Page 93
Counseling and Prayer

Make sure that you spend time in your sessions in prayer. Lead by example in this. While it may not be an integral part of many seminary and Bible school training regimens in the classroom, our desire is to model the spiritual nature of intellectual work.

Therefore, never consider it an overly familiar or unnecessary thing to ask the students if they need prayer for someone or something connected to the ideas and truths presented in the lesson. Prayer is a wonderfully practical and helpful way to apply truth; by taking specific needs to God in light of a truth, the students can solidify those ideas in their soul, and receive back from the Lord the answers they need in order to be sustained in the midst of their ministries.

Of course, everything is somehow dependent on the amount of time you have in your session, and how you have organized it. Still, prayer is a forceful and potent part of any spiritual encounter and teaching, and if you can, it should always have its place, even if it is a short summary prayer of what God has taught us, and a determination to live out its implications as the Holy Spirit teaches us.

5
Page 94
Reading Assignment

These articles are of particular usefulness on the power of penetrating networks of relationships which may be virtually impenetrable from the outside. God is doing unique things today in winning people within frameworks of relationships in very difficult fields. These ideas are somewhat controversial but highly important for discussion and understanding within the class.

MENTOR'S NOTES 3

Planting Urban Churches
Tending

📖 1
Page 99
Lesson Introduction

Welcome to the Mentor's Guide for Lesson 3, *Planting Urban Churches: Tending*. The overall focus of lesson three is the explanation and outline of the second main phase of church planting, *Equipping*, through the idea of *follow-up*, or incorporating new disciples into the Church. In this lesson we will argue forcefully that the local church is God's means of bringing new Christians to maturity. Disciples are born and raised in the context of the local church, which itself is considered a household of God. In the materials that follow, we will provide the students with a clear outline of the central elements in the practice of following up new believers in Christ. In the second segment of the lesson we will go further in the development of new Christians by taking a fresh look at the practice of discipling growing believers. Again, we will consider these practices in the context of and how they relate to the local assembly of believers. We ought not define Christian discipleship as a characteristic of being alone, in isolation from the body of Christ. Discipleship is demonstrated in the everyday working out of loving relationships with others in the body of Christ.

Here is a sampling of the abundant Scripture admonitions in the NT that are addressed to us in the context of the body, "one another," "each other," and so on.

> John 13.34-35 - A new commandment I give to you, that you love one another: just as I have loved you, you also are to love one another. [35] By this all people will know that you are my disciples, if you have love for one another.

> John 15.12 - This is my commandment, that you love one another as I have loved you.

> John 15.17 - These things I command you, so that you will love one another.

> Rom. 12.10 - Love one another with brotherly affection. Outdo one another in showing honor.

> Rom. 12.16 - Live in harmony with one another. Do not be haughty, but associate with the lowly. Never be conceited.

> Rom. 13.8 - Owe no one anything, except to love each other, for the one who loves another has fulfilled the law.

Rom. 14.13 - Therefore let us not pass judgment on one another any longer, but rather decide never to put a stumbling block or hindrance in the way of a brother.

Rom. 15.7 - Therefore welcome one another as Christ has welcomed you, for the glory of God.

2 Cor. 13.11 - Finally, brothers, rejoice. Aim for restoration, comfort one another, agree with one another, live in peace; and the God of love and peace will be with you.

Gal. 5.13 - For you were called to freedom, brothers. Only do not use your freedom as an opportunity for the flesh, but through love serve one another.

Gal. 5.15 - But if you bite and devour one another, watch out that you are not consumed by one another.

Eph. 4.2 - with all humility and gentleness, with patience, bearing with one another in love.

Eph. 4.32 - Be kind to one another, tenderhearted, forgiving one another, as God in Christ forgave you.

Col. 3.9 - Do not lie to one another, seeing that you have put off the old self with its practices.

Col. 3.16 - Let the word of Christ dwell in you richly, teaching and admonishing one another in all wisdom, singing psalms and hymns and spiritual songs, with thankfulness in your hearts to God.

1 Thess. 5.11 - Therefore encourage one another and build one another up, just as you are doing.

1 Thess. 5.15 - See that no one repays anyone evil for evil, but always seek to do good to one another and to everyone.

Heb. 3.13 - But exhort one another every day, as long as it is called "today," that none of you may be hardened by the deceitfulness of sin.

Heb. 10.24-25 - And let us consider how to stir up one another to love and good works, [25] not neglecting to meet together, as is the habit of some, but encouraging one another, and all the more as you see the Day drawing near.

James 4.11 - Do not speak evil against one another, brothers. The one who speaks against a brother or judges his brother, speaks evil against the law and judges the law. But if you judge the law, you are not a doer of the law but a judge.

James 5.9 - Do not grumble against one another, brothers, so that you may not be judged; behold, the Judge is standing at the door.

James 5.16 - Therefore, confess your sins to one another and pray for one another, that you may be healed. The prayer of a righteous person has great power as it is working.

1 Pet. 1.22 - Having purified your souls by your obedience to the truth for a sincere brotherly love, love one another earnestly from a pure heart.

1 Pet. 4.8-10 - Above all, keep loving one another earnestly, since love covers a multitude of sins. [9] Show hospitality to one another without grumbling. [10] As each has received a gift, use it to serve one another, as good stewards of God's varied grace.

1 John 3.11 - For this is the message that you have heard from the beginning, that we should love one another.

1 John 3.23 - And this is his commandment, that we believe in the name of his Son Jesus Christ and love one another, just as he has commanded us.

Our focus on this lessons is underscoring this abundant NT data with a clear understanding that discipleship occurs in the context of the local church, and that all of us, in one way or another, can play a real and significant part as model, mentor, and friend to new and growing believers.

This is the heart and soul of this lesson, and you ought to do all you can to help the students recontextualize in their minds the *place* where follow-up and discipleship occurs. All too often the literature on helping new Christians has emphasized the

individual side of helping new converts to grow. In this lesson we want to focus on the reality that disciples are grown in the greenhouse of faith, the Church. This is why *Equipping* is connected to the *Assemble* and *Nurture* phases of church planting. To separate these practices from the local church ensures defeated and isolated converts.

Attempt to draw these principles and perspective out in this lesson. Notice again how the objectives are clearly stated, calling for your ongoing emphasis of them throughout the lesson, during your review of the key points, and through and interaction with the students.

This devotion focuses on the intimacy that the apostles had in raising their children spiritually. With the same kind and intensity of passion, wisdom, and care that good physical parents provide each day to their children, so the apostles provided to those under their charge in the Lord. This spiritual parenthood, this intense loving tenderness on behalf of newborn Christians is deeply characteristic of all vital church planting in both the *Assemble* and *Nurture* stages. Look at some of the texts which underscore this important truth:

> 2
> Page 100
> Devotion

> 1 Cor. 4.14-17 - I do not write these things to make you ashamed, but to admonish you as my beloved children. [15] For though you have countless guides in Christ, you do not have many fathers. For I became your father in Christ Jesus through the Gospel. [16] I urge you, then, be imitators of me. [17] That is why I sent you Timothy, my beloved and faithful child in the Lord, to remind you of my ways in Christ, as I teach them everywhere in every church.

> 2 Cor. 12.14-15 - Here for the third time I am ready to come to you. And I will not be a burden, for I seek not what is yours but you. For children are not obligated to save up for their parents, but parents for their children. [15] I will most gladly spend and be spent for your souls. If I love you more, am I to be loved less?

Gal. 4.19 - My little children, for whom I am again in the anguish of childbirth until Christ is formed in you!

Titus 1.4 - To Titus, my true child in a common faith: Grace and peace from God the Father and Christ Jesus our Savior.

Philem. 1.10 - I appeal to you for my child, Onesimus, whose father I became in my imprisonment.

1 Tim. 1.1-2 - Paul, an apostle of Christ Jesus by command of God our Savior and of Christ Jesus our hope, [2] To Timothy, my true child in the faith: grace, mercy, and peace from God the Father and Christ Jesus our Lord.

This imagery of raising spiritual children is a fitting and potent vision of the character of follow-up and discipleship in the local church. Help the students understand the kind of *feeling* and *connotation* that is communicated in the "button-busting" pride that a parent has in an obedient child, along with the trepidation and pain for a disobedient one. We are called to raise spiritual children in Christ, and to do so with the same passion and intensity that Paul had for his spiritual children, both individually and as a congregation.

3
Page 116
Student Questions and Response

Is it critical to understand the role of the local church in follow-up and discipleship, for once this is understood, the kinds of loving impact that caring individuals can have become even more plain. In the questions below concentrate with the students on the key data which undergird the objectives set forth in the first part of the lesson. This last video segment highlights the importance of follow-up in the context of the local Christian community. Concentrate on ensuring that the students understand the answers in light of the lesson aims of the first segment with its focus on the local church. Keeping the role of the body in the light during your discussion will prevent the discussion from turning to purely issues of individual preference and methods in establishing new Christians *separate from their ongoing welcome and membership in a local assembly.*

While we have emphasized the role and place of the local church in follow-up and discipleship, it will be important in these case studies to see that not all churches are edifying and Christ-honoring. The need is immense for us to train our students to be aware of the variance that exists in the quality of Christian discipleship being displayed in churches. Assure the students that discernment and wisdom are critical skills and gifts to be employed, even as they seek to find the best places and methods to equip the new believers who have responded to the Gospel through their evangelism and *oikos* penetration. It is certainly one thing to know that the local assembly is God's means for catechesis, growth, and spiritual development; it is another matter entirely to plant churches which reflect this depth and substance.

4
Page 136
Case Studies

By the end of this second class session, you ought to begin to emphasize with the students the need for do the spadework to plan their Ministry Project. Also, by this time, you should have emphasized their need to select the Bible text for their Exegetical Project. These projects are done with far better thought and excellence when students prepare for them as early as possible. Make sure that you remind them of these facts for, as in all study, students usually are preoccupied with a number of thing, and unfortunately at the end of the course many things will become due. It is a rare student indeed who does not begin to feel the pressure of getting a number of assignments in at the same time, all which are due within a short period. Any way that you can remind them of the need for advanced planning will be wonderfully helpful for them, whether they realize it immediately or not.

5
Page 139
Assignments

Because of these circumstances, we have found that you help your students greatly if you insist on their work at the times that you say they are do. As a matter of fact, we even advocate that you consider docking a modest amount of points for late papers, exams, and projects. While the amount may be nominal, your enforcement of your rules will help them to learn to be efficient and on time as they continue in their studies.

Planting Urban Churches
Reaping

MENTOR'S NOTES
4

📖 1
Page 143
Lesson Introduction

Welcome to the Mentor's Guide for Lesson 4, *Planting Urban Churches: Reaping*. In this lesson we concentrate upon our role in helping new churches progress toward independence through *Empowerment*, and the final phase of urban church planting: transition. The PLANT acrostic highlights in step-by-step fashion the steps in planting a church in the city: *Prepare, Launch, Assemble, Nurture*, and now in this lesson we look at the processes surrounding *Transition*. In this lesson we concentrate on the theme of leadership and the transferring of leadership over to the newly formed fellowship. By all accounts, godly, servant leadership that is willing to provide ongoing shepherding care to a local church is its greatest asset and most important weapon against heresy, division, and stagnation.

In one of the students textbooks, *A Biblical Church Planting Manual*, Marlin Mull provides twelve reasons for starting a new church from the Book of Acts. Here is that list:

1. A new church brings the Kingdom of God to earth (Acts 1.3; 8.12; 14.22; 19.8; 20.25; 28.23; 28.31).

2. A new church helps fulfill the Great Commission (Acts 1.8; Matt. 28.18-20; Mark 16.15-16; Luke 24.46-49; John 20.19-22).

3. A new church provides a place of prayer to meet God with others (Acts 1.14; 4.31; 12.5).

4. A new church provides another public preaching place (Acts 9.20; 10.42; 14.7; 16.10; 20.20).

5. A new church is the most effective evangelistic tool (Acts 2.38-39; 14.21).

6. A new church teaches the Bible (Acts 4.2; 5.19-21; 5.42; 8.4; 11.25-26; 18.11; 20.20; 28.31).

7. A new church offers another place for Christian service (Acts 6.3; 9.36; 11.25-26; 11.29-30; 17.15).

8. A new church trains lay leaders to become preachers (Acts 6.10; 14.23).

9. A new church crosses cultural barriers (Acts 8.35; 10.1-48; 16.9; 22.21).

10. A new church mentors new believers (Acts 9.26-28; 20.20; 20.31, 36; 20.34-36; 20.27).

11. A new church supports worldwide missionary activity (Acts 13.2-3; 16.9-10).

12. A new church starts other churches (Acts 13.2-3; 16.9-10).

In looking at this list, all of them assume leadership. The church that brings in the Kingdom of God possesses men and women who know God and love God, are surrendered to Christ and represent his kingdom interest with integrity. These leaders seek to enable the members of the fellowship to contribute to the fulfillment of the Great Commission in their neighborhood, and these leaders organize prayer and preach and teach the Word of God. Through follow-up and discipleship, they turn whatever place the church meets into a place of ministry and service, and equip lay leaders who can join them in crossing cultural barriers and mentoring new believers. They lead by example in their support of worldwide missionary activity, and lead the fellowship in reproducing itself. It is hardly possible to imagine one of these reasons being devoid from godly, servant leaders who selflessly serve the Church as under-shepherds of Christ, who purchased it with his own blood (Acts 20.28).

Please note again the emphasis of these ideas in the objectives that are listed here. Seek to understand these concepts and truths as well as you can so you will be in a better position to emphasize them as you lead the discussions with the students.

At the end of these questions is an excerpt from Ed Stetzer's important recent work on church planting, *Planting New Churches in a Postmodern Age*. After you have answered the questions to review the key concepts covered in the last segment, it would be good to look at his SHAPE acrostic for identifying potential church planters, and see how they relate to the notions of commission, character, competence, and community. This kind of cross-pollination of ideas is good, for it helps your students to see the kinds of criteria that many are accepting today as

2
Page 163
Student Questions and Response

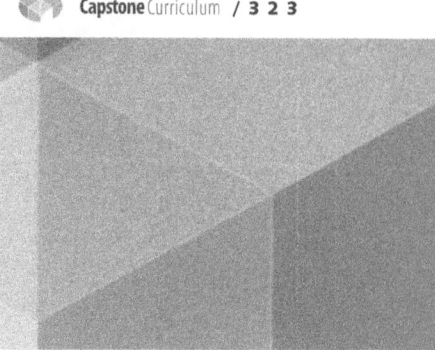

norms for those who would go on to plant churches. Always, of course, be aware of the cultural and class issues that affect our understanding of planting churches in the inner city or among the poor. These concepts will need to be filtered through that particular lens in order to be properly understood relative to city life, both its promises and its perils.

📖 3
Page 178
What are Church Planting Movements?

One of the most important things to talk with your students about is the possibility and the need to not only plant a single healthy church, but a movement of churches. David Garrison has written an important book recently on this subject entitle *Church Planting Movements: How God is Redeeming a Lost World*. Included in the Student Workbook is his definition of Church Planting Movements, and his explanation of each clause in the definition. Spend time thinking through with your students the implications of this kind of thinking for the *Empowerment* phase and the *Transition* stage of church planting. It can spur them to think in new ways about multiplying the impact of their ministry, and going to fields which are truly furthest from us.

📖 4
Page 183
Assignments

Your work as an instructor and grader begins in earnest now. Make sure that you have commitments for the ministry projects, exegetical projects, and other data together as this will be important for you to determine the student's overall grade. Again, your discretion regarding late work can easily determine whether you dock students of points, resulting in letter grade changes, or give students an "Incomplete" until the work is finished. However you adopt your standard regarding their work, remember that our courses are not primarily about the grades that students receive, but the spiritual nourishment and training these courses provide. Also, however, remember that helping our students strive for excellence is an integral part of our instruction.

www.ingramcontent.com/pod-product-compliance
Lightning Source LLC
Chambersburg PA
CBHW080729300426
44114CB00019B/2522